The Tenants of East Harlem

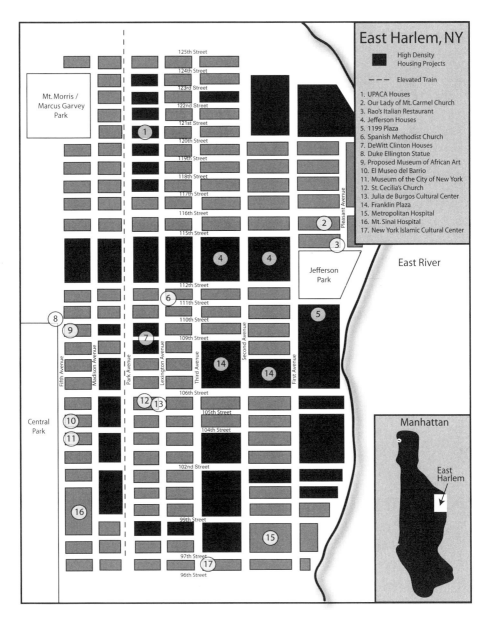

Map 1. East Harlem

The Tenants
of East Harlem

RUSSELL LEIGH SHARMAN

UNIVERSITY OF CALIFORNIA PRESS
Berkeley   Los Angeles   London

University of California Press, one of the most distinguished university presses in the United States, enriches lives around the world by advancing scholarship in the humanities, social sciences, and natural sciences. Its activities are supported by the UC Press Foundation and by philanthropic contributions from individuals and institutions. For more information, visit www.ucpress.edu.

University of California Press
Berkeley and Los Angeles, California

University of California Press, Ltd.
London, England

Library of Congress Cataloging-in-Publication Data

Sharman, Russell Leigh, 1972–.
    The tenants of East Harlem / Russell Leigh Sharman.
        p.   cm.
    Includes bibliographical references and index.
    ISBN-13: 978-0-520-24427-6 (cloth : alk. paper), ISBN-10: 0–520–24427–3 (cloth : alk. paper)
    ISBN-13: 978-0-520-24747-5 (pbk. : alk. paper), ISBN-10: 0–520–24747–7 (pbk. : alk. paper)
        1. Sociology, Urban—New York (State)—New York.   2. Urban anthropology—New York (State)—New York.   3. Ethnicity—New York (State)—New York.   4. Community development, Urban—New York (State)—New York.   5. Gentrification—New York (State)—New York. 6. East Harlem (New York, N.Y.)—Social conditions.   7. East Harlem (New York, N.Y.)— Economic conditions.   8. East Harlem (New York, N.Y.)— Social life and customs.   I. Title.

HN80.N5S53   2006
305.8'009747'1—dc22 2005021225

Manufactured in the United States of America

15	14	13	12	11	10	09	08	07	06
10	9	8	7	6	5	4	3	2	1

This book is printed on New Leaf EcoBook 60, containing 60% post-consumer waste, processed chlorine free; 30% de-inked recycled fiber, elemental chlorine free; and 10% FSC-certified virgin fiber, totally chlorine free. EcoBook 60 is acid free and meets the minimum requirements of ANSI/ASTM D5634–01 (*Permanence of Paper*).

Seek the peace of the city to which I have sent
you . . . for in its peace, you will have peace.

Jeremiah 29:7

People in communities, whether it's Manhattan,
Bronx, Queens, they have the history of New York.

Lucille

Contents

Acknowledgments

When Cheryl and I first arrived in East Harlem, there were two families that quickly adopted us as their own, showing us kindnesses that could never be repaid. This book is dedicated to all the residents of East Harlem, past and present, but special thanks are reserved for the Chapelles and the Riveras. Many others in my neighborhood inspired and facilitated the writing of this book, whether they know it or not: Norma Ojeda, Debbie Quinonez, James de la Vega, and David Givens, to name just a few.

I also thank all those who took the time to encourage the project along the way. Stan Holwitz, at the University of California Press, championed the idea of *The Tenants of East Harlem,* then trusted me to see it through. Philippe Bourgois, Ken Guest, and Michael Blim read various chapters, and the writing group led by Steven Steinberg was instrumental in encouraging the earliest drafts. The anonymous reviewers for the University of California Press gave insightful and constructive critiques. In addition, the final few months of work on the manuscript would not have been possible without the generosity of Brooklyn College and the Whiting Foundation, as well as the forbearance of my colleagues in the anthropology department.

Finally, two individuals deserve special consideration. Michael Blim, without whom I would not be an anthropologist, is a mentor whose intellect is rivaled only by his generosity. And Cheryl, whose gift for writing I can only hope to dimly reflect, brought me to East Harlem in the first place; this book is hers more than it is mine.

Preface

Located in a somewhat infamous corner of upper Manhattan, East Harlem is hemmed in by 96th and 125th Streets, Fifth Avenue and the East River. It has always been distinct from the better-known Harlem, at least in the eyes of its inhabitants, though it has not always been considered a specifically *Spanish* Harlem. Germans, Irish, Italians, Jews, and African Americans all took up residence before the arrival of Puerto Ricans. But the Puerto Ricans staked the most recent claim, overwhelming every other ethnic group by sheer numbers so that East Harlem became Spanish Harlem, which would fight a losing battle with the *other* Harlem for municipal attention and economic development.

By the 1980s and 1990s East Harlem had become one of the most stigmatized communities in the city. With the introduction of crack cocaine to the informal urban economy, 40 percent became the magic number for

East Harlem's misery: 40 percent of its residents lived below the poverty line (compared to 19 percent for New York City); 40 percent of families living there resided in public housing projects; and 40 percent of East Harlem households had no wage or salary income.

A decade later East Harlem continues to attract new immigrants who slowly transform the community in the subtle, ongoing work of putting down roots. Mexicans join the well-entrenched Puerto Ricans to radically realign the nationalist divisions of the Latino community. West Africans along Third Avenue confuse notions of African, American, and black. Asians link the urban space in a network of restaurants and bodegas, working behind bulletproof Plexiglas. And, finally, the gradual appearance of downtown money and upwardly mobile but cash-poor whites signals the latest and most pervasive migration yet.

I suppose that's where I come in. I arrived in East Harlem in summer 1999—married, unemployed, and determined to establish an art education organization in an economically marginalized urban community. It took less than a month to settle on East Harlem, a vibrant Manhattan neighborhood with a burgeoning art scene. In less than a year we were incorporated there as a nonprofit organization and teaching art classes to a couple hundred children in a local community center.

In those first few years, I was teaching part-time at a half dozen different campuses around the city and spending the rest of my time at community board meetings and neighborhood events. But for all my involvement in the community, I could not shake my association with the increasing number of white folks snapping up overpriced apartments that were still cheaper than those on the Upper East Side. I was not an individual; I was part of a group with very specific racial, political, and economic implications for the neighborhood.

My realization that this was true of everyone in East Harlem was the inspiration for this book. East Harlem has always suffered the indignities of racial essentialism—the belief that the Italians, the Puerto Ricans, or any other ethnic group was somehow monolithic and usually hardwired for social dysfunction. This idea was often associated with specific sections of the neighborhood: east of First Avenue was Italian Harlem; south of 110th Street was Spanish Harlem. Common sense would suggest that

PREFACE xiii

any individual might diverge from the collective stereotype, or indeed that no single individual would match the stereotype at all.

And yet each individual is invariably connected to a particular identity, bound by geography as much as genealogy. Our lives move in and out of the stream of experience that feeds that identity, and each of us, regardless of intention, stands in for the whole.

What follows is an unusual style of ethnography—unusual because modern monographs generally have little ethnographic depth. We allow theory to run roughshod over the experiences of individuals, the true subjects of our inquiries. There is no introductory chapter that abstracts a theoretical perspective or lays out a disciplinarily acceptable polemic (these few prefatory remarks aside). That approach may inspire the like-minded, but too often we lose the student and the nonspecialist—readers with whom we should be most concerned. Instead, I embed a set of theoretical perspectives in the text, allowing ethnography to do the work of theoretical abstraction. I have followed several guiding principles: poverty *and* gentrification result from macro-economic forces and institutional and environmental racism rather than simply individual rational choice; race and gender are both individually constructed and socially constrained; ethnic identity powerfully constrains individual agency but is not monolithic; urban space is an interpretive field, open to a mutually constitutive process of meaning production.[1] By privileging ethnography over theoretical abstraction, I hope to guide the reader to a more nuanced understanding of these critically important contributions anthropology has made to social theory. There will always be a need for theoretical monographs, but if we subordinate ethnography to theory, if we lose the empirical thread found in the stories of our informants, our theories become "thrice removed from reality, nothing more than semblances, easy to produce, with no knowledge of the truth."[2]

The style of ethnography I follow, if unusual, is nonetheless familiar because individual experience, particularly in the form of life histories, has long distinguished anthropology from other social sciences.[3] The life histories presented here are collaborative documents.[4] As products of my writing process, they are not strictly autobiographical. Even my own history, as presented in the final chapter, is subject to the parameters that I established for this project. I situate each of our stories in a historical and social framework by pinning the narratives to broad themes that emerged from interviews and the flow of events around East Harlem from the 1920s to the present. Scholarly and archival data reinforce the content of each narrative, just as each narrative guides the collection of external data. The result is "neither native nor nonnative history but simply history—in this case the history of a particular present."[5]

As a history of a particular present and an "ethnography of the particular,"[6] this book offers the stories of those who have settled in and carved out a space for themselves in one of the most diverse districts in New York City. Like Sidney Mintz's "Taso," none of the individuals in this book are public figures or famous. "In fact," except for their unique stories, they "might be described as quite average in nearly every way."[7] It is a contradiction, unique versus average, that can be resolved only in praxis, in the living out of myriad overlapping identities that constitute any given individual. Pete, José, and Lucille were all born in East Harlem. Maria, Mohamed, Si Zhi, and I were not. But all of us have lived through some portion of the story of East Harlem, and so certain themes will emerge: housing, education, population change, crime, and employment.

All of us, too, have lived out particular constellations of identities, and so no one story will stand in for all. There will be no easy generalizations, at least not those based on ethnic difference, which is why I have organized the chapters around demographic essentialisms—the Italians, the Puerto Ricans, the African Americans, the Mexicans, the West Africans, the Chinese—an intentional conflation of nationality, race, ethnicity, and regional identification meant to challenge our assumptions. The heart of each chapter is one individual, one tenant of this community, standing in for the whole but navigating a life that is both unique and representative. In these stories you may find the whole of human existence reduced to a single gesture, but more likely, you will find seven small strands of a much larger story that is still being told on the streets of my neighborhood.

ONE East Harlem

East Harlem sustains two ongoing and often competing narratives of urbanism: one inscribed in concrete and the other in flesh. People conform to the built environment just as the built environment conforms to people over the course of generations and centuries. The story of East Harlem is written in the sidewalks and storefronts, the abandoned buildings and corner bodegas, the public school yards and project courtyards as much as it is written in the lives of Puerto Ricans and African Americans, Italians and Mexicans, new immigrants and old. To understand East Harlem, one must understand how these two narratives fit together, how people transform the streets and how the streets transform the people.

Between 96th and 125th Streets, Fifth Avenue and the East River, East Harlem lies just beyond the printed boundaries of most tourist maps and the imaginations of most Manhattan residents. There, in little more than two hundred city blocks, live more than one hundred thousand people. Italian, Puerto Rican, African American, Mexican, West African, Chinese, and more than two dozen other national and ethnic groups constitute one of the most diverse communities in New York City.

What follows is a biography of the neighborhood, a dual narrative of place and people that extends through time but is limited to a very specific space. The people introduced in each chapter model the ethnic distinctions that divide the neighborhood. There is the old guard: Pete,[1] one of the last Italian holdouts on the same block as Rao's famous Italian restaurant; José, a second-generation Puerto Rican resident who fled the crime of the 1980s, only to return more committed than ever to El Barrio; and Lucille,[2] an African American living in the shadow of the *other* Harlem and standing up to the daily demoralizations of public housing. There are more recent immigrants who seem likely to change the face of the community as drastically as earlier arrivals: Maria,[3] an undocumented Mexican who has run the gauntlet of La Frontera, twice, to be a hairstylist in East Harlem; Mohamed, who came to New York from Guinea to open his own store just down the avenue from the mosque on 96th Street; and Si Zhi, a civil engineer from China whose night-shift job in the lobby of a Times Square hotel paid for his own building in the neighborhood. Finally, there are the newest immigrants to East Harlem, upwardly mobile whites fleeing downtown rent increases and settling in the newly renovated buildings that anticipated an expanding market. The new migration is most visible in the refurbished buildings, new commercial franchises, and new upscale restaurants featuring live jazz. But urban renewal comes at a price as Pete, José, Lucille, Maria, Mohamed, and Si Zhi face the looming uncertainty of market fluctuations and their ability to hang on in a moment of cataclysmic change.

East Harlem is a community defined by the attachments of its inhabitants. The life stories that I present explore how roots sink so deep so quickly in a community that has always hosted the city's most recent arrivals, how new immigrants challenge the claims of the old, and how that cycle is now threatened as never before by the specter of gentrification. But first, let us take a tour of the neighborhood.

BLOCK BY BLOCK . . .

An oversized concrete mosque dominates the corner of 96th Street and Third Avenue. Still unfinished but obviously thriving, the mosque is one of several institutions that mark the physical boundaries of the neighborhood. A few blocks away, between Second and First Avenues, stands Metropolitan Hospital, a large public institution that serves the majority of residents who have little or no health care coverage. On the opposite border, nestled in the most affluent corner of East Harlem on Fifth Avenue, lies Mt. Sinai Hospital. Mt. Sinai is an even larger voluntary hospital, serving the well-to-do of the Upper East Side and the few well insured of East Harlem. These buildings at the southern border of East Harlem mark off the barrio and stand out from the largely undifferentiated low-slung buildings of the neighborhood.

Standing next to the mosque, at the top of the hill on 96th Street that descends down into East Harlem, you can tell it's Friday by the black Lincoln Town Cars triple-parked along Third Avenue. The cars, lined up like a UN motorcade or a dignitary's funeral procession, wait for their owners to finish their afternoon prayers. They are the "gypsy cabs" that serve East Harlem and neighborhoods like it. The ubiquitous yellow taxis of Manhattan rarely cross the border at 96th Street without a paying customer already inside, usually headed for La Guardia Airport via the Triboro Bridge at 125th Street and First Avenue. Instead, the streets of East Harlem teem with the dark sedans of gypsy cab drivers, tapping their horns at each intersection to interest potential customers. The gypsy cabs are driven mostly by entrepreneurial West Africans who have managed to save enough cash to buy a car and work as illicit "wholesale" vendors on the streets. They offer reliable car service to local residents based on negotiated rates. With no meters and little regulation, the gypsy cabs are as illegal as street vendors, but the city has long abdicated control over this niche of the informal economy.

North along Third Avenue, past the mosque and Metropolitan Hospital, the street level is dominated by the thriving commerce of 99-cent stores, corner bodegas, discount clothing stores, and fast-food restaurants. Sidewalks, split by weather and speckled with spit and chewing gum, are crowded with merchandise spilling from the open doors of discount stores and the folding tables of temporary merchants. Sweat suits and evening gowns, underwear and overcoats hang on racks and lie in bins, selling two for one and guarded by employees lounging in chairs held together with duct tape and speaker wire. Music tumbles from windows above and cars below—salsa, soul, rap, and reggae—blending with the Spanish, English, Mandarin, and Wolof spoken and catcalled from the vendors and customers. The smells of snow cones and *bacalaito*, uncollected garbage and fresh-cut flowers combine. Jewelry stores, pawn shops, hardware stores, dry cleaners, liquor stores, and pharmacies mark the distance from one block to the next. There is now a McDonald's every seven blocks from 96th to 125th Street.

And there, at almost every corner, often obscured by dumpsters and scaffolding, are the public galleries of urban art. Some bear the scars of turf wars, the "tagging" of graffiti writers, but most display a more discrete mural art aesthetic. Many mark buildings with the portraits of entertainers, an homage to the rap artist Biggie Smalls or the salsa king Tito Puente. Others carry explicitly political themes, declaring Puerto Rican independence or protesting the bombing of Vieques. One artist dominates this genre, a young Puerto Rican named James de la Vega who has left his mark in religious, pop cultural, and art historical iconography throughout the neighborhood. But the most common form of public mural art is often the most transient, the RIPs, or Rest in Peace murals, that mark the sites of violence. The colorful collages of the deceased's likeness along with the symbols of the person's passions or an ode composed by a loved one serve as semipermanent reminders of loss. Most of these are charred by the soot of temporary altars fashioned from cardboard boxes, votive candles, and liquor bottles.

Above, the skyline is a low-lying, seven-story maximum, occasionally disrupted by the towering public housing projects at 98th, 106th, 110th, 112th, and 125th Streets. The lower buildings display an arresting array of color above the bacchanal of commerce at street level. Old tenements of green, blue, red, and white form orderly canyons, guiding the streets and avenues as they neatly dissect the neighborhood. Rising high above are the housing projects. The drab, muddy brick monoliths seem naked and unfinished, like foundation posts for some impossibly larger building. And the taller, more obtrusive buildings not only disrupt the riot of color; they also disrupt the orderly grid the older, smaller buildings work so hard to maintain. Organized around so-called superblocks, the housing projects razed micro-communities and closed off streets to create building complexes centered on green spaces. Heralded as a miracle of modern urban planning and a model for democratic housing, the projects were given names like Jefferson, Washington, and Johnson. But with no stores and no restaurants, the superblocks killed off the street life and quickly turned their green spaces into some of the most fearsome real estate in the city.[4]

The steady march north past short blocks and narrow streets is arrested at 106th Street, the first of two wide, two-way streets that intersect the neighborhood. On the corner of 106th Street and Third Avenue there are the telltale signs of relatively recent economic investment: KFC, Blockbuster, and a shiny new chain pharmacy. But there are also the indelible marks of the Puerto Rican community, the midcentury immigration trend that turned East Harlem into Spanish Harlem and El Barrio. La Fonda Boriqua sits just behind Blockbuster Video, serving up Puerto Rican comfort food to the local literati. And just down the street, at Lexington Avenue, is the heart of Puerto Rican East Harlem.

The 197-A Plan to revitalize East Harlem developed by the community board, calls the intersection of 106th Street and Lexington Avenue the "Cultural Crossroads." On one corner stands the Julia de Burgos Cultural Center, a somewhat controversial private enterprise that houses an upscale art gallery, music studio, and performance space. On Thursday nights the renovated public school building plays host to "Julia's Jam," an open mike event for Bomba y Plena music and Nuyorican poetry. Just next door is the spiritual anchor for the Latino Catholic community, St. Cecilia's Church. The large, ruddy red brick building dominates the block and still offers most of its services in Spanish. St. Cecilia's also houses Opus 118, the violin program made famous by Meryl Streep's film *Music of the Heart*. Across the street is Metropolitan Studios, new home to Black Entertainment Television. Facing St. Cecilia's Church and the Julia de Burgos Cultural Center, Metropolitan Studios is a physical reminder of the African American presence in the community, most notably in its highly rated video music program, "106th and Park."

West of the Cultural Crossroads, at 106th Street and Park Avenue, a third of East Harlem is sliced off by the elevated Metro North railway. Bursting from underneath the streets of the Upper East Side at 98th Street, the chunky granite and steel viaduct carries office-weary workers north to Westchester and beyond. Gliding across the cityscape at the roofline, commuters are carried swiftly over and through the neighborhood that was founded in part to house the workers that built the tracks. Down below, the arches carved through stone at each intersection gape like forbidden caves, daring pedestrians to enter their unlit murky passageways. Stalactites of unidentifiable ooze hang overhead, and the stench of human waste hurries most against the light and into oncoming traffic.

Back into daylight and on toward the western border, the institutional buildings of public housing, public schools, and the hinterlands of Mt. Sinai Hospital mark the way toward the northern edge of Central Park and the famed Museum Mile. On the right, a public school yard is an assault of color. The graffiti "wall of fame" was designed to channel the creative energy of so-called urban vandals. A rotating mishmash of style and theme, the ball court–turned–outdoor gallery stands as an open-air, contested counterpoint to the institutionalization of art and "culture" awaiting at Fifth Avenue.

Fifth Avenue, known as Museum Mile because of its elite institutions, includes the Guggenheim and the Met. But two museums mark the western boundary of East Harlem at Fifth Avenue: the Museum of the City of New York at 104th Street and El Museo del Barrio at 105th Street. Like the mosque and the hospitals that guard the southern border, these two institutions of history and art face the western approach. Both occupy grand buildings on the avenue, and both face the Conservatory Garden, one of the most secluded and peaceful gated gardens of Central Park. But each has its own relationship to the neighborhood: one a museum of New York that blurs the line between city and community; the other a museum of the community that redraws the lines of division through art and performance.

A few blocks north of the two museums, a small brick plaza redirects traffic around the corner of Fifth Avenue and 110th Street. Lifted high above the street on a platform supported by figures of nude women, Duke Ellington stands regally next to a baby grand piano. The monument anchors the southwest corner of Central Harlem, the capital of Black America, where Duke Ellington reigned as most influential musician. But Duke does not face Harlem. He gazes across the other half of that traffic circle, which remains starkly empty of any similar memorial, into East Harlem. When Tito Puente died just three years after the installation of the Duke Ellington statue, Puerto Ricans were quick to rename 110th Street Tito Puente Way, and plans were set in motion to erect a statue, facing Duke, of Tito and his timbales.

A few blocks east, past the trestle of the Metro North railway at Park Avenue, is the intersection of 110th Street and Lexington Avenue, perhaps the most infamous corner in East Harlem. In the 1980s this was the epicenter of the crack cocaine catastrophe that rocked New York City. Made infamous by Philippe Bourgois's book *In Search of Respect*, the corner has long been known by locals as a haunt for drug dealers and violence. Even the post office located at the intersection seems to echo this mystique with the ominous "Hell Gate Station" emblazoned above its entrance.

Since the beginning of the 1990s, the intersection of 110th and Lexington has made a slow climb out of disrepute. Thanks in part to an improved economy and more effective policing, the area has witnessed a few more of its abandoned buildings–cum–crack houses transformed into restaurants, grocery stores, and bodegas. Even the public library on 110th got a much-needed face-lift. Though drugs now change hands out of sight for the most part, the corner remains a constant reminder that East Harlem is a few subway stops and a world away from the rest of Manhattan.

Up the narrow canyon of Lexington Avenue, the thick odor of deep-fried food fills the air. Local *cuchifritos* entice pedestrians with greasy clear plastic facades filled with stacks of deep-fried fare distinguished only by size and shape. Chinese restaurants, most no wider than the door itself, serve up lo mein, chicken wings, and fried plantains to go, trying to keep up with the tastes of the neighborhood. And there is the ever-popular fast-food knockoff, like Kennedy Fried Chicken with its oddly familiar red-and-white logo, that offers the eponymous poultry along with pizza, burgers, and the occasional egg roll, all prepared behind the safety of Plexiglas. Plexiglas does a thriving business in East Harlem.

Nowhere is this more apparent than in the liquor stores that are as common in the neighborhood as intersections. Open later than most businesses, liquor stores are easy to spot at night, casting their fluorescent glow onto the sidewalk and street, collecting three or four loiterers like moths to a flame. Inside, the retail stores have the feel of a wholesale distributor, their wares displayed in bulk behind a wall of Plexiglas. Customers mill about in one or two lines, waiting for their turns at the plastic lazy Susan that spins away their money and spins back a bottle of Hennessey, Pisco, or wine.

Farther up the street you will likely find another mainstay in the local small business economy, the botanica. One-stop shopping for syncretic Catholicism, botanicas cater to the Old Country beliefs of older Puerto Rican immigrants. Window displays are public folk art museums, with effigies, icons, amulets, and artifacts. Inside, a busy Caribbean market brought indoors, bins full of herbs, pots for potions, and all manner of incendiary magic crowd the narrow aisles. Votive candles, slender glass holders filled with colored wax and painted with images of worship, are on offer for every occasion—one for a prayer to the Virgin Mary, another for St. Jude, and even one with a space for filling in a lottery number with a magic marker.

But the true mainstay of the East Harlem economy, the barrio equivalent of the general store, is the corner bodega. Entry-level operations in the formal economy, bodegas in East Harlem, as elsewhere in New York, are the last vestige of the mom-and-pop store in the homogenized city. They are the touchstones of micro-neighborhood identification.There is hardly a block without at least one bodega, hardly a bodega that doesn't serve one discrete, circumscribed urban space. They are the proscenium of storefront socialization. But for all their support of the individualized entrepreneurial spirit, bodegas thrive on their uniformity as much as Starbucks, Blockbuster, or KFC. They have the same colorful facades, announcing the same assortment of wares under the same emblem, the

"Deli Grocery" (don't look for the word *bodega* on the signage), the same racks of 50-cent snack food, the same cases of soda, the same deli counters, the same aisles of cleansers and toilet paper. And the same rules of exchange apply at each Plexiglas cashier's window: the wordless pantomime between customer and owner; prices dictated by the whim of the teller; and no need to form a line; if you know the price, just make sure the cashier can see your money laid out on the counter.

As you move from 110th Street up Lexington Avenue, you pass through the three-block-wide swath of public housing that was carved out of East Harlem from First Avenue to Lenox Avenue in Central Harlem to 116th Street, which marks the second of the two main east-west thoroughfares in the neighborhood. To the west, the elevated Metro North continues its trek along Park Avenue sheltering the defunct La Marqueta, a once-thriving Puerto Rican produce market. To the east, a noticeable shift in the street aesthetic begins to take hold. The red, white, and blue flags of Puerto Rican stalwarts give way to the green and red banners of Mexican newcomers.

If 106th Street marks the cultural crossroads of Puerto Rican East Harlem, 116th Street is the new nexus of Mexican East Harlem. Specialty groceries bathed in green and red offer imports from provincial outposts in the home country. Restaurants like La Hacienda let the ballads of northern Mexico fill the street, drowning out the salsa music from apartments upstairs. Travel agencies advertise one-way rates to Mexico City, Oaxaca, and Guadalajara. And just one block north stands another mark of Mexican East Harlem, a massive mural in the great tradition of Mexican muralists dedicated to the Zapatista movement in southern Mexico.

Farther east, 116th Street is brought up short against the concrete retaining walls of the FDR Parkway and the East River beyond—but not before crossing Pleasant Avenue, the last truncated stretch of concrete before the eastern border. From Jefferson Park at 114th Street to the Wagner housing project on 120th, Pleasant Avenue is still considered the Italian section of East Harlem. Here, in the quietest corner of East Harlem, the numbered streets dead-end into the parkway or the ruins of the abandoned wire factory that spreads over several blocks awaiting a new Home Depot and Costco wholesale club.

The stores at this eastern edge of East Harlem are a mix of commerce, but many still bear the marks of Italian Harlem: Ray's Italian Ice, Morrone's Bakery, or the original Patsy's, which still lures downtown pizza fetishists to its brick oven. Rao's remains the most famous landmark of a fading glory. Its thick red facade welcomes many of New York's elite, their limousines waiting to whisk them back safely to civilization after the second seating. Legend surrounds the place, rumors of a six-month waiting list and connections to the Genovese crime family, but most locals have never seen the inside. The stories themselves are probably more satisfying.

Despite the lasting fame of its eateries, the most defining features of Pleasant Avenue and its paved tributaries are its churches. A few neo-Gothic temples of Catholicism that once served an overcrowded Italian enclave now minister to the new wave of Latino faithful. Our Lady of Mt. Carmel remains the patroness of Pleasant Avenue, drawing back thousands of Italian Harlem expatriates for her annual feast day in July. Next door to her shrine on 115th Street, the new red brick National Museum of Catholic Art and History is set to replace the storefront version in the near future. But even the enshrined Catholicism has had to give way to Pentecostalism springing up in the shadows. The tumult of tambourines, guitars, and glossalalia crowds the solemn soundscape on Sundays and dominates during irregular prayer meetings throughout the week.

At 120th Street, Pleasant Avenue runs into Wagner Houses, a public housing project nestled in the shadows of the Triboro Bridge. Just the other side of its abandoned green space and seldom-used common areas lies 125th Street, the northern border of East Harlem. This is the last of the busy thoroughfares that divide the community into ten-block increments, and like its counterpart at 96th Street, it marks a palpable boundary between one world and the next.

West of Fifth Avenue, 125th Street, also known as Martin Luther King Jr. Boulevard, is Central Harlem's economic artery and cultural center. It is also the center of Central Harlem's economic development and urban renewal. Magic Johnson's movie theater and the Starbucks coffee shop formed a bulwark for future investment, and soon chain stores anchored the intersections of Malcolm X, Adam Clayton Powell, and

Frederick Douglass Avenues. It was and is a socioeconomic revolution that spread to Central Harlem's housing market and produced what some have called a second Harlem Renaissance. Unfortunately, for many, it has meant an erosion of African American influence over an eerily familiar frenzy of real estate speculation.

On the other side of Fifth Avenue, the East Harlem side of 125th Street, this trend is visible in the changing face of the built environment. The Metro North station at 125th Street, where the railway makes its last stop in Manhattan before heading out of the city, is a renovated art deco homage to the economic changes. One block east, a behemoth Pathmark supermarket caters to every need, leaving the bodegas and 99-cent stores to wither and fade, and a shiny new office complex waits in joyful hope that commuters will find the 125th Street station as convenient as Grand Central.

From 96th Street to 125th, Fifth Avenue to the East River, East Harlem block by block, bodega to liquor store, tenement to project. From the transformation at 96th to the transformation at 125th, the neighborhood is a study in contrasts, an assault on the senses that is unrelenting and always changing.

. . . AND PERSON BY PERSON

East Harlem cast in concrete is only half the story. Running alongside and often counter to it is the other half, the flesh and bone that has inhabited this rectangle of urban space day after day for the past few centuries. Inasmuch as this book is the story of those streets, it is also the story of these people. Moving in and out, over and under the sulking buildings and sagging sidewalks, the tenants of East Harlem have carved a life from this place, a life for themselves and for their neighbors.

Dividing up the streets into micro-communities, residents have long dug in and held fast to their corner of the neighborhood, filling each niche with the social clubs and restaurants, murals and flags that defend the claims of Italians against Puerto Ricans, of Puerto Ricans against Mexicans, of old-timers against newcomers. The streets, of course, know the bitter irony. The turf so zealously guarded by some today will be just as important to others tomorrow. It's a running joke among the silent participants, the buildings themselves: the concrete endures, but the people rarely last.

In these pages you will meet Pete, José, Lucille, Maria, Mohamed, Si Zhi, and me. We are the players: one life story for each of the streets and avenues that play host to a self-selected collective; one life story for each of the self-defined ethnic and national groups that dominate East Harlem.

In "Pleasant Avenue: The Italians," you will meet Pete, a third-generation Italian who was born on 114th Street near Pleasant Avenue in the 1920s. He's a small man with a shock of silver hair and the toothless grin of unassuming wisdom. His memories tumble out in vignettes of his mother sewing leather gloves in the basement, of his gang, the Seahawks, and their social club, of his building razed to make way for public housing projects, of his neighborhood changing before his eyes. Now Pete presides over 114th Street, just a block from his long-forgotten tenement birthplace, in his plaid-striped, folding lawn chair. Balanced precariously over the broken sidewalk in front of his building, Pete reads his *Daily News* and regales the non-Italian youth with stories of his East Harlem, Italian Harlem. "This used to be all Italian, only Italian," he will say from his chair, watching the children play in Jefferson Park across the street, "not like today."

Italians were the first dominant ethnic group of the twentieth century in East Harlem. As Pete likes to brag, "There were more Italians on 112th Street between First and Third than anywhere else in the country." German and Irish Catholics, who had settled earlier, were ruthless in their discrimination against the southern Italian immigrants,[5] but by the 1920s their numbers overwhelmed every other ethnic claim to the neighborhood. Many of the German and Irish Catholics, as well as European Jews, began to flee East Harlem.[6] This Italian territorial victory would not last long, however, as African Americans moved into the vacancies left by Europeans fleeing the Italian "invasion," and, just a decade later, the unprecedented influx of Puerto Ricans overwhelmed even the Italian claim to the neighborhood.

Today most of Pete's Italian neighbors and all of his family have long since died or moved away. Indeed, Pete's story demonstrates, perhaps more clearly than elsewhere, the complete cycle of intracity migration, from early influx to permanent settlement to upward mobility and abandonment. Part of this story is the story of public housing in New York—how visionary urban planners turned a thriving community into a demographic dumping ground in less than a decade. Pete is a witness to that transformation, but he is also a witness to the early history of Italian settlement along this avenue and its tributary streets, from the youth gang rumbles to the aging social clubs, establishing the well-worn pattern of ethnic immigration that echoes in each of the stories that follow.

In "106th Street: The Puerto Ricans," you will meet José. A scrappy Puerto Rican kid, José grew up, dodged gangs, and met his wife on the streets of East Harlem. After a tour in the army as far away as Staten Island and a brief sojourn in Florida during the crack cocaine epidemic of the 1980s, José returned to the neighborhood with his wife, Cecilia, to raise their children. Wearing a Day-Glo Jets jacket and carrying a digital camera, he is a permanent fixture on the streets around 106th Street now. José maintains a website for the community, www.east-harlem.com, an evolving ode to a patch of New York real estate that, for all intents and purposes, was annexed by Puerto Rico after Puerto Rico was annexed by the United States.

José was born in the 1950s, the decade of legend in Puerto Rican East Harlem. In the era after World War II, hundred of thousands of Puerto Ricans were encouraged to leave the island for the United States, New York City in particular. In the first year after the war, 39,000 Puerto Ricans made the journey, with an annual average of 50,000 in the next decade. Another 586,000 Puerto Ricans would leave the island for New York City in the 1960s.[7] It was a mass migration that rivaled that of the Italians before World War I, with two crucial differences. Since 1898 the United States has maintained an ambiguous claim on the island, and since 1952 Puerto Rico has remained in political limbo, neither wholly independent as a nation nor fully incorporated as a state.[8] The Puerto Ricans arriving in New York in the twentieth century were not immigrants like the Italians; they were southern migrants, no different in legal terms from

African Americans moving north after the Civil War. In addition, unlike turn-of-the-century immigrants who took advantage of a booming industrial economy, Puerto Rican settlers entered the labor market at a time when North America, especially New York City, was shifting from an industrial to a service-based economy.[9] This left many thousands of Puerto Rican newcomers at a distinct disadvantage.

José's story explores the institutionalization of Puerto Rican identity along the broad stretches of 106th Street, chronicling the transformation of East Harlem from an Italian to a Puerto Rican community and the way in which Puerto Rican newcomers managed to become the old guard in a few short decades. Unlike Italians, Puerto Ricans were citizen immigrants, a peculiar paradox that would haunt them into the twenty-first century. José's story focuses on the process of Puerto Rican entrenchment, playing on the ambiguous nationalism that stirs most of the local residents to shore up the boundaries of their community in the face of yet another wave of immigration. José is the face of these changes, born on the streets of East Harlem and fighting to hold on to El Barrio.

"125th Street: The African Americans" is Lucille's story. Sitting in the lobby of UPACA Gardens, Lucille presides with embittered optimism over the slow decline of public housing in the neighborhood. Born on 117th Street in East Harlem, she played double Dutch in the shadow of the elevated train, innocent of the struggle undertaken by her mother and grandparents in their move from the South. But when her mother died quietly in a Harlem social club, she was swept into a subsidized existence of welfare and public housing. A young woman with a daughter of her own and two brothers to care for, Lucille refused to take help for granted. She created a youth center in the basement of her building and more than thirty years later still sits tenant patrol in the evenings. The tenements of her childhood are all gone now, replaced with upscale townhouses and priced out of reach, but she can still see what once was—street life as community, the extended family of neighbors and friends.

African Americans settled east of Fifth Avenue long before the first housing projects were built in the 1940s and before Puerto Rican migration began in earnest. The post-Reconstruction mass migration of African Americans out of the southern United States and into the industrialized

North radically transformed the demographics of cities like New York, and upper Manhattan became an enclave community from the first years of the twentieth century. The reputation of Central Harlem as the capital of Black America is now well ensconced, and at the turn of the century Fifth Avenue was not the discrete boundary it is today. East Harlem, though at the time already considered a European ghetto with thousands of Irish, German, and Italian settlers, was close enough to the excitement of the Harlem Renaissance for thousands of African Americans to put down roots. Indeed, Central Harlem remained the center of African American attention, even as Italians and then Puerto Ricans established the Fifth Avenue boundary throughout the twentieth century.

Lucille represents the African Americans who have long debated the Puerto Ricans as to the ethnic character of East Harlem and its relationship to Central Harlem. Since 1990, with urban renewal driving more and more African Americans out of Central Harlem, non-Hispanic black residents have added more than six thousand newcomers, while Puerto Ricans have actually lost more than seven thousand.[10] This leaves East Harlem Puerto Ricans at a numerical disadvantage compared to non-Hispanic black residents for the first time since the 1940s. Lucille's story examines this slow-burning rivalry between African Americans and Puerto Ricans, revealing the cultural abdication from East Harlem by many African Americans who still feel a stronger connection to Central Harlem and exposing the peculiar constructions of racial identity that blur the boundaries between two groups bent on division.

"116th Street: The Mexicans" introduces Maria. An eager young woman with an eye to the future, she scrambled across the Arizona desert in the mid-1990s to earn funds to build her mother a home in Mexico. After a brief stint as a housekeeper in New Jersey, Maria moved in with friends in East Harlem. She leased a chair in a neighborhood barber shop and began putting a decade of salon training to use. Now she shares a one-bedroom apartment off Second Avenue with two brothers, a cousin, and a husband she met in the neighborhood. The steady stream of relatives through their cramped apartment joins the larger flood of Mexican immigrants to East Harlem—a promising sign for Maria's business as non-Mexicans in the neighborhood often refuse to sit in her chair.

Since 1990 the Mexican population in East Harlem has increased by more than 350 percent, while the Puerto Rican population has decreased by 17 percent. Based on the latest census, there are now more than ten thousand Mexicans living in East Harlem, which does not include undocumented migrants who refused to participate in the count. This is only part of a citywide phenomenon of Mexican immigration in the past couple of decades. Between 1980 and 1990 Mexican immigration to New York more than doubled. Between 1990 and 2000 it more than tripled. Most of these new immigrants come from southern Mexico, a region known as Mixteca, but the newest trend in Mexican immigration is from an area near Mexico City called Ciudad Nezahualcoyotl, or "Neza." In 1992, 15 percent of Mexican migrants came from Neza; today the figure is closer to 25 to 30 percent.[11] In East Harlem undocumented migrants from Mixteca and Neza fill the remaining tenement buildings, and resourceful entrepreneurs have concentrated their Mexican groceries, restaurants, and record stores on 116th Street.

Maria's story examines the new and ongoing process of settlement for one of the neighborhood's newest immigrant groups, bringing a discrete Latino nationalism that competes directly with the Puerto Rican claim to the "Spanish" of Spanish Harlem. Her story allows for a thorough treatment of undocumented migration and the clash of inter-Latino identities that characterizes much of contemporary urban demographics in the United States.

In "Third Avenue: The West Africans," I introduce Mohamed, who arrived in New York from Guinea in 1991. He is a tall, mustachioed man who looks much younger than his forty years. Always ready with an easy smile, Mohamed's natural countenance is a studied seriousness that is always looking to the future. Like most men his age, he left West Africa to secure a place in the burgeoning traders' market of New York. Tribal tradition encouraged an educated profession, medicine or law, but Mohamed broke with his lineage and the past to enter business. Starting out as a messenger on the streets of lower Manhattan, Mohamed eventually opened his own 99-cent store on Third Avenue in East Harlem.

West African immigration is one of the most recent events in the demography of New York City. The devaluation of the West African franc in 1994 reduced the standard of living in the Francophone nations by 50 percent almost overnight, forcing professional traders to liquidate inventory and set off for more lucrative markets. The West African population in New York doubled between 1990 and 1996, and though they are still far fewer in number than other immigrant groups, West Africans have become a visible presence as vendors on the streets of the city.[12] Like Italians at the turn of the twentieth century, many West Africans at the turn of this century are transient tradesmen, spending three to six months in the United States before returning for a similar period in Africa. Unlike the Italians and most other groups, West Africans have not established a concentrated urban settlement but rather follow a dispersed pattern of residence throughout the metropolitan area. This is a result in part of the diversity of West African points of origin. Most arrive from Ghana and Nigeria, but many more are arriving from the Francophone countries of Senegal, Guinea, Mali, and Niger. Though some West Africans have taken up residence in East Harlem, most commute to their businesses on Third Avenue from Central Harlem, Queens, or New Jersey.

Mohamed's story reflects the lives of West African commuters and settlers, probing their connections to the community and their hopes for the future. For many, Third Avenue is one great pedestrian mall, worth the commute after being pushed off 125th Street by the city and by African American store owners who resented the competition. For others, those who have moved from the folding table to the storefront, East Harlem is home, the crucible of the American Dream conceived years ago and thousands of miles away.

"Second Avenue: The Chinese" presents Si Zhi's story. Si Zhi is thin and wiry, with a generous smile. His thick Shanghai accent obscures his English only half as much as he thinks it does, but then he is a perfectionist. Si Zhi built ships as a civil engineer in Shanghai, and he brought his precision and attention to detail, along with his wife and daughter, with him when he arrived in New York a dozen years ago. But the language barrier precluded a career in engineering, or even unionized construction, and he found work cleaning out dirty ashtrays in the sleek lobby of a Times Square hotel. As with many of his compatriots, his first apartment was in an overcrowded tenement building near Chinatown.

After several years of hard work and sacrifice, he was able to buy a three-family townhouse in East Harlem, part of a real estate initiative to make home ownership easier for low-income families. He still works the night shift at the hotel, and during the few daylight hours he enjoys, he is still busy perfecting his new home.

Chinese settlement in the United States is older than that of most of the groups represented in these chapters. Thousands of ethnic Chinese migrated to the West Coast in the nineteenth century, mostly as manual labor for the growing industrial economy. New York did not see comparable numbers of Chinese settlers until well into the twentieth century. A change in immigration law in the 1960s removed quotas on specific sending regions, and this turned the tide of Chinese immigration to New York City. Documented immigration from China, Hong Kong, and Taiwan jumped from 110,000 in the 1960s to 445,000 in the 1980s. In the 1980s and 1990s there were an average 12,000 new Chinese immigrants settling in New York City each year. Chinatown, on Manhattan's Lower East Side, once contained almost all ethnic Chinese New Yorkers in ten square blocks, but after the 1960s Chinese settlers spread beyond the boundaries of Chinatown and into all five city boroughs, especially Brooklyn and Queens. By the 1990s new immigrants were arriving from nontraditional areas in mainland China, including Beijing and Shanghai, which historically retained its residents.[13] Global economic restructuring and changes in Chinese politics loosened the flow of migrants. Si Zhi left from Shanghai just after the Tiananmen Square standoff in 1989.

Si Zhi's story offers insight into the impact of these new trends in immigration from mainland China and the strategies for creating a sense of place in a nontraditional settlement area. East Harlem is not a Chinese enclave. In fact, their numbers compared to those of the other groups included in this book are quite small. But their presence is felt in both housing and small business ownership. In telling Si Zhi's story, I explore how he and others like him maintain a sense of community that reaffirms transnational ties without abdicating a connection to their host country. Si Zhi manages this paradox quite well: he recently purchased a condominium in a luxury high-rise in downtown Shanghai for his annual trips "home," and in 2002 his daughter enrolled at West Point Academy.

The last chapter, "Urban 'Renewal' and the Final Migration," is my story, for I am the face of what could be the final migration. I moved to East Harlem with my wife in 1999. Together we started a local nonprofit organization, and I taught part-time around the city. East Harlem was the ideal site for our vision of cooperative art education and, we hoped, the ideal site to put down roots in a city notorious for spitting out young idealists. But it was not intended as a research site.

Not long after settling into the neighborhood, I became involved with the local community board and began to establish a network of contacts for our nonprofit. We were committed to local leadership and put together a board of directors from local residents. Our insular focus proved, in the end, a fiscal disaster, but in terms of our own attachment to the community, it was an overwhelming success. Neighbors became friends, and friends became confidants as we all struggled to make a place for ourselves in the always-changing neighborhood. I began to see the contours of ethnic allegiance through the individuals I knew on the streets, in the stores, and on the community board. Their stories became more and more compelling, and eventually, writing them down was unavoidable.

Through it all, we were seldom made aware of our own ethnic difference. The occasional "Evening, officer!" called out by a group of teenagers hardly bothered me, and I could even ignore the more rarely mumbled "Fucking white people" as we walked past. But as the 1990s became the new millennium, it was harder to ignore the more frequent sightings of white folks moving into the neighborhood. East Harlem was still a gritty, urban space, but even that was changing as new restaurants and chain stores slowly began to appear.

East Harlem has changed significantly since the startling increase in crime reported by Bourgois in the 1980s.[14] Indeed, crime has actually dropped by as much as 64 percent. With less open violence, reinvestment was inevitable as developers sought to "reclaim" a corner of Manhattan, arguably the most desirable real estate in the country. As one real estate agent recently explained, "It's the rock, the green rock!" Most streets still boast at least one derelict building, but these are being replaced by new businesses and upscale or mixed-income residences at a quickening pace. One census tract in particular, consisting of four square blocks in the southwestern corner of the neighborhood, tells the story. With a per capita income of $53,039, the residents of census tract 160.02 earn more than four times the East Harlem average, and its residents, 63 percent of whom are non-Hispanic whites, do not look like the rest of the community. While most East Harlem residents can still point out bullet holes in cracked facades and still speak of the previous decades in the weary tones of veterans, all agree the neighborhood is changing.

This chapter tells my story and that of others like me who are caught in a paradox of urban renewal that makes way for the upwardly mobile by displacing the recently settled. I met Maria at the barbershop on my street, Mohamed runs the 99-cent store on my corner, and Si Zhi is my landlord. These are my neighbors, and I represent an economic force that could change everything. My role in the drama completes the cycle of street-level contradictions in East Harlem, how roots sink deep without the strength to hold firm and locals form attachments in this always-changing community.

Our stories are as representative as any; that is to say, none speak for all, but all of us speak with authenticity, with the authority of experience. In each you will find the cords that tether our stories to the stories of those we represent, the history of our entrenchment and the hopes for our future. In each you will find the ties that bind us all to East Harlem, the story of one community in one city that is as unique as it is universal.

TWO

Pleasant Avenue

Pete is in his office. On a folding lawn chair just a few feet from the curb, the *Daily News* tucked into a low-hanging branch above his head, he watches children hurry home after school to change into their costumes. It's Halloween, and though it is still early in the day, the October sun has descended behind the towering housing projects on First Avenue. Pleasant Avenue and 114th Street turn cold in the shadow of the pale brick structures.

A few feet away, a crowd of young men, primarily Puerto Rican and African American, gather in front of Danny's, a small clothing shop on an otherwise residential street. Pete doesn't pay much attention, glancing only now and then when one or another turns up the stereo in a parked car or yells an obscenity. Danny, the round, dark-skinned proprietor, regales a few young men with political diatribes but mostly sits in his swivel chair watching them hang out on the stoop.

Farther down the block, the Holy Tabernacle Church is setting up for a prayer meeting. Well-heeled parishioners make their way up the steps and into the outsized building, sandwiched between nineteenth-century tenements. Most of the faithful have driven in for church, as few members of the African American congregation actually live in the neighborhood.

Pete shifts his chair to face Jefferson Park across the street, turning his back on the distractions of Danny's and Holy Tabernacle. Behind him, Nancy, well dressed and in her early forties, ambles down from First Avenue with her six-year-old daughter, Carolanne. Stepping quietly behind him, Nancy taps Pete on the shoulder.

"Oh!" Pete shouts with a start. He turns and rasps, "How are you!?"

His voice strains against his age, like a rope that's frayed but still strong. The words tumble over his few remaining teeth.

"My goodness, all I did was touch you. Am I so electrifying?" Nancy snorts.

"Oh, you are. Just the thought of you is electrifying! How are you? You gonna have a party tonight?" Pete's thick neighborhood New York accent complements Nancy's Puerto Rican lilt as the two banter back and forth.

"No, I'm taking the girls just around here. I'm gonna dress them now."

"Oh yeah? I'm gonna be on the run tonight so . . ." Pete smoothes the lapels of his double-breasted blazer.

"Oh yeah? You looking really sharp today," Nancy says encouragingly.

In fact, Pete has just returned from a funeral. Another friend from the neighborhood passed away in his sleep, and Pete, as usual, paid his respects. His tousle of hair has been combed back and weighted down, and his autumn stubble has been shaved away. His clear, blue eyes stare out through oversized glasses, and his two or three teeth jut out at odd angles when he smiles, but all told, Pete does look sharp today.

"Are you just gonna hang out in the neighborhood tonight?" Pete asks.

"Yeah."

"Maybe I'll hang out tonight. I could go downtown maybe later. I'll catch up with you tomorrow."

Pete stands to retrieve his paper from the tree branch as Nancy herds Carolanne toward the door to their building. Once the barracks of Italian Harlem, the few remaining prewar buildings now house the relative newcomers, Puerto Ricans and African Americans, along with the even more recent West Africans, Asians, and whites.

Pete barely looks up from his paper when Fannie, another Italian hold-out from the old days, steps onto the sidewalk in her housecoat to see the day turn to dusk. Children crowd the street now, dressed up in flimsy costumes from the 99-cent store around the corner and filing between Pete and Fannie in their quest for sweets. Fannie smiles and waves at a few of them before retreating inside. Pete lets the paper rest in his lap and watches the miniature procession.

.   .   .   .   .

"My folks came in 1922," Pete explains, leaning in close for effect. He repositions his large blue-framed glasses and rubs his chin, but it's his singular voice that grabs your attention. Raw and overused, it is the thick accent of an old matinee mobster, even as he waves to the children that wander past.

Pete's parents arrived in New York as husband and wife in the dwindling years of southern Italian migration. Years before their arrival, Italians and European Jews had outpaced the Irish and Germans as the dominant immigrant groups. Between 1880 and 1910 the number of Italian immigrants in New York City climbed from just 12,000 to more than 340,000—about 80 percent of them from southern Italy. By that time Italian and European Jewish immigrants made up almost one-fifth of the total population of New York. In fact, one-fourth of all Italian immigrants to the United States settled in New York City in the first decade of the twentieth century.[1] Many of these new arrivals found the Lower East Side already overcrowded and made their way north to East Harlem, known then as Italian Harlem.

Pete's mother had enjoyed a comfortable life in Naples. "My mother's family, they had a business of all manufacturers. My mother had a hairdresser every morning. They had it good. One of the brothers went to Sardinia, practically ran Sardinia." But despite the good life his mother enjoyed, most Italians were burdened with a new wage-labor economy, escalating taxes, and little access to farmland. It was Pete's father who decided to move his new bride to the United States, to join most of her brothers, who had found their way to New York as early as 1911.

"My uncle was the patriarch. He started here in 1911, then went down to Mott Street. He moved out to Ozone Park." Ozone Park? Pete offers a dismissive wave toward the East River. "Out that way, over in Queens. The youngest brother, on my mother's side, opened a big distributorship, cheese and oil, on Mott and Grand."

Ask Pete why his parents settled in East Harlem instead of with a brother on Mott Street or in Ozone Park, and he'll tell you, " 'Cause everybody came to East Harlem!" By the 1920s most new immigrants went directly to upper Manhattan or Brooklyn, areas described as "secondary settlements," though they were as isolated and neglected as Mott Street or the Lower East Side.[2] Pete's parents moved immediately to 112th Street. By 1937 the Mayor's Committee on City Planning called East Harlem "probably the largest Italian colony in the Western Hemisphere."[3] Pete's parents quickly contributed to the growing number of Italians: his older sister was born shortly after their arrival.

Two years after Pete's parents arrived, the Johnson-Reed Immigration Act of 1924 radically transformed the openness of the United States to the huddled masses of distant shores. As early as 1911 legislators had been pushing for an ethnicity-based quota system for immigration as recommended by the United States Immigration Commission in its forty-one-volume report of that year. In 1921 a temporary, one-year measure was passed that set the first numerical limits for all immigrants, including Europeans. That law was extended two years, until the more comprehensive and restrictive Johnson-Reed Immigration Act was passed in 1924. The law codified the xenophobia of post–World War I America, limiting immigration to 2 percent of the total population of each immigrant nationality according to the census of 1890.[4] In the following years, the formula would be tweaked according to the politics of international relations, but the overall effect was an abrupt end to the massive numbers of European immigrants arriving in New York during the turn of the last century.

For forty years, the United States would strictly control the flow of migrants, making few exceptions and allowing Italians to settle into a seldom-contested cultural dominance over East Harlem. One of those exceptions was Puerto Rico, an island of legal citizens of the United States and a force for change in East Harlem that would eventually supplant the Italian claim on the neighborhood.

By the time of the Johnson-Reed Immigration Act, Pete's parents and sister had moved to 114th Street, the same street Pete presides over now in his folding lawn chair. Pete was born on the ground floor of a tenement building on 114th Street between First and Second Avenues, a spacious apartment for that era that his father rented from a fellow Neapolitan immigrant.

Pete's family was fortunate in their living arrangement. As he explains, "The landlord loved my father, my family. We had the whole first floor." Pete has a wistful gleam in his eye whenever he speaks of the neighborhood before World War II, especially the buildings: "When I was a youngster I had my own room. That's the way it was, that building. That particular building was like that. We had separate bathrooms, almost seven rooms."

As late as 1930, housing in East Harlem consisted of Old Law Tenements, with shared bathrooms and no running water.[5] While developers were busy replacing most of Manhattan's housing stock with New Law Tenements and high-rise apartment buildings, most residents of East Harlem were still surviving without central heating or private bathrooms. "Yes, we used to have shared bathrooms," recalls Pete. "It was a shared bathroom, but it was sealed, then we had our own bathroom they made. Sometimes you had bathrooms in the hallway. I was small, but I remember."

By 1930 New York City had already passed several Tenement House Acts designed to regulate the infamous living conditions of the vast majority of residents.[6] The earliest, the Tenement House Act of 1867, legally defined a tenement as any building occupied by more than three families or by more than two families per floor. The law required such basic safety and health provisions as fire escapes and at least one water closet for every twenty tenants. But the law was seldom enforced, which led eventually to a much more stringent revision, the Tenement House Act of 1879. It required that no new building occupy more than 65 percent of a standard 25-by-100-foot lot, and this proved far more controversial than fire escapes or water closets. The costs associated with land purchase and construction made any design under 80 percent coverage untenable. The compromise between developers and the city resulted in enforcement of the old law, producing the familiar Old Law Tenements that still stand throughout East Harlem and other niches of Manhattan.

Another radical attempt to regulate housing construction in 1901 produced the New Law Tenement, which strictly enforced no more than 70 percent lot coverage, as well as running water in every apartment. The new law forced more creative solutions in architectural design, including the development of three or more lots at once to provide the most efficient use of space. These larger building projects attracted more established architectural firms, which produced higher-quality housing. But the Tenement House Act of 1901 applied only to new construction, and there was little enforcement of new building codes in older buildings, especially in neighborhoods like East Harlem.

Pete still remembers the days before central heating, when he had to carry drums of kerosene to the stove for heat in the winter: "You made your heat, oil burners, coal stoves. We had a kerosene stove, which was dangerous. I had to go get five gallons of kerosene. Stoves were made for that purpose. Steam came in 1940 where I was." But despite these anachronistic living conditions, the concrete fabric of the place always moved him. "That building had tile floors, marble, brass pipes. They were beautiful brownstones, with stoops and brass railings." The few remaining Irish and Germans, those who hadn't yet moved on to Long Island or New Jersey in the cycle of upward mobility, were often landlords themselves if not prominent businessmen. Pete still remembers how many cared for their properties in a way seldom seen today: "I used to see those Germans polishing the brass."

Sights and sounds come flooding back. Pete remembers the horse and wagon of the milkman. "You used to hear them at two o'clock in the morning. The horses and their hooves. And La Guardia made them put rubber around the wheels because they were making too much noise when people were sleeping."

Most of Pete's childhood was colored by the Great Depression of the 1930s. With the halcyon memory of childhood, Pete remembers even the hardship with a kind of fondness: "We used to go swimming in the East River, and it was dirty, a sewer pipe used to run out in there. We were kids, what did we know? There were barges in the middle of the river. Coal barges were anchored there. Guys used to swim to it, to the barge. There were big water rats. Water rats, not one, packs of them. Down here, by the sewer. It was a pier, a concrete pier, that's all it was. These conditions were all over New York at the time."

Pete's world did not stretch very far beyond 114th Street, Second Avenue, and the East River. Though there was the occasional journey to see his maternal uncles down in lower Manhattan or Queens, Pete stayed close to the front stoop of his tenement. Pete saw those who traveled outside Italian Harlem, like his father, as the adventurers, the intrepid journeymen who sailed from port out into the unknown. But this is more than a metaphor. Pete still remembers the old ferry port around the corner from his apartment: "There was a ferry on 116th. It went to the island. People were working. I used to sit there and watch the people get on the boat, watching the boat go back and forth, watching the people get on and off. They were working on that island someplace. I was a kid, what did I know?"

Work at that time was a scarce commodity. For many immigrants in East Harlem, consistent, gainful employment could be as strange and mysterious an activity as it was to Pete sitting on the pier. Work was short term and low paying, employing the unskilled for weeks or, more often, days at a time. Everyone, it seemed, was looking for an angle. "We used to have to put money into the meter for Con Edison to get electricity, and they took advantage of the people. Guys in the service of Con Edison used to come and take coins out of the box and say, 'You owe more money.' 'No, I put it in.' 'No, you were cheating.' They were vicious."

Women especially found it difficult to contribute to the domestic coffers. Those who could work did so as seamstresses on a piecework basis.

Making paper flowers or sewing dresses provided a few extra cents each week and often allowed them to stay at home with their children. Even before the depression years, more than a third of Italian women did industrial homework.[7] Pete's mother was no exception.

"My mother was a glove maker," he explains, "She made gloves. We had the machines in the rooms, off the kitchen and everything. You had to improvise, you have to make room. They were works of art, those machines." Pete still remembers the clatter of the cast iron machines, surely a rare capital investment for any woman at the time. He also remembers serving as an employee in his mother's enterprise: "We all used to pitch in. I used to put the thumbs together, and my sister did stitching. I used to bring them to the factory and everything." In the hushed tone of deep reverence, he talks about his mother's talents: "Now when I say my mother was a glove maker, these were special gloves, elegant, ladies' gloves. My mother used to teach people how to make gloves. My mother used to sing, all day. I still remember the songs. My mother was a good singer. Beautiful, the old days."

His father, though somewhat of a mystery to Pete, worked where and when he could, like most men in the 1930s. "My father? Driving around the country trying to make a living. He got into the cheese importing business, cheese and olive oil. At the time he had a truck. He drove to California and back. Covered the states. Then he went into the fruit and vegetable business. I went with him when I was a baby. He had some tough times."

There were tough times, but there was always the consolation of his mother's family. His father's family, most of whom remained in Italy, were distant and hazy relations, but his mother's brothers were intimately involved in his enculturation. Well established and financially secure throughout the depression years, Pete's maternal uncles were his most vivid experience of Italian familial loyalty.

Pete recalls, "In Ozone Park, the clan used to meet. My uncle had a dining room table like the knights of old. It was made of tile, massive and oak. A big backyard, fig trees, peaches, plums. The house is still there. He was the oldest brother of my mother. They all congregated there. He used to take people off the street to come in. He was very benevolent. People used to come from all over to visit him."

This stateside patriarch, Pete's eldest uncle, attained such a regal life in no small part because of his experience as a skilled laborer in Italy. As a mason, he and another brother were immediately more employable than the vast majority of unskilled labor that was migrating from Italy at the turn of the century. As Pete explains, "They were masons. My grandfather used to build churches, he was suppose to be 'it' in Naples. They say my uncle was superior than him, that he could have carved your picture out of stone." Whereas most newly arrived Italians found what work they could in construction and manufacturing, Pete's uncles joined the older population of Irish and German laborers who had moved up the ranks of skilled employment. According to Pete, "He and another uncle of mine took part in [the] building of the Empire and the Chrysler. They worked on the Empire State Building and the Chrysler Building."

.   .   .   .   .

From his chair on 114th Street, Pete waves hello to Lynn, another neighbor. Children in their Halloween costumes are wending their way back home, loaded down with candy, their parents in tow. Lynn asks Pete, "You mind watching my kids while I run upstairs?"

The kids are two boys under ten playing in the backseat of a parked SUV. "Sure thing, Lynn," Pete replies and shuffles over to the truck. "She's the wife of a friend of mine," Pete explains. "That son over there, when he don't see me, he sees my chair, he comes and hugs the chair, 'Pete's chair!'" Pete laughs. "When they went upstate, they came back and got me a little pumpkin."

Pete watches the other children file past, keeping one eye on his temporary charges. "When we were between First and Second, I always used to come down this block. Come down here, go to Pleasant Avenue, and go to the Colonial Tea Room there on Pleasant Avenue. Everybody in the city used to go there. Used to be hundreds of people out there at night. It was at 116th off of Pleasant Avenue. It's no more. I used to be in there morning, afternoon, and night. When I was a young man."

The Colonial Tea Room, Sloppy Mike's, Aida's—these were the neighborhood hot spots of the 1940s, thriving social institutions before the advent of public housing and the scourge of slum clearance. As a young man, Pete socialized on the streets. "Me, I was all over this neighborhood. I was everybody's son. I mingled with the people down there, the girls and everything and whatnot. They see me, and I was their son too. The old woman may be sitting outside, I was one of their sons." Like most of his friends, he haunted the candy stores, social clubs, and lounges of Italian Harlem. "One time, my mother says, 'Where is he? Where is he? Where's my son?' Pop says, 'Aw, go to sleep. Don't worry. I can hear him from over here, he's singing in Aida's.'"

But for all his wide-ranging familiarity with the neighborhood, Pete stayed close to the all-important block. On 114th Street, between First and Second Avenues, home spilled out the front door of the tenement, down the stoop with polished brass railings, into the candy store, social club, or street, to include all the young people on the block.

Pete remembers, "Each block had their own stickball teams, had their jackets and everything. They were the Seahawks, they were the Eagles, they were the Falcons. We had our own. We were the Seahawks. We had a jacket and everything." The Seahawks presided over 114th Street from Second Avenue to First and had their own official headquarters in a storefront social club. "I got the picture somewhere of me standing alongside the club. It was a storefront, it had a jukebox. You paid dues. What was it? One dollar, two dollars. You paid the landlord the rent. The rent was negligible. For the time, you know. You had a jukebox in there, maybe a little pool table, cards and everything."

The social clubs of the infamous youth gangs of Italian Harlem were the fonts of much-publicized delinquency and, eventually, it was said, of organized crime. Certainly some of the young people crowded into Old Law Tenements would turn to crime in later years, as evidenced by "Fat Tony" Salerno and the Genovese crime family that operated out of a storefront social club on 115th Street as late as the mid-1980s. But much of East Harlem's reputation was built on the sensationalism of overeager journalists, and there were far fewer street rumbles or youth riots than newspapers seem to portray.[8] The social clubs of Pete's youth were more like extensions of overcrowded apartments, a space over which young people could have some real control.

The innocence of street life at that time is illustrated in the other street-bound hangout, the candy store. "Across the street there was a candy store. I was sixteen, seventeen. The candy store was the hangout. In the old days in the candy store we used to have potbellied stoves we used to stand around to keep warm. But candy stores we had, we had one, two, three candy stores up that block. It was a lot of guys, lot of girls, lot of people on the block."

When Pete wasn't on the street or helping his mother stitch together ladies' gloves, he was in school. Like most teenagers, Pete was ambivalent about his classes, but education proved one of the most galvanizing issues for the Italian immigrant community in East Harlem and its relationship to the city. This would be true for African Americans and Puerto Ricans throughout the second half of the twentieth century, as East Harlem played host to the ongoing debate over public education in New York. But at the time Pete entered school, one Italian led the charge. His name was Leonard Covello.

Covello immigrated with his parents from southern Italy to East Harlem in the late nineteenth century. After years of hard living on the streets of the neighborhood, Covello placed his considerable energy and talents at the service of the community. "Leonard Covello said we need a high school for the people in this neighborhood," Pete explains. "He opened an annex on 108th Street, now it's a residential building on 108th near Second Avenue. On 109th Street you can see it. It says Leonard S. Covello Senior Citizen's Center now, but that was the school."

With the help of local politician-cum-mayor Fiorello La Guardia, Covello secured funding for Benjamin Franklin High School in East Harlem. Fighting against a prevailing sentiment that the working poor of East Harlem could do no better than a vocational training school, Covello established a school with "all the dignity of a seat of learning."[9] After several years in storefronts and annex buildings, Benjamin Franklin High School was opened in 1942 on Pleasant Avenue between 114th and 116th Streets, just around the corner from where Pete sets his chair. "I came here when this was completed. That was Benjamin Franklin High School."

The brick and concrete domed building still sits regally on the East River, looking west down 115th Street past Mt. Carmel Church toward St. John the Divine Cathedral and Columbia University several avenues away. "I took a walk in there a couple of years ago," Pete recalls. "They took one look at me and said, 'You must have gone here.' I said, 'I most certainly did.' "

The building looks the same when Pete revisits now and then, and in some ways, so do the students. There are fewer Italians walking the halls, but the overall ethnic diversity of the school today was at the heart of Covello's vision for Franklin High School. And by the 1940s East Harlem was becoming more and more diverse.

"There was a lot of tension between Blacks and PRs [Puerto Ricans]. There was tension between Italians and, not so much in this immediate area, you know, but there was a lot of tension between Italians and PRs."

Pete did not live in fear of race riots or violent gangs organized around discrete ethnicities. Youth gangs were street based, which may or may not have been predominantly Italian, Puerto Rican, or African American, and they rarely provoked the violence for which East Harlem and similar immigrant neighborhoods are famous. According to Pete, "There may have been conflict, you know, in times past," but violence usually occurred because of "individual provocations," not ethnic gang warfare.

Pete recalls isolated incidents, however, moments when ethnic difference marked clear divisions in the community. "Back around somewhere in the forties, I was on Lexington Avenue. Some blacks corralled me on 116th and Lexington Avenue. They said, 'What are you doing here?' I says, 'What are you, a wise guy?' He says, 'Answer me.' I can still see his face. I says, 'You looking for trouble, you wait right here. I'll be back.' And I went down to the movie house. That was in 1944, I think, or '43."

Pete also remembers an incident with some Puerto Ricans at Sloppy Mike's, the prewar lounge frequented by Italians. "These two guys come in with girls. Guy turns around, and says, 'Nice girls, huh?' And I says, 'Yeah they're nice.' So he says I'm provoking him, 'You don't like my girl?' I says, 'Look fellow, you can't just have a nice time? Enjoy yourself. She's your girl. I have no eyes for your girl.' One thing led to another, and it went out to the street." The incident still troubles Pete, and at least in this case, the easiest explanation is rooted in ethnic mistrust and stereotypes. "I mean, what are you provoking something like that for? They were Spanish. Whacko. Great provocateurs. Trying to force their girls on me. I mean, this was uncalled for."

But by the 1940s Puerto Ricans were the new Italians, and Pete found himself in a position of power over a new immigrant population by virtue of his tenure. He can still remember a young Puerto Rican girl and her cousin who found themselves on 114th Street: "They were afraid. They were Puerto Ricans, and her and her cousin were afraid, you know, 'Those Italians are gonna hurt us.' And they turn around and says, 'Look at that fellow by the candy store. He's standing in the front, the one with the big hat with the brim, he won't let nobody touch us.' That was me, in the hat."

These confrontations were nothing new. Ethnic succession often precipitates ethnic conflict. Irish and German settlers were relentless in their discrimination against early Italian immigrants, and in turn, Italians defended their turf from newly arrived African Americans and Puerto Ricans. Some of Pete's earliest memories are of confrontations with non-Italians: "When I was a little boy, I was skating around over there by the library on 110th Street. I was about nine or ten years old. These black kids came up to me, and says, 'Take off your skates.' I says, 'You want my skates?' I bent down, I took off one skate, I hit the guy, and with the other skate I ran up the library steps, and I says, 'Mister, these colored guys they want to take my skates.' He came out, they were gone."

The library in which Pete sought refuge on 110th Street was Aguilar Library, another monument to ethnic succession in East Harlem. Established in 1899, the library, despite its misleading name, is not connected to Puerto Rican settlement. It was named for Grace Aguilar, a poet, theologian, and Sephardic Jew.[10] Jewish organizations from New York's Lower East Side founded the library in East Harlem to serve the growing community of Russian Jews moving north out of their own immigrant ghetto. By the time the Aguilar Library opened, Russian Jews constituted 12 percent of the population south of 110th Street and east of Fifth Avenue.[11]

In the first few decades of the twentieth century, tens of thousands of Russian Jews formed a well-established enclave in Central and East Harlem. With thriving synagogues and small businesses, the Jewish population maintained a strong connection to the community. One of the clearest examples was the large, open-air market at Park Avenue and 116th Street under the elevated train tracks. Pete can still remember accompanying his mother to the market, where Jewish vendors knew enough Italian or Spanish to make a sale.

Eventually, the market would become known as La Marqueta, the name "Aguilar" on the library would make it seem like any other Spanish institution, and the Jewish presence would fade. It took less than a decade for Harlem's Jewish population of 178,000 to decrease to a mere 5,000 by 1930.[12] This was a result of intracity migration, a combination of postwar housing construction and the rapid influx of African Americans. Pete would never know the story of Grace Aguilar, or remember very much of the Russian Jews who came before him, but her library was a welcome sanctuary from the threatening demographic changes around him.

In the late 1940s a letter arrived at Pete's 114th Street tenement. The New York City Housing Authority (NYCHA), which had become his family's landlord a few years earlier, was condemning their building to make way for a new public housing development. "They had purchased the buildings from everybody by the right of eminent domain. People weren't getting nothing for their houses! Used to have to go to pay the rent on 113th and Third Avenue, the city set up an office. Well, the city let us know that they were condemning and we had to be out by a certain time."

By the time Pete's family received their letter, NYCHA, along with the Public Works Administration (PWA) of Roosevelt's famous first hundred days and eventually the United States Housing Authority (USHA), had built several massive housing projects in Manhattan and Brooklyn. In fact, New York had pioneered subsidized public housing, erecting First Houses on the Lower East Side in 1935 before the federal government had established the USHA. This was followed by projects in Williamsburg, Brooklyn, and Harlem, which, despite the ongoing struggle over adequate housing for the city's exploding population, used federal money set aside for the PWA to "create employment and stimulate the building industry."[13]

Before World War II, East River Houses was built just ten blocks south of Pete's building. The project, completed in 1941 between 102d and 105th Streets along the East River, was the fifth public housing development in New York City and the first such development to use high-rise towers. At the time, it was a hard-won victory for many residents in East Harlem who had organized against the substandard housing that seemed to plague the neighborhood more than most sections of the city. Leonard Covello wrote in his autobiography that "the idea of compact units with thousands of families living in comfortable apartments, each with independent toilet and bath, was wonderful to contemplate and fight for."[14] Fears over real estate speculators grabbing up riverfront property to develop into high-priced apartment buildings motivated the community to rally around subsidized housing as an anchor for the working poor of East Harlem. Community meetings, demonstrations, and petitions flooded NYCHA, claiming: "We, the . . . tenants of East Harlem, living in one of the worst slum areas in the city, urge you to allocate funds for a low-cost housing project."[15]

The construction of East River Houses demolished several city blocks to create one large "superblock" and erected high-rise buildings surrounded by green space. It was in many ways exactly what the residents of East Harlem were fighting for, and it represented the cutting edge of housing design at the time. Inspired by urban planning theorists such as Ebenezer Howard in England and Corbusier in Paris, the high-rise towers surrounded by parkland were part of a utopian vision of city life that grew out of disaffection with the short blocks and low-rise buildings of industrial cities.[16] It was also part of a systematic plan to rid the city of troublesome slums. New construction on the outskirts of the city would leave a decaying interior, while slum clearance in neighborhoods such as East Harlem allowed NYCHA to use existing infrastructure and make a clean slate of substandard housing.[17]

East River Houses became the model for East Harlem public housing and much of public housing throughout the city. But the enthusiasm of local residents for the "tower in the park" design was short lived. As more and more sites were marked for demolition and development, the short-comings of the design came into focus. As Pete recalls, "After the war, things started going. The signs were in the air. People seemed different."

By the late 1940s Pete's building was slated for demolition. "In 1951 they started to tear them down. We were hanging on, but you'd see buildings going down here, buildings going down there." By the time Jefferson Houses was completed in 1952, 114th Street between Second and First Avenues was gone, replaced by a superblock of high-rise towers. "We all lost," says Pete. "Depressing. It was depressing. Everybody says, 'They had to knock those buildings down! We would have still been there.' They changed everything."

Criticism of the high-density "tower in the park" design in public housing quickly spread to theorists and politicians. Jane Jacobs, in her landmark critique of urban planning, *The Death and Life of Great American Cities,* wrote: "Low-income projects [have] become worse centers of delinquency, vandalism and general social helplessness than the slums they were supposed to replace."[18] In the late 1960s one researcher compared two contiguous housing projects in Brooklyn, one low-rise and one high-rise, and found 50 percent more reported crime in the high-rise development.[19] Today almost one-third of East Harlem real estate consists of high-rise public housing projects.[20]

"A lot of people left," recalls Pete. "There were no apartments around. It wasn't the same. There was no cohesiveness. There was a mass exodus in the late fifties and sixties." As the tenements were razed, many of the Italians of East Harlem followed the route of Irish and German settlers of previous generations to the outer boroughs, Long Island, or New Jersey. Even Pete and his family tried to leave: "We were going to go to Queens. We made all kinds of attempts to go to Queens. They wanted a lot of money for those days. In 1951 they wanted a lot of money, an awful lot. I think it was $103. That's an awful, awful lot of money."

"But still I stayed," he says now. By then, Pete was working downtown as a salesman for his own line of tinware and jewelry. "I wanted to stay downtown, and Pop was down there working as a foreman." So the family moved one block east, still on 114th Street, between First and Pleasant Avenues. "All I know is, we had to pay five [$500] under the table, to the landlord. And it cost us $2,200 to fix it up at that time." The

building, where Pete still lives in the second-floor apartment, was a renovated Old Law Tenement that escaped the wrecking ball of NYCHA.
Standing now in the shadow of Jefferson Houses, the squat red brick
building has lost some of its original charm but still reminds Pete of how
things used to be: "It was a pretty building. Oh, no, no! You should have
seen it then. Oh yeah! Pretty building."

·　　·　　·　　·　　·

A flash jolts Pete from his reverie. He stands halfway, scanning up and
down the sidewalk for its source. A mother with a disposable camera
snaps another photo of her two children, and Pete settles back into his
chair with a faint scowl.

"Somebody takes a picture of me, I don't like it," he says.

For another hour, Pete keeps one eye on the corner of 114th Street and
Pleasant Avenue, where Rao's Italian Restaurant sits half a block away.
He smiles at passing children or waves hello to their parents, but there is
a restlessness about him. Twice he lunges out of his chair midsentence,
without warning, and takes a few furtive steps toward the corner. "I'm
waiting for a guy," he explains halfheartedly as he settles back down.
Finally, another lunge, and he is scampering down to the corner. Five
minutes later, he emerges from the garden-level restaurant at the corner
carrying two brown paper bags.

"What's in the bags, Pete?"

"So where were we?" he asks, blithely ignoring the question.

Pete's secrecy only adds to the mystique of Italian Harlem after the
tenements came crumbling down. Those Italians who did not join the
exodus out to Long Island or New Jersey seemed to consolidate around
Pleasant Avenue and its connecting streets, a last stand against a relentless enemy. Rao's Italian Restaurant, from which Pete appeared with his
brown packages, became the celebrated headquarters of Anthony "Fat
Tony" Salerno, and as East Harlem settled into the 1960s and 1970s, Italian Harlem settled into a stigmatized association with organized crime.

Much of Pete's adult life during this time passes in a blur. He was, for
most of his working years, involved in "wholesale distributing" downtown. "I used to make and do things, [with] metals, everything. I'm good

at what I done. Nothing like it. Nothing like it. Doing something with your hands. The knowledge that you have. Always pursuing it. More than forty years. I was a kid when I started. A little kid."

But uptown, back in East Harlem, life was changing. The new public housing projects dominated the local real estate and radically altered the demographics of the community: "It started getting more tension around in the late fifties, early sixties. People were moving out. I call it social regimentation. It brought in an eclectic bunch. You see the changes. Friends are drifting. Not coming around no more. Guys used to take the train from Parkchester to come around here every Saturday. Stopped coming around. There was nowhere to go."

Life on the streets around Pleasant Avenue, however, seemed as alive and vibrant as it had when he was a boy. Those Italians, like Pete, who remained and commuted to careers downtown helped to secure the remaining few blocks of Italian Harlem. The social clubs of Pete's youth became the social clubs of Italian men, and nickel cards were traded in for high-stakes poker. "Casino, I used to play casino. I was a bum at poker and pinochle, I hated poker. Pinochle, poker, forget about it. Those games, they were card sharks. I've seen pinochle games become quite expensive. Lose $5,000 and everything."

Mickey, a friend of Pete's, stands out in his memory. He was a first-rate card player who did quite well gambling among the local social clubs. "My friend Mickey was a good player. He used to be $1,400, $1,500 at a pop. They played right here on a table on the street." But Mickey also represents those who could not adapt to the new life of the neighborhood and, eventually, lost everything. "There was a guy who used to travel around, he was a card gambler. He wanted to take Mickey, he liked the way he played. I told Mickey, 'It's a lousy life. Town to town, here to there. You don't want to do that.' I says, 'Stay in the Bronx, you want to gamble, you gamble up there.' I haven't seen him in a number of years. He took a beating in a card game one time over here. He walked out of the block, I haven't seen him since. I don't know where he is."

Pete did well enough for himself downtown, and there is little reason to believe he ever became involved in the real source of Italian Harlem's reputation for organized crime. According to Pete, "They ran the neighborhood, but these housing projects knocked them all out. It really weakened them. But there was crime families here. Rao's is the only place left from that time. Rao's has been in the family over a hundred years. You wouldn't believe who goes in there if I tell you."

Rao's has been the target of FBI investigations into organized crime for generations. Vincent Rao, the former owner, was convicted in 1979 on money-laundering charges that linked him to the Genovese crime family.[21] One of five Mafia families in New York City, the Genovese organization was run by Salerno in the 1980s before he was imprisoned on racketeering charges in 1986. He continued to exert considerable control over the fading organization from his prison cell, where he died in 1992.[22]

Rao's is not the only institution in the Pleasant Avenue section of East Harlem to become associated with organized crime. In June 1983 the FBI planted listening devices in the Palma Boys Social Club on 115th Street across from Mt. Carmel Church. After two years federal agents had enough evidence to convict Salerno and prove he "shifted the focus of the family to the Palma Boys club, which sources say, served as the headquarters for his multimillion-dollar loan sharking and lottery operations."[23]

Today Rao's is owned by Frank Pellegrino, Vincent Rao's nephew, whose only apparent connection to organized crime is playing a part from time to time in mob movies. The restaurant, despite the occasional setback (it was torched by unknown arsonists in 1995, and two men were shot there in 2003), remains the most elusive reservation in town.[24] Pete has always been a fixture in the kitchen and at the bar in the ten-table restaurant.

"I used to rub elbows with, uh, Anthony Quinn. Warren Buffet goes there. Get this, one night, Warren Buffet and Bill Gates were there. It was in the night, they were singing a duet, 'My Girl.' I've been there many times with that kid, John Kennedy. He was such a nice kid. He came one night all alone on a rainy night on a bicycle. They said, 'John, why the heck you didn't take a cab!' They put the bicycle in the garage and locked it up, so not everybody would pass by and want to take it. He used to sit at the front table. I liked that kid. He was a nice kid. He sat with his back to the door. Who is gonna touch him there? He knew he was where everybody has his eye on him."

When Pete wasn't at Rao's or watching the poker games in the local social clubs, he was at home caring for his aging parents. His sister had long since married and moved to Long Island, and though he tried to move away, Pete could not bring himself to abandon his father and mother.

His father was the first to show signs of failing health. Since the war he had had steady work as a shop foreman for a tinware company on the Upper East Side. "They made good tinware. The building is still up. They loved him. They loved him. The boss loved him. The workers." But in 1962 he suffered a stroke from which he would only marginally recover.

"Pop was always looking for me. You know, 'Where's my boy? Where's my boy?' He was very smart, but when he got that stroke, he didn't know nothing. It affected his brain. After a while, I brought him down to the sidewalk for a couple of years, to move around and everything. I taught him how to read and write again, how to write, how to spell, how to count. Don't ask me how I done it. Don't know what got me to do it. Bring him out into the hallway, by the banister to hang on and walk up and down, to learn how to shuffle his foot."

Then, in summer 1967, shots rang out in the street in front of Pete's building. "They were running in the streets shooting, and everybody was sitting out." Partially paralyzed from his stroke, Pete's father could not take cover. "So, my mother, she didn't want him out anymore. She said, 'No, take him up. How's he gonna move?' " Pete's father sat in the second-floor window watching the street until his death in 1972. "I used to put him in front of the window and give him a newspaper and tell him to watch the car. And he would say, 'Okay, I'll watch the car!' And I would leave him there while I went to work, and my father would sit there and watch the car."

After his father's death, Pete's mother began a slow descent into illness. She went out less often and became more alienated from the street below. "I was in bed one night. My mother said, 'Pete, they shooting!' I said, 'Ma, don't go near the window.' And she stayed in the bed."

Pete eventually quit his business to care for his mother full-time. Throughout the 1980s, the last full decade of her life, she never left the apartment. It was a self-imposed confinement, one that other aging Italian immigrants chose in response to their changing environment. Leonard Covello wrote of his mother: "My Mother was always tired now. . . . She lost all desire to go out into the street or to see anything new."[25] Neighbors still remember Pete's mother standing at the window of their apartment. A ghostly image of an ailing woman, and the only evidence that she was still alive.

The agony of that time is reflected in one simple and sorrowful event that serves as a daily reminder. One night, after years of caring for his mother, a time of deep sorrow and, by his own account, the darkest years of his life, Pete was feeding her dinner. Watching her frail body unable to perform the simplest task, Pete was overcome with the tragedy of her decline. Gnashing his teeth, he heard a loud crack and felt a piercing pain. Within months he lost all but three teeth.

His mother died in 1992. Pete has not touched her room since. One day, in 2003, he pulled out his mother's slippers from beneath the bureau. After eleven years, they were coated with dust. "I tried to clean out under there, it was all full of dirt, but I just couldn't do it. Every once in a while I will pack up a box of her things and give it to someone to get it out of the apartment, but not very often. It's very difficult."

He was missing for three months after his mother died. He just disappeared. "People were banging on the door, people from Rao's, people from around the block." He won't say where he went, but he has been restless ever since. "I can't stay in the apartment, I have to be on the move."

·   ·   ·   ·   ·

It has been almost two months since Halloween, and the weather has turned bitter in New York City. Wind whips through the high-rise towers and down into the canyons around Pleasant Avenue. Pete has put on a scarf and a winter growth of thick white stubble, but he is still out on the sidewalk with his *Daily News*.

"They cut off the hot water!" he exclaims. "There's been no hot water, no nothing, for over a week now. Even though these landlords are getting away with all these high rents and everything. It's all that Wall Street money that makes these high rents. They showed on TV, an apartment rented for $22 million. What are they, crazy? You could buy the whole neighborhood!"

Roseanne steps past Pete to enter the building and waves a quick hello. Pete calls after her, "When that hot water comes back on, you take a long hot soak. You don't want to get sick."

"All right, Pete, don't worry about me," she calls back before disappearing inside.

"Of course I worry, these are like my kids."

But Pete doesn't have any children, not his own, only those who have grown up under his watchful eye on 114th Street. "I never married," he offers, "but that was 'cause of me. I could have gotten married many times. It was me. I don't think I could be married. Great father, 'cause I like kids. I knew some nice girls, too. I don't know. You know, many, many years back, everybody says the first guy to get married would be me. I see them all go. And they say, 'He's still around.' I used to know a lot of girls then, at the time. I had people planning on how my wedding was going to be, too."

His sister, and only sibling, married decades earlier, giving Pete two nephews and a niece. They are grown now, and none of them live in the neighborhood. His sister is older and in failing health. She lives with one of her sons on Long Island, and Pete doesn't see her as much as he would like. His niece used to call more often, even when traveling as far away as Hawaii or Australia. She lives in Georgia now.

A nephew lives in Seattle. Pete smiles broadly and explains, "He calls me all the time, on the road in the car, he pulls tricks on me all the time. He's a good kid. He has a group called Randy and the Rainbows. It's a musical group. He's compiling an anthology of the music they've made. They're terrific. I'm proud of him, just the way he is. My nephews are good kids. They never got in trouble where I had to run and go see somebody. They were around here when they were small, and then out to the island."

It's a common refrain for Pete. The friends and family he remembers all seem to end up moving "out to the island," and then perhaps to New Jersey, Florida, or California. "Years back, everybody used to go down to Florida right after the New Year. Over here in this neighborhood. I didn't go. They used to go down for about a month."

Pete never left, and he rarely traveled, though friends continue to try to coax him away from the old neighborhood. "I got a call from down in Florida this morning, wanting me to come down. They said, 'You should come down, we got a house and everything.' You know, he says he sent his son up to see me a lot of times. But his son has not been able to get in touch with me, to contact me. His three sons, I'm like their uncle. We were together many, many years. Him and I. They're old friends. He left here, I'd say, late fifties. He went to the Bronx, and then he went to Long Island. He bought something out on the island, fabricated it, then he left the island and went down to Florida. He calls me all the time, but this area, they knocked it down, and a lot of people had to go to all different places."

When asked why he stays, Pete replies, "I don't know. I got my mother in a cemetery on Long Island. You know what I mean? I was going to go out there this week. I used to go a lot. I was out there before nine o'clock one morning, in a storm. Just to see what it looks like. I forgot to put a blanket on her. I keep thinking about that. When it's cold weather, I says, 'Ma, I didn't put a blanket on you.' You know, to keep her warm. I should have done it that morning. I thought of it afterward. She's laying in a nice solid bronze casket. So is Dad."

Perhaps it is the memory of his parents that keeps him rooted in East Harlem and not just the preservation of their memory but the fear of what uprooting can do to the soul. As Pete reflects, "In times past, it was proven, that when people are displaced from their natural habitat, in other words, where they had been living for hundreds of years, and this pertains to this country as well where people were settled in certain areas. Anyway, it was proven that people got sick. The same thing happened to neighborhoods like this. When the city took this property by the right of eminent domain, people got sick and withered and passed away, heartbroken. This was their life."

In a whisper, Pete adds, "I saw it a lot."

For Pete, the monolithic housing projects bear the guilt of destroying Italian Harlem and in some ways, perhaps, of killing his parents. His daydreams now are what East Harlem could have been if left to its own devices. "The stores would be modernized and everything, upscale. People would come and be happy and raise their children and whatnot. Probably even better than the Upper East Side. The people were starting to climb the ladder. They had money. Some of them were building houses in the neighborhood. These brownstones that were here were mansions! You got no idea what they tore down! I still got that vision of them, I says, 'What are they doing!?' The stoops coming up to big marble pillars with the columns on them holding up this fortress. I saw that hammer breaking them down. They tried to stop them, but it was too late. From here they went below. 106th, 107th, 108th."

The changes now are irreversible, and even Pleasant Avenue has lost its hold on Italian Harlem. Pete's neighbors now are Puerto Rican, African American, Mexican, West African, and Asian. He regrets not buying into the neighborhood when he had the chance, before the demographic changes that have overwhelmed his sense of place. "I could have bought this building then, and if I had, I probably would have kept the apartments above me as storage. It would have been quiet. I am very quiet."

Jacko lives upstairs now, but Pete gets to keep his peace and quiet. "He comes from Benin, Africa. He's a gentleman. He lives on top of me and does everything not to disturb me." Jacko has helped to shape Pete's perspective on the new ethnic diversity of East Harlem. "I tell you something, the Africans keep to themselves. They don't bother nobody. They don't bother with the blacks. There will always be a division. They don't consider them. They won't have anything to do with the Africans that were here. Jacko, he's a good guy. He also speaks French. Very good. I hear him on the phone sometimes. French cooking, too. He works for a real estate company."

Some of the older settlers in East Harlem are harder for Pete to understand. Despite his reluctance to characterize the arrival of Puerto Rican immigrants in midcentury as cause for violence or overt resistance, he still seems befuddled by the new Latino dominance in the neighborhood. "I went to the bank this morning, you had this Spanish in there, Puerto Rican. One was having an argument with the other one. She must have been the supervisor. Spanish they talked. You talk to a Spanish person right now, they start talking in Spanish. Which is an affront to you. They do that all the time. Why they do this, I don't know. They won't speak English."

This frustration often leads too easily to stereotypes and unfounded explanations of escalating violence in East Harlem. According to Pete, "Puerto Ricans don't want to tangle with the Mexicans, don't want to be near them. It's the same way why they don't want to be near the Dominicans. A Puerto Rican told me one time that they weren't nice, and violence has cropped up like mad lately. You see these guys running through the streets, over here shooting at one another. That's something they didn't do in the fifties and sixties. Not then. They kept to themselves. They're getting more wild."

One specific event still haunts Pete. Shortly after his mother died, he was in bed when he heard shots in the street below. "Boom. Boom. And I says, 'Oh, those were shots again.' I come down and the super at the time, he was hosing down the sidewalks. And he says, 'Pete, I got to clean the blood off over here. They killed a guy over here.' I says, 'I know, I heard the shots.' He says, 'He still had his hat on.' Right over here it was. About ten years ago, after I lost my mom. The guy was cleaning the blood off."

That kind of physical violence, according to Pete, keeps the daydreams of East Harlem's advancement unreachable. The idea that the neighborhood could ever be like the Upper East Side seems impossible now. "You got that housing project here, you got 105th, you got 122nd. You know, these public houses. You gotta have it. Who wants to live in public houses? It was a mistake to build them in the first place. It was so nice before. You had some nice buildings there."

Rumors that developers may convert the federal housing units into private co-ops offer little hope for Pete and reveal his misgivings about another, newer immigrant group. "I've been hearing this for ten years now. Where are these people going to go if they privatize? For ten years, I've been hearing this. I even heard that some Chinese were supposed to be buying them. If the Chinese ever bought them, you'd have to run out of this neighborhood. They'll run you out, like they done down on Grand Street. They've been doing it down on Mott Street, too. You're not familiar with Grand Street, what it was like. They took over everything. The same thing would be here. You already got some of them who have been going into Franklin Plaza. They're in there. It's on Second Avenue, it's not a city thing, it's a kind of a complex."

The idea that Asians are plotting to "take over" East Harlem is less about ethnic stereotypes and outright prejudice than it is a reflection of the bitterness many Italians feel about losing their cultural and economic dominance in the community. This is poignantly, if not offensively, demonstrated in one particular comment from Pete: "Koreans got the fish places. They got one on 119th. Chinese, Koreans, whatever they are. They got one on 120th. I told somebody about ten years ago, 'How come we didn't think to put a market like that?' This guy grew up in the fish business. He says, 'Right, Pete. How come?' The Korean place on 119th, they got everything. They know that business."

.   .   .   .   .

"I keep thinking back, I don't know why. The events of the past are coming back to me. Little incidents, my old friends and everything." Pete is in his chair, huddled close to the brick steps of his building. His pale blue eyes water against the wind, and he pulls his London Fog jacket close around him. No one else is out on this crisp late autumn day. Winter is only a few days away, and some of the upstairs neighbors have strung Christmas lights from the fire escape.

This time of year, Pete must rely on his memories. Fannie, who lives a few doors down, stays inside during the winter. Friends and family prefer to wait for warmer months to visit the old neighborhood.

"In July friends come back. For the Giglio, guys come up from Florida to carry it, and Mt. Carmel."

The feast of Our Lady of Mt. Carmel has long been an important event in the lives of East Harlem Italians. The church, on 115th Street just off Pleasant Avenue, was built by Italians in what was the Irish and German section of East Harlem in the late nineteenth century. New Italian immigrants were made to worship in the basement, a powerful symbol of discrimination. It wasn't until 1919, when Italians had successfully supplanted Irish and German cultural dominance in the Pleasant Avenue section of the neighborhood, that Italians emerged from the basement to worship in the sanctuary. They brought with them the statue of la Madonna del Carmine sent from Polla, Italy, in the 1880s, to be placed in the seat of honor at the altar. Crowned by decree of Pope Leo XIII in July 1904, the church on 115th Street became one of only a handful of sanctuaries dedicated to the Virgin Mary in the United States.[26]

Documented in detail by Robert Orsi, the feast day of la Madonna is celebrated each July with an elaborate procession that winds through the neighborhood the night before and the next day, interspersed with masses at the church, a fair on 115th Street, and, more recently, the ceremonial lifting of the Giglio, a two-ton wooden tower complete with brass band. Over the decades it has been a time for Italians in East Harlem to reconnect with their place in the geography of the neighborhood, especially after the postwar exodus of many Italian residents. Since the 1960s July is a time to return to Pleasant Avenue, say hello to old-timers and hangers-on, and remember life on the streets when it was still Italian Harlem.

But this, too, has changed.

In the 1980s Italians returning to celebrate la Madonna were joined by a handful of Haitian worshipers. Standing apart and singing their hymns in French, they were a curious addition to the evening procession and midnight mass. As the years wore on, that handful became a crowd, eventually outnumbering the Italians themselves. Our Lady of Mt. Carmel is also an important figure in the pantheon of Haitian Catholicism, and word quickly spread of its celebration in East Harlem.

Today the feast of Mt. Carmel is sharply divided, night from day, Haitian from Italian. During the day, the Italians march through the streets with the altar and statue, singing hymns and waving flags. In the afternoon, the Giglio is hoisted on the shoulders of a hundred men, each offering their burden as penance to la Madonna. The evening procession through the streets of the neighborhood is dominated by Haitian worshipers, crowding the altar that holds the statue of la Madonna as they sing French hymns to an Italian brass band. After the procession, thousands of Haitians fill the church for midnight mass, now given over completely to the newcomers with a Haitian priest officiating in French.

The waves of French hymn singing that swell in the air of a hot summer night, spilling out the door of the sanctuary, seem to shake the very foundations of the century-old church. Outside, the sounds of worship mingle with a Frank Sinatra tune piped through loudspeakers hung above the Italian street fair. Carnival rides and sausage stands compete with the reverence of worship.

"There is going to be a celebration of the coronation this coming year," Pete explains. It's still six months away as Pete chats from his chair on the sidewalk, but the hundred-year anniversary of the coronation of la Madonna del Carmine is a momentous occasion. "The cardinal might come up, too." But Pete knows that even this cannot bring back what has changed forever. "They wanted people to volunteer to plan, and I walked away. I was at the parish council meeting, I didn't even say anything, I just kept quiet. I says, 'I'm not up to anything anymore.'"

With the tenements of his youth long since exchanged for high-rise public housing, the very street he grew up on obliterated by government bulldozers, and now even the feast of Mt. Carmel given over to new immigrants, what remains of Italian Harlem?

With a sigh, Pete adds, "I used to stay, but then I been going to other places."

THREE 106th Street

Hands jammed in the pockets of his green and white New York Jets jacket, José rounds the corner at Third Avenue and 106th Street. A new year has turned, and the fall colors have faded into a monochrome winter gray that seems to sink into the pavement, buildings, and sky, hardening them into a frozen tableau. The streets are mostly empty, and José's short, stocky frame bends against the chill. Ignoring the outposts of downtown commercialism—Blockbuster Video, KFC, and Duane Reade pharmacy—he heads west down 106th Street, the boulevard of his barrio, the "cultural corridor" of Puerto Rican Harlem. He is hungry and longing for some good old-fashioned Puerto Rican soul food.

In the distance, he can see the Julia de Burgos Cultural Center, St. Cecilia's Church, the Metro North railroad tracks, and Mt. Sinai Hospital. But a few steps past Third Avenue, just behind the Blockbuster Video and before the bodega, he lays a hand on a glass door and pushes inside La Fonda Boriqua. The establishment is all steam, music, and chatter as he steps past the lunch counter and the bins of rice, beans, chuleta, chicken, pernil, and soup. Tossing a few greetings in hesitant Spanish to the young waitresses behind the counter, José saunters to the back room. Booths molded from polished wood line the yellow walls, and José picks one underneath a massive canvas produced by a local Puerto Rican artist.

José pulls off the bulky nylon jacket and falls into his seat. The tight curls of his short-cropped hair no longer appear a uniform black against the deep copper of his skin. Flecks of gray betray his nearly fifty years, but there is still a youthful exuberance in his frequent gesticulations and fast-paced, clipped diction. If he were standing outside, or sitting in the two-bedroom apartment he shares with his wife, Cecilia, and their three children, he would doubtless have a Newport cigarette to distract some of that excess energy.

José is at home here, not just in La Fonda Boriqua. Born and raised in East Harlem, there is no place he feels more comfortable. He has spent no more than seven years outside her boundaries, and each has indelibly marked his allegiance to El Barrio. "Going downtown" still means a string of stores on 86th Street, and even when he must travel longer distances he refuses to fly—as if afraid such efficient transportation could take him too far away.

"Hey, José! ¿Como le va?" A round, clean-shaven Puerto Rican, one of the owners of the restaurant, greets José with a firm handshake.

"Bien, gracias. How you been?" José shifts awkwardly into English, still unsure of his Spanish. "Listen, I've got those pictures and I'll get them to you in a couple of days."

"No problem, yeah, that's okay," replies his friend as he backs away to greet other customers.

José adjusts his glasses to study the menu, reading over the list of Puerto Rican delicacies such as roast suckling pig and sopa de mondongo, a soup made from a cow's stomach lining. A young waitress interrupts his meditation and asks in hip, slurred Spanish if he is ready to order. José does his best to flirt in a language he stopped using several decades earlier, and finally settles on the soup.

.   .   .   .   .

"I was born on December 11, 1955, at Mt. Sinai Hospital." José speaks a cartographic language, spinning out tangents on how buildings, blocks, and the barrio have changed to give context to his memories. "It was just one building then. A small building, three- or four-story building, where that big monstrosity sits now."

José sits back, lets the soup steam clear from his glasses, and places his youth. "We lived on 104th Street between Lexington and Park Avenue, in the tenements there." With a pause, he adds, "I remember that time period."

The 1950s, East Harlem. Piri Thomas and the mean streets of Puerto Rican Harlem, Spanish Harlem, El Barrio. José was just a child, but he can still remember the feel of the streets around Lexington Avenue and 106th Street before the monoliths of public housing swallowed up the tenements and the ubiquity of mass-market consumerism blotted out the local businesses.

"I remember being in those tenements, and I remember the layout of the apartment we lived in." He stares into his bright orange bowl of broth and spongy tripe and adds, "I had a very intense childhood, maybe that's why."

Migration from Puerto Rico to the U.S. mainland began almost imperceptibly in the years following the Spanish-American War of 1898. By 1910 there were little more than 1,000 Puerto Ricans living in the United States. By the time José was born, there were more than 600,000 Puerto Ricans in New York City, and 60,000 of them lived in East Harlem.[1] That trend would continue until the 1970s, when economic recession discouraged Puerto Rican migration to mainland urban centers and new immigration policies brought new competition for low-wage employment. By 2000 Puerto Ricans would slip to just below 35,000, or 32 percent of the East Harlem population.

Two important pieces of federal legislation were in large part responsible for this radical population shift that would forever change the fields of Puerto Rico and the streets of East Harlem. In 1917 Congress passed the Jones Act, which extended U.S. citizenship to all Puerto Ricans. In that year alone, almost 11,000 Puerto Ricans left the island, more than in the previous seven years combined.[2] As citizens, Puerto Ricans were no longer immigrants, but they still faced stiff competition for scarce resources from the flood of European newcomers, such as the southern Italians who settled around Pleasant Avenue. The second legislative watershed occurred in 1924, the Johnson-Reed Immigration Act, which would all but cut off the flow of competition from Europe and leave Puerto Rican migration unchecked to fill the pre- and postwar segmented labor market.

Both of José's parents were born in Puerto Rico around the time of the Johnson-Reed Immigration Act. Both experienced the push of island overpopulation and the pull of economic opportunity in Nueva York.

"My mother came alone, originally," explains José. In fact, she left Puerto Rico to escape an unstable and destructive relationship. "She got married in Puerto Rico. I think she got married to get out of the house, which is a bad idea 'cause this guy was a womanizer, a drinker, and he would beat people." Leaving her daughter in the care of relatives, José's mother followed the tens of thousands of island-born Puerto Ricans leaving for New York City each year, hoping to save enough money to eventually send for her only child.

José's father arrived in the company of his parents, a family, like most, in search of stable employment. Settling first in Queens, his father enrolled in vocational school to learn the welding trade. But soon, like many newly arrived Puerto Ricans, he was drawn into the emerging world war and became a merchant marine.[3] "He was on the merchant vessels during World War II, crossing back and forth from here to Hawaii. So he could have been torpedoed at any time." There is more than a hint of pride in José's voice. Thirty years later, José, too, would join the military and serve for almost a decade. "My father was a war hero. I like that. He didn't chicken out."

The industrial boom after José's father's tour in the merchant marine led to work building batteries for nuclear submarines. With the ensuing cold war, the new company flourished and moved the entire operation out of the city and into the northern suburbs. "They were going to pay for a move and a house, so my father had the choice to buy a house and we could have grown up in the suburbs. My father didn't want to because he didn't want to drive, so we stayed in East Harlem."

It was a decision that José would come to appreciate, though he still wonders how life might have been different in the suburbs. "My aunt took the opportunity, and my cousins all grew up in the suburbs. They would look down on us, like, 'You people live in the ghetto.' Everybody lived in East Harlem, though, all the Puerto Ricans." With more pity than disdain, he adds, "My cousins are not very Puerto Rican actually, but they are doing well."

Not all of José's extended family found their way to the suburbs. Like many Puerto Ricans who settled in East Harlem, they became a conduit for migrating relatives and maintained close ties to José's grandparents. It was his father's mother who left the clearest impression. "She was a *santera.* This is why I say my childhood was intense."

Santera is the common name for a practitioner of Santería, a catchall European label for any number of religions born in the crucible of Spanish Caribbean slavery. The best known is the Afro-Cuban Regla de Ocha, known as Lucumí in the United States. Lucumí, derived from Yoruba religion, was cast by colonizers and social scientists as a form of "folk" Catholicism, but this obscures the more likely subversive character of Lucumí practice. Indeed, it seems the Yoruba *orisás,* or spirits, took on the identities of Catholic saints as protection against repression but never lost their sense of discrete power.[4]

Though Cuba remains the center of what is popularly known as Santería, Puerto Ricans developed their own practice of Catholic subversion through Yoruba orisás. Known as Puerto Rican spiritualism, the practice differs subtly from its Afro-Cuban forebear and seems to have developed most prominently among the diaspora of New York City.

José remembers his grandmother's talents with both awe and incredulity. "She used to do things, you know, santera things for us, and my mother would bring us to her and she would get rid of this pain and you know." He remembers the thick cigars she smoked constantly, and the clandestine rituals she often performed for her illness-prone grandsons. "We would go to her house to do it, in her basement, that's where her altar was and all that. I don't think she did it for anyone else, she did it for family. My mother would take us because my father would say, take them over there. My father was a believer, too, but my mother was not."

José's mother, a devout Catholic who would not even take communion until her first husband died, thus absolving her from the sin of remarrying after a divorce, was not as amused by her mother-in-law's beliefs. José believes the conflict was more than theological: "They didn't really get along. It was something about my grandmother being real dark and my mother being light."

Race and theology take on a syncretism of their own in the social history of Santería—a fact that has colored the perception of the practice in all its manifestations and may account for José's mother's mistrust. Its roots in Yoruba religion, as well as other religions of Nigeria, Benin, Cameroon, and the Congo, entwined its practice and its practitioners with the pseudoscientific racism of the early twentieth century. Any persistent expression of African identity, whether in religion, music, or phenotype, was proof of a "primitive" inability to adapt. According to José's mother, a light-skinned Puerto Rican woman who had already "married down" by marrying a dark-skinned man, José's grandmother fit all the tropes of blackness by performing her basement rituals. Though the orisá known as Changó might be protected in the guise of Santa Barbara, José's grandmother could do little to hide her link to Puerto Rico's African ancestors.

This recurrent issue of race within the Puerto Rican community was often as divisive as it was confusing. On the island, there had long been a struggle between the perception of racial interconnectedness and the experience of a color hierarchy.[5] This was most obvious in the nationalist promotion of a tripartite identity consisting of white, black, and Indian for all Puerto Ricans and the ongoing denigration of darker-skinned compatriots. "Our mothers grew up telling us, 'Don't marry a black guy,' 'cause, I don't know, you're suppose to improve the hair of the race, not make it worse. For real. Marry some white guy, but never marry a black guy. Mothers were always telling their daughters that. It's built in. And that comes from Puerto Rico, too."

This confusion was only made worse in the trip north, where mainland U.S. society allowed only for clear racial categories based largely on phenotype, skin color in particular, precluding even the perception of interstitial categories of racial mixing. Mainland-born Puerto Ricans such as José still struggle to reconcile island identity politics with mainland racism. "In Puerto Rico a lot of people are dark-skinned, but they're Puerto Rican, they're not black. My grandfather was white, light-skinned and Puerto Rican, but white. My father is dark, darker than me. He doesn't look black, he's Puerto Rican black." It's the same tortured knot of phenotype and identity that Piri Thomas tried to undo for his brother in *Down These Mean Streets:* "Poppa thinks that marrying a White woman made him White. He's wrong. It's just another nigger marrying a White woman and making her as Black as him. That's the way the paddy looks at it. The Negro just stays Black. Period. Dig it?"[6]

.   .   .   .   .

José turns the key in the lock of the green iron gate that separates the stoop of his building from the sidewalk. A row of fresh, almost faux-tenement buildings line up along the narrow street—new construction providing home ownership for low- to middle-income families. But unlike their architectural ancestors, these four-story, narrow buildings are divided in thirds, one apartment per floor, with a garage for the owner-landlord's car. After several decades in the projects, José is back in private housing—paying "market" rent that is four times higher than his parents, who still live at DeWitt Clinton Houses four blocks away, pay.

José locks the gate behind him and moves slowly up the dozen steps of the front stoop. His knee is weak from the added weight of approaching middle age, so he rests at the door to take one last drag from his Newport. Standing at the top of the stoop, he can see DeWitt Clinton Houses towering over the tenements that still line Third Avenue. Fishing out his digital camera, he snaps a photo of the scene in the fading light. Tomorrow morning it will grace the home page of his community website,[7] but for now he is content to lean against the front door and watch the sun go down behind his parents' building.

Behind him, the raucous sounds of construction are fading as work on new housing nears completion and thick-set, dust-covered men walk off the job and head home for Brooklyn, Queens, and New Jersey. José has seen this before, the clash of development in his neighborhood. Before turning into his fourth-floor walk-up, he says, "You can always take a chance with the private housing, but unless you move everyone out of the projects it doesn't change."

In June 1957 a headline in the *New York Times* read: "Harlem Changed by Public Housing: 137 Acres Are Being Razed East of Madison Avenue in Attack on Slums."[8] The article describes East Harlem as one of the worst slums in the metropolitan area and touts the clearance of 137 acres to provide for a dozen new housing developments. The plan would create the highest concentration of public housing projects in the city.

To be fair, the attack on slums began in the 1930s; by the late 1950s it was full-scale war. Pete had already moved down 114th Street with his parents, and by 1957 Jefferson Houses would stand as a low-rise, seven-story tombstone to his old tenement block. Jefferson, like five other projects, was federally funded, making it the most heavily subsidized of the new housing at $10 per room. New tenants of Jefferson Houses had to qualify with an annual income limit of $4,000 and a $100 allowance for each child. Other projects were subsidized by the state and city, and slightly more expensive.

"In 1957 my family moved to Jefferson projects on the First Avenue side facing the pool, on First Avenue and 112th," José says, sitting, half eaten by his overstuffed couch, in the living room of his top floor apartment. "In those days you moved into the projects, you weren't in the ghetto anymore. People would say that."

Despite the current iconic status of public housing as state-subsidized slums, José remembers the early years of life in the projects as halcyon days far from the madding crowds of tenement life. Families who for years fought landlords and superintendents over substandard conditions in the old tenements found themselves in a smoothly efficient high-rise of clean and well-maintained apartments. José remembers routine house visits and strict rules maintaining a welcome sense of order. "You weren't supposed to hang anything on your walls. You weren't supposed to paint without their permission. They would come in and paint every three years whether you liked it or not. They looked at everything, the pipes. They would check the kitchen, make sure the stove was still in shape, that you didn't mess up the refrigerator. That there weren't more people than you said were supposed to be in there."

But the overcrowding of tenements, like traffic on city streets, would not be solved by adding more space. Since the end of World War II as many as fifty thousand Puerto Ricans a year were making the trip north, and by the mid-1950s East Harlem was described by some as one of the world's most densely populated areas.[9] Migrants availing themselves of social networks in their move to the mainland continued to use their relatives' apartments as transitional housing. "We had a few cousins and uncles, mostly uncles come through and stay and get a job. They would come from the island, and we would get bumped from our rooms. I remember for a year or two not having my own room because my cousin lived in there. Within a half a year they would get a job and then they left."

Life on 112th Street and First Avenue was several blocks and a world away from the heart of Puerto Rican Harlem along 106th Street. José's family, along with several hundred others stacked seven stories high, was living a frontier existence on the leading edge of Puerto Rican dominance over the streets of East Harlem. Across the avenue was Jefferson Park, still known as Italian territory, and despite their shrinking numbers, Italians still claimed the surrounding blocks as their own.

"What I saw as the boundary was 116th Street," José explains. "When we went to do the laundry at 116th Street, we saw all the Italians." But even a child could see the fading presence of the once-dominant ethnic group: "They looked like shoddy, old Italians. They were mostly old men."

116th Street remained one of many seemingly intransigent boundaries of ethnic difference in the neighborhood. The 1950s were, after all, the same years of Piri Thomas's violent sojourn on the streets of Spanish Harlem, when turf wars between youth gangs inspired sensational headlines and often overwrought accounts of racial conflict. José remembers Italian youth stalking the streets, "ripping the antennas off the parked cars." "They would snap it off, and they were on their way. And my mother would drag us upstairs quickly because they were on their way to fight some Puerto Rican gang."

However, not unlike Pete in his account of life on 114th Street, José dismisses much of the lore that accumulated around gangs and violence in the early days of Puerto Rican settlement. As he explains, "I never saw them fighting, I just saw them on their way to the fight. My fear was based on my mother having this fearful look on her face. We'd be playing right there on the grass, and she would say, 'Come on, come on!' If I would see that now, I wouldn't even move my kids from the street. They're going to fight someone three blocks down. They're not going to do anything to you. My mother overreacted."

José's mother employed a number of strategies to safeguard her children in an increasingly alien environment. From the streets around Italian Harlem to the hallways of her building, she did her best to ward off anonymity and the danger that came with being unknown. "My mother worked quickly to get to know her neighbors, and that was good. There were only seven stories. You got to know everybody, especially the Hispanic people." According to José, that was relatively easy, considering the de facto segregation of each building in the new development: "In fact, there weren't any African Americans in that building at all. They were in the other building."

When the first of the three phases of construction for Jefferson Houses was completed in 1955, tenancy in the 468 apartments was 47.5 percent white. Two years later the second phase was completed, and José's family moved into one of 324 new apartments where 90 percent of the tenants were Puerto Rican or African American.[10] In October of that year, Mayor Robert Wagner promised to pass "a real good anti-bias housing bill" and declared, "We are on the way to wiping out the last vestiges of discrimination in our town."[11] In September 1958 NYCHA hired Madison Jones, a "full-time race relations expert" who wanted "to kill the idea that public housing is minority housing."[12]

By 1959 more than half of New York City's public housing tenants were African American or Puerto Rican (39.3 and 17.3 percent, respectively).[13] In that year the third phase of Jefferson Houses was completed, opening 701 new apartments. The Housing Authority moved African American and Puerto Rican families from the first two sections to the new building and redistributed white tenants to all three in a proactive attempt to create racial balance.[14] But forced desegregation could not mollify the conflict between residents accustomed to the clear ethnic divisions of preproject street life.

This was made glaringly apparent to José after a traumatic altercation in the courtyard of a neighboring development. "One day we were walking with my mother's cousin in another project behind us. Two guys came up and picked up my mother and her friend and felt them up and then ran away, a quick feel. My mother was screaming." Their attackers were described as black, and according to José, "She immediately wanted a transfer out of those projects because of that one thing. I mean, I would of thought, hey, it's very unlikely to happen, it was like two buildings away, but she no longer felt safe there."

Despite NYCHA's publicly announced efforts to integrate developments such as Jefferson, José, like many others, assumed the opposite. "I'm just guessing, but maybe they were putting more black people in the projects." Some whistleblowers at the time accused NYCHA of doing just that. In one report, a former assistant public relations director for NYCHA accused his employer of orchestrating a complex tiered system for regulating access to specific housing projects, essentially giving preference to white tenants in lower-rent, more centrally located developments and forcing black and Puerto Rican tenants to take up residence in higher-rent, less desirable locations.[15]

Regardless of NYCHA's stated policy on desegregation, after the trauma of the attack in the courtyard, José's family wanted out. "They just said, we want to get out of here." Within a year they retreated to DeWitt Clinton Houses at 108th Street and Lexington Avenue, the heartland of Puerto Rican Harlem. They moved in just three months after Malcolm X was fatally shot on February 21, 1965, while giving a speech at the Audubon Ballroom not too far from East Harlem in upper Manhattan. "It was May 25, 1965," José recalls of his move to DeWitt Clinton. "I remember because it was brand spanking new and everything. I loved it. That's where I feel I grew up."

·   ·   ·   ·   ·

José bites into an oversized burger from the steakhouse around the corner from his apartment. The aluminum container perches precariously on his knees, as he perches on the edge of his couch. "This is the best burger I have had in years," he says between bites. "My kids will die when I tell them what I am eating. They found a cockroach in their food there once and won't eat there anymore."

The living room is bright and as sparse as it can be for a family of five. As in any New York apartment, most stationary objects perform multiple functions. A table, with the chairs pushed against a wall, is covered with papers, books, and plants and seems to get little use as a dining table, and a few bookcases filled with paperbacks also hold dozens of family photos. In one corner, hundreds of plastic figurines, comic book heroes, and science fiction aliens crowd a dining nook, lining the walls and reaching the ceiling; they are the joint collection of father and son. For the first few years, the living room was also where José and his wife slept on a sofa bed.

The apartment is quiet at the moment; Cecilia and the kids are visiting José's parents. It's a weekly ritual, one José periodically rebels against. He appreciates his parents' proximity, but he also jealously guards his time away from work. Most weeks he enjoys visiting them, especially since it places him closer to the heart of childhood associations with East Harlem. Much of that centers on 106th Street.

"East Harlem started on 106th Street," José says. "The name 'El Barrio' started there and Spanish Harlem." José remembers the courtyard playground in his new building that he was allowed to go to unattended. "As soon as we moved into DeWitt Clinton, my mother let us go down by ourselves."

The fear associated with life in an "integrated" building on the cusp of Italian Harlem subsided as the family settled deeper into Puerto Rican Harlem, and José enjoyed a newfound freedom. From their window in the new high-density, high-rise building, they could see the lush treetops of Central Park and as far south as 96th Street, the boundary of East Harlem. "This time we were on the sixth floor, 6H. And she would watch us from the window and make sure we were playing where she could watch us."

He spent the afternoons of his preadolescence on the playground of DeWitt Clinton Houses and at the Aguilar Library two blocks away on 110th Street. Three decades earlier Pete escaped certain death, or at least the loss of his precious skates, by seeking refuge in the incongruous grandeur of the library. A generation later José escaped the embarrassment of being held back in school by reading every book on the sparse shelves.

José attended a private parochial school in the grand old Catholic institution St. Cecilia's, on 106th Street. St. Cecilia's Church had long been the repository of community faith among Puerto Ricans. Though serving a diverse congregation before and after Puerto Rican settlement, it became a refuge for Puerto Ricans. José recalls, "Back then St. Cecilia's was half Hispanic Puerto Rican and half Italian and Irish. We were moving in and they were moving out. So I got to see that transition." Its immense red-hued facade and neo-Gothic convent building swallowed up three quarters of the city block and was packed with religious and social services, including classes for the immigrant community. "The Sisters of Atonement and the Sisters of Mercy were both in the same building on 106th Street. I went to the Sisters of Atonement nursery and then St. Cecilia's grammar school, they were the Sisters of Mercy."

Atonement and Mercy, a heady contradiction for a young man in a sea of transition and difference: "The nuns weren't too sensitive back then. There were fifteen of us Puerto Rican kids in that first class, and they would tell us, 'You're stupid. You're going to fail this year.' And we did fail, they left back fifteen of us. It was along color lines, except for like two people who were white."

José worked hard to redress the educational discrimination that he felt held him back so early. But the damage to his sense of self and community was done, leading to disaffection with the world beyond tight-knit Spanish Harlem on 106th Street. By the time he entered high school, the streets were neat boundaries of difference—competing Harlems, competing worlds that threatened perpetual intrusion on hard-won collective turf: "From there I went to Power Memorial High School, which is no longer there. It was a private Catholic high school for men over by Lincoln Center, run by the Irish Christian brothers. We figured out we could walk to the train at 110th and Lenox and take that. The only thing was we had to walk all the way to Lenox. It's long and you don't know what's going to happen and there's people there. Things weren't that bad, but it was Harlem. I was thinking, 'These people are animals.'" Even now José cringes at his own ignorance. "God punishes me for thinking this stuff, you know."

By the 1960s, despite the more than half a million Puerto Ricans who arrived in the United States from the island during that decade, the great wave of Puerto Rican migration was slowing. In 1965 new legislation opened the doors to a host of other immigrant groups. As they had for centuries, many settled in East Harlem, competing with each other and those already entrenched to force further shifts in the ethnic mélange of neighborhood street life. In 1965 Puerto Ricans held a slim majority with 41 percent of the population, and African Americans were close behind with 38 percent. The median family income in East Harlem was $3,700, about 38 percent lower than the median for New York City. One in three pregnant mothers received no prenatal care, and infant mortality was 37 per 1,000 live births compared to the city average of 26. Even then, East Harlem was home to more public housing projects than anywhere else in the city, with one in three residents living in them.[16] José, like most Puerto Ricans, felt the shift and braced for the changes to come.

"There are people with guns in the church!" José's mother rattled through the three-bedroom apartment one morning in mid-October 1970. José's father turned on the television to watch the drama unfold. A small group of Latino youth known as the Young Lords had barricaded themselves inside the Spanish Methodist Church on 111th Street—for the second time.[17]

In summer 1969 the Young Lords, a street gang with ties to the Black Panther movement that started in Chicago and spread to other cities, including New York, had garnered media attention for dumping garbage at traffic intersections along Park Avenue in East Harlem.[18] Protesting the perceived deficiency in municipal attention to El Barrio, the Young Lords successfully made a name for themselves in the local press. Then, on December 28, 1969, after months of animus between the Young Lords and the Cuban pastor of the church who refused to host a breakfast program for local children, the Young Lords seized the Spanish Methodist Church on 111th Street. For eleven days, the Young Lords held teach-ins, rallies, and press conferences from inside the church, refusing to vacate until they were given permission to run their breakfast program. On January 8, 1970, 105 members of the Young Lords agreed to leave the building and end the standoff.[19]

Several months later a member of the Young Lords was found dead in his jail cell after an arrest for attempted arson. A funeral procession ended at the same Spanish Methodist Church on October 18, 1970, and two hundred Young Lords once again seized the church. This time they were heavily armed and demanded an inquiry into what they called the assassination of their fellow member at the hands of prison officials. They would remain barricaded in the church for almost two months.[20]

The Young Lords were tapping into the nascent angst of a new generation of Puerto Rican youth. No longer a huddled mass of migrants, desperate for steady work and decent housing, these children of newcomers found themselves citizens of a nation that still considered them freeloading immigrants. The Young Lords, like many young Puerto Ricans in East Harlem and throughout New York City, rejected the second-class nature of their citizenship and rallied around a new nationalism, a Puerto Rican nationalism linked to the ongoing struggle for Puerto Rican independence from the United States.

Inspired by the radical movements of the late 1960s, the politics of the Young Lords may have resonated with mainland sympathizers and island revolutionaries, but not all East Harlem Puerto Ricans were eager to sever the link with the United States. Many in the older generation of devout Catholic and politically conservative Puerto Ricans favored the status quo of commonwealth status or even full-fledged statehood.

José's parents made clear their distaste for the Young Lords' tactics and instilled a palpable fear in their fifteen-year-old son. "When they took over the building, I was so afraid. I thought, 'We can't even walk through the neighborhood, there are people with guns.' I didn't want to go outside. I experienced the Young Lords by virtue of fear," José explains. He was shielded from much of the activity taking place only a few blocks away, zealously protected by his mother. "I only got to see it over the news on TV. But I knew it was right there. I could look down the street and see the cop cars."

José's mother could not keep him inside for long. Whether inspired or repulsed by the actions of the Young Lords, he soon found himself enmeshed in the tangled web of neighborhood politics. It was perfect timing.

"I came out of hotline," José recalls. In 1970, not long after the Young Lords seized the church and local headlines, a young man named Ralph Flores started a telephone counseling service in some spare rooms at

Washington Houses.[21] "Ralph and a group of teens came up with the idea after one of the teens died of an overdose. He said, 'We need to intervene.' So they came up with the hotline as a crisis intervention by phone." A few years later José joined the group as a teen counselor. "I thought it was a great idea, helping people over the phone, saving lives and so on. As it turned out, as I came in, all the kids who were there before were leaving for college. So I was the only worker for a year. He gave me the key to the space and a row of four phones."

José's work at the hotline led to a number of lasting relationships with East Harlem neighborhood activists, including Norman Eddy, who had helped to negotiate the surrender of the Young Lords during their church-bound standoff. "Politics in the 1970s was black and white for some of us. I was in Norman Eddy's group, and we were the reformers."

In the decades leading up to the 1970s, political power in New York City was centralized and largely detached from the concerns of local communities. The Civil Rights and other social movements had begun to challenge the consolidation of power around political machines, and by the time John Lindsay took office as mayor in 1966 the stage was set for one of the most sweeping political decentralizations in urban America.

In 1968 Lindsay proposed local law 39, which redefined and empowered community planning boards established in the 1961 city charter revision. This allowed a school decentralization bill to be passed in 1969 that created local school boards with the power to appoint superintendents and administrators. In 1971 Lindsay established the Office of Neighborhood Government, which connected community planning boards with his Urban Action Task Force.[22] The cumulative result was that two years after Lindsay left office, many of his reforms were written into the 1975 city charter revision that created the current community board system, including community board 11, which represents East Harlem.

Against the backdrop of Lindsay's decentralization and a looming fiscal crisis, José and his political mentors fought against what they saw as endemic corruption among local politicians. The principal target was Angelo del Toro, a Puerto Rican representative to the New York state assembly throughout the 1960s and 1970s. As a teenage political idealist, José was unconcerned about ethnic loyalties and pushed for del Toro's

eviction from office. Del Toro's brother, William, was eventually convicted of bribery charges in 1974, but when he was later released from
prison and paid back salary by his own nonprofit organization, José was
outraged. "I called up the paper and made a big stink and they wrote
about it. And the Hispanic community was pissed at me. But I was very
upset that my community would be looked at that way."[23] José was nineteen years old.

While José was busy sorting out his place in neighborhood politics, his
mother was following in the footsteps of Pete's mother and countless
other women in the garment worker's trade. "My mother was a seam-
stress," he explains. "She was part of the International Ladies Garment
Workers Union." Entering the labor force in the 1950s, José's mother took
advantage of a still-thriving industrial economy in New York City.
Though this would not last into the next decade, even at its peak, the
work was arduous and often dangerous. "It was a sweatshop. My mother
got paid by the piece; if she didn't show up, she didn't get paid."

The working conditions made an impression on José: "She would take
us to work, because she was not going to miss work. All the friends that
came to their parties actually worked with her. And they would always
talk about school. I remember the guy who used to iron, he used to say,
'Make sure you stay in school and go to college so you don't have to do
what I am doing.'"

For a time, José followed the advice of his mother's coworkers, and in
1975 he graduated from Power Memorial High School. By then New York
City was well on its way to an economic and social implosion. Recognizing the signposts of a radical new economy, José broke the mold of typical
East Harlem Puerto Ricans and enrolled at Fordham University, intent on
completing the full circuit of Catholic education. But, after three and a half
years, José walked out of the high-rise university at Lincoln Center just
one semester short of his degree. "You get tired in school after a while."

It was an ill-timed fatigue. By 1975 the city ledgers revealed a stagger-
ing array of fiscal failure: a budget deficit of $2 billion, an accumulated
debt of $13 billion, and an unemployment rate of 11 percent.[24] Hardest
hit was the already diminishing industrial sector of the New York metro-

politan area, which in 1960 represented 12 percent of all manufacturing employment. By 1983 industrial labor dropped by half in the city, and close to 450,000 workers lost their jobs.[25] It was a precipitous descent for a region that in 1960 was responsible for a third of the nation's financial sector.[26]

Of course, the early 1970s were lean times for all Americans. In 1973 oil prices soared, taking inflation and interest rates with them. But given the disproportionate share of the nation's economy carried by New York City, these difficult times became truly insurmountable for the overburdened metropolis. Fearing for the solvency of the city, banks began raising interest rates for loans to the city and began selling off city bonds. By April 1975, with no credit to continue borrowing, the city stood on the precipice of bankruptcy. Mayor Abraham Beame appealed to President Gerald Ford for federal assistance but was denied, prompting the October *Daily News* headline: "Ford to City: Drop Dead." A month later politics prevailed, and with federal support New York began the slow climb out of economic ruin.

But the deathblow had been dealt to the industrial economy, the mainstay of Puerto Rican employment, not to mention the dreams of tens of thousands of new immigrants arriving at JFK airport each year since the mid-1960s. The factory work that welcomed new arrivals in the 1930s and 1940s taught a generation of laborers to devalue higher education, which many believed would only delay entry to the labor force.

José remembers the experience of his sister, twelve years his senior, before the economic upheaval of the 1970s: "My sister graduated from Julia Richman High School, and the next day she went to work. And in those days there were a lot of jobs. As soon as you came out of high school that was the thing. Not that many people went to college. You went from high school to a job, but there were jobs for you. They were mostly in manufacturing. My cousin from Puerto Rico got a job putting heads on a doll in a factory. There were a lot of those jobs available in the city then." When a new service economy replaced manufacturing, education became the key to advancement, leaving the children of factory workers with few options for legitimate employment.

"After the economy changed my mother didn't work in the garment district anymore. She opened her own bridal shop. She shared an office with a lawyer who did nothing but curse. It was terrible." Like Pete's mother sewing gloves in their Italian Harlem apartment, José's mother adapted to her place in the local economy. If factory work was unavailable, she put her textile skills to entrepreneurial use. "She put together gorgeous dresses. My mother, being like myself, was not a good businessperson. She would do the wedding dress but then do all the bridesmaids dresses for free, because she felt bad."

.   .   .   .   .

José's daughter, Jessica, has arrived home before the rest of the family. José has eaten the last of his burger and taunts her with its infamous origins.

"What, you didn't have your daily roach requirement yet?" Jessica asks.

José laughs a deep, throaty laugh—a sound you hear often in his company, especially with his kids. Jessica is a freshman at Hunter College, on 68th Street and Lexington Avenue.

Soon Cecilia arrives with José, their eldest, and Letticia. "Hey!" José brightens perceptibly as they enter. His son says, "Hey, Dad," as Letticia helps Cecilia with food left over from José's parents.

"You want some spaghetti with Spam?" Cecilia asks.

"Spam meatballs, a Puerto Rican delicacy," José says. He then sheepishly admits to the burger, and Cecilia gives him a long look. "It was good!" he protests, adding, "Except for the roaches."

Letticia wrinkles her nose. She is the youngest and still in high school. Cecilia slumps into a chair, replacing a stray strand from her bobbed hair.

"Whew, sorry, but my feet hurt and I'm tired," Cecilia exhales. A recent ankle injury still bothers her, made worse by frequent double shifts as a supervisor of the Metropolitan Hospital switchboard.

José says, "That was fast."

"Hello, your sister wasn't there." Cecilia rolls her eyes and engages a pantomime that belies her professed fatigue, "We went, 'Love you, Mami. You ate? Okay, great. Kiss. Kiss. Bye. We're gone.'"

José fills the room with another smoky laugh. "You're the best. I wouldn't trade you for anything."

ummary[...]

José started dating Cecilia when he was a student at Fordham. "At a sweet sixteen party, I walked in, and Ceci's sitting on some boy's lap. She was all of fifteen. And she had this red outfit on, red shirt, red pants, everything was red. But I knew who she was. Her mother would come buy dresses from us. And we started dancing and we just hung out."

By the time he dropped out of college and joined the military, José had asked Cecilia to marry him. He joined the navy in an administrative position and was commuting to his posts first in Staten Island and then Brooklyn. His father's pride at having a son in the military competed with the disappointment of friends and mentors in the community who saw the military as an agent of U.S. imperialism, particularly against Puerto Rico. Norman Eddy made no secret of his frustration at José's career choice. "Norman was upset at me for joining the military, because you know he was a liberal and he was like, 'You shouldn't join the military!' And I said, 'I need a job.' I did what I had to do. I joined the military, and it was great. It got me out of here, and I got to see different parts of the world, different states anyway."

New Jersey, at least. His first post was in Bayonne, just across the port from Staten Island on the New Jersey shore. José, Cecilia, and their newborn son, José, settled into married housing to await two more daughters. From Bayonne, the growing family was shipped to Albany. And for the first time in his life, José had a house with a yard. "It was nice to have a house. My kids kind of grew up there. They went from being three years old to about seven there. From there I decided to leave the military, 'cause they were really working me, twelve-hour days. And I came back to East Harlem to do the community work that I always wanted to do."

In all, José spent a little less than a decade outside his beloved East Harlem. But when he and his new family returned in 1989, it was to an East Harlem far different from the one they left. "That's when the crack epidemic hit, when I was outside the neighborhood. It was a noticeable change. Coming back, you were a little fearful. I noticed people were more skittish, now people were actually looking around and seeing who was in the elevator with them, who's walking by them, who's behind them."[27]

East Harlem was still a predominantly Puerto Rican community in 1989. Puerto Ricans constituted 82 percent of all Latinos in the neighborhood and 46 percent of the total population. Median household income in East Harlem in the year José returned to the neighborhood was $9,371, 44 percent lower than the New York average. The astonishing transformation of New York City from an industrial center to a service-based economy in the wake of the fiscal crisis of the mid-1970s left generations of Puerto Rican skilled laborers with little hope for gainful employment. Millions had traveled north to take advantage of the strongest industrial economy in the hemisphere at midcentury, only to find factories closed and jobs gone.

Disillusioned young people in East Harlem scrambled to generate income in an exploding informal economy that included hand-to-hand sales of crack cocaine. Few were completely removed from that downward spiral of criminalized activity, as José points out: "My uncle was one of them. He was a hoodlum, a user, probably a part-time dealer. He was always in jail. He got on methadone, and then he stayed on methadone. He never had a job. He never worked a day in his life. I think he worked harder trying to beat the system."

Despite the quagmire of unemployment and escalating public violence, José was determined to return to East Harlem. "I still wanted to come back. By the time it was '89, it had already peaked and was on its way down."

Throughout the 1990s crime decreased precipitously in New York City, and East Harlem was no exception. From 1993 to 1997 violent crime in the neighborhood decreased by 37 percent. By 2002 violent crime had decreased by 61 percent over the previous decade.[28] This much-publicized decrease occurred in spite of the continued economic hardship faced by East Harlem residents: 38 percent still lived below the poverty line; 40 percent of households still reported no wage or salary income; and the median income remained 44 percent lower than the city average.

The decrease in crime inspired nascent community activists to focus their attention on persistent economic problems. José joined community board 11, which serves East Harlem, and became an outspoken advocate for the Puerto Rican presence in the neighborhood. He reconnected with Norman Eddy, joined Eddy's Metro North Association, and used his political capital to persuade New York state senator Olga Mendez to help him find an apartment in public housing across from his new job at Metropolitan Hospital.

As East Harlem found its feet again, so did José. Both survived a decade in the wilderness, José in the military and East Harlem in the pit of municipal neglect, and both emerged in the 1990s with a renewed commitment to self-improvement. "My supervisor at Metropolitan Hospital said, 'You have to finish college.' And I saw the truth in that, and went over there and asked if they would take me back, and they said yes. And it was the same person that got me in the first time! It was the same woman, she was African American and a very nice person. So all of that is a miracle. It was so painful, but who cares. I finished college first, I was the first one in my family to finish college after doing ten years in the military."

.   .   .   .   .

"I wish I was going to be thirty again. It goes so fast." José sits hunched over the open chassis of a homemade computer. Stray wires and odd-shaped components lie strewn about the double bed in one of the two bedrooms of his apartment. Cecilia saunters in with a dish of potato chips and a glass of soda for José.

"Careful, Ceci," he cautions as she holds the full glass over the open chassis. Cecilia retreats in silence, and José returns to his hobby.

"My sister will be fifty this year. That's like, wow, man, you're middle-aged." José shakes his head and takes a sip of soda. "She's the one who convinced me to move to Florida. I told my wife we have to live there, my sister had convinced me." José sags under the weight of his regret and adds, "I really wish she hadn't."

Like the Irish, Germans, Russian Jews, and Italians before him, José joined a seemingly endless cycle of immigration and slow upward mobility that had steadily transformed East Harlem from one enclave into another. As those before had moved to the Bronx, Long Island, or New Jersey, Puerto Ricans steadily left El Barrio. Some returned to Puerto Rico, fulfilling the dreams of parents or grandparents, but most stayed in the United States, searching for that iconic image of American prosperity, home ownership.

So, in 1997, José and Cecilia liquidated their accumulated pensions and began searching for real estate. Home ownership in New York proved out of reach, and his sister's testimonials about life in Florida were persuasive. "By then I had done almost ten years of community work, and Ceci had put up with a lot, meetings and me not being home, and things like that. So I thought this was something I could do for her, even though it meant leaving the community that I love. At least she could have her house, that she wants, and I could give something to my wife."

José quit his job at Metropolitan Hospital and traveled to Florida with $20,000—the entire sum from their pensions. After living a few weeks with his sister, he rented a house and sent for his family. But living with his sister and trying to adjust to the car culture of Florida had taken its toll. "By the time I had picked out that house, we had paid $3,000, a month's rent and two months' security. The airfare was $1,000. Moving our stuff over was $4,000. The car that I bought was $5,400. Before I knew it, all I had left was $6,000. I thought, 'No!' And I told my sister, 'Something tells me that this is not going to work.'"

It did not take long for Cecilia to see the futility of their plan and agree to return to East Harlem. They had already given up their apartment in public housing, so they had to move in with José's parents until they could resettle. "I was in Florida five months, Ceci was there three and a half. And the money was all gone, $20,000. And it hurts coming back here and telling people. Because everyone said, 'Wish you luck,' and then to come back and have them ask, 'What are you doing back here?' And have to say, 'It didn't work.' It's embarrassing. What still hurts to this day is to lose that much money and not have anything to show for it."

Cecilia managed to get back her job at Metropolitan Hospital, and José eventually found work at the newly opened Upper Manhattan Empowerment Zone, an initiative of the Clinton administration. In the time they were away, a coworker at the hospital had become the owner-landlord of a triplex townhouse in a new housing development.

"I remember saying good-bye to Maria, she was a renter then, knowing she was going to buy this and saying good luck. I never knew that we would end up living with her." José and his family were able to rent Maria's top-floor, two-bedroom apartment, but the arrangement exacerbated José's frustration over losing $20,000. "When Maria explained how much she needed for the house, we had exactly that. We had the right amount of money to buy one of these, and I could have been a home owner. And it makes a difference, someone could be paying my mortgage. And there is security in that. I'm a tenant. And the place is really too small for us."

Still, sitting in his cramped bedroom, peering into the chassis of the unfinished computer, José can reminisce about Florida with the beginnings of a smile. "We did love that house. I loved having a backyard where I could sit and read the paper and just be at peace. That's what I miss, the backyard. It means a lot to me to have a place like that."

.   .   .   .   .

Someone urinated in the elevator. A small pool of liquid, forcing fellow residents to press against the walls, surrounds the carcass of a soggy, half-smoked cigar. José presses the button for the sixth floor and pretends not to notice.

It's his mother's birthday, and the family has gathered in their apartment in DeWitt Clinton Houses to celebrate. Only a few weeks before, she spent several days in Mt. Sinai Hospital after her latest episode of heart trouble. José, like the rest of his family, wonders how much longer she will be around.

The elevator doors slide apart, and José expertly avoids the puddle of urine to enter the fluorescent haze of the sixth-floor hallway. Cream cinder blocks run up the walls, punctuated by pale green doors. Around a corner, down the hall, and José pushes into 6H.

"Hello," announces José in a happy singsong.

His elder sister appears in the doorway of the kitchen, two feet from José, and asks, "You hungry?"

To the left, a long hallway leading to three bedrooms carries the laughter of José's children and their cousins playing in a back room. Cecilia is working a double shift and will not make it to the party. To the right, through a narrow doorway, José's frail mother rests lightly in a heavy black wheelchair in the middle of the small vinyl-covered living room. A plastic tiara sits atop her head, and the tray strapped to the arms of her chair is weighted down with gifts waiting to be opened. On the couch, a rotating group of family, José's sister and brothers and some of their children, sits patiently engaging the matriarch with brief chats in Spanish. Across the room, José's father sits in a recliner wearing a sleeveless T-shirt, boxer shorts, and slippers. One hand rests on his pot belly, the other grasps a remote control that flips between the Mets and the Yankees playing on separate channels of the large television.

"My mother is sick, and she is not going to last much longer, and I am not sure what is going to happen when my father is by himself." José's concern is less about his father's well-being than it is about the fate of his childhood home. "Already they have tried to get people who had families but are now by themselves to move out. 'Cause the truth is families need those three bedrooms. But the sad part is, if that happens, how do I have access to that in the future? It's important. People grow up in a home, and the family still owns the home, they have every confidence in the world that you are going to be able to go back there."

The narrow corridors of their beehive apartment have been home to José and his family off and on since 1965. The sadness over losing his connection to the tattered public housing unit is tempered only by his ongoing alienation from the building itself. The changes that prompted their shift from Jefferson to DeWitt Clinton are not far from his calculations. "If I could move into DeWitt Clinton, except for the animals in the building, I would—I am talking about the people, *los animales.* You know, the animals. It wouldn't be safe for my kids, in the elevator all the time. But at some point we will probably lose the apartment, unless I get it somehow."

After an hour of pleas from the younger children, José's sister unveils the ice-cream cake purchased for the occasion. José's parents remain in the living room, father in his recliner and mother in her wheelchair. Candles are lit, and the sing-along begins with family drawn close to the withered woman. The lyrics are familiar, but the rhythm shifts midway into an unmistakable Latin beat. The ice-cream cake starts to lean and dribble as it melts under the heat of the candles. The close-knit group dances and jiggles to the Nuyorican stylings of "Happy Birthday."

"When you move someplace, and you form an enclave, people naturally stick together, whereas back on the island they would probably never hang out." José has only visited Puerto Rico once or twice, though he still has plenty of extended family living there. His sense of being Puerto Rican comes from the vibe in that room, the transplanted nature of an ethnicity on the move. As he says, "But once you are far from your old homeland, that has a dynamic all its own. Once you have those shared values, you tend to coalesce and stick together more than if you were on the island."

Perhaps that is what feeds his turf-based approach to local politics. This approach works diligently to mark the boundaries of El Barrio regardless of the ongoing turnover of its tenants. In fact, according to the 2000 census, non-Hispanic black residents outnumber Puerto Ricans in East Harlem for the first time since the 1940s, with Mexicans gaining on their position among Hispanics. Still, as far as José is concerned, "I think every seat in this district should be Puerto Rican. The assemblyman should be Puerto Rican. The council member should definitely be Puerto Rican. The state senator should be Puerto Rican. But the Puerto Ricans don't vote, that's our biggest problem. If 90 percent of us voted, we could control whatever we wanted, but we don't."

That a Puerto Rican fills none of the political positions enumerated by José is a constant frustration for him, especially in regard to the community board that represents East Harlem. In 2001 he published reports on his own community-based website accusing the community board of disproportionately African American representation and criticized as too "Afrocentric" the entertainment chosen for the night that new officers were installed. "Community board members are volunteers, they don't get paid, they give of their time. They should be applauded. But the people who appoint, the borough president and city council representative, by appointing African Americans they can get things through that are not really for East Harlem, but are more for Harlem. There's no differentiation between East Harlem and Harlem for them, it's just the 125th Street strip."

José's accusation of insensitivity to the history of community boundaries applies not only to the community board but also to many of the cultural institutions that mark the identity of Spanish Harlem. "Cultural institutions survive because they adapt to the population," he explains. "They are like buoys in the sea telling you who is here. We have a lot fewer institutions, so what I am saying is we want to have a presence here forever. A marker to say, 'Hey, we were here.' In that respect, don't take away our institutions." Unfortunately, that is exactly what José and other community activists feel is taking place.

The clearest example is El Museo del Barrio. It began in 1969 as a Puerto Rican art museum and educational institution in the heart of the neighborhood. The fledgling Museo occupied several locations around 104th Street and Lexington Avenue and has asserted itself as a distinctly Puerto Rican institution. In 1977 it moved to a new space on Fifth Avenue and 104th Street. The same year, El Museo joined the Cultural Institutions Group of the City of New York, and a year later, it became a founding member of the Museum Mile Association. But in the years since its move to Fifth Avenue, El Museo has expanded its original mission as a Puerto Rican art museum to exhibit art from across Latin America.[29]

The more inclusive agenda offended many Puerto Ricans who had worked so hard to create an institution to serve their community. This sense of disconnection was exacerbated in 2001 when the museum announced its intention to hire a new director, most likely from outside the community. José and others joined a campaign to put pressure on the museum to hire a Puerto Rican director and return to its roots in the community. But in November 2002 El Museo announced the appointment of Julian Zugazagoitia. Born and raised in Mexico, Zugazagoitia not only is El Museo's first non–Puerto Rican director but also represents a connection to that other burgeoning Hispanic population in East Harlem—one that has already met with strong resistance from the Puerto Rican community.

José is philosophical about the setback, ceding defeat without giving ground to the immigrant newcomers. "They didn't do that because of Mexicans. They did it because of money. Because there are more people of Central America and South America in the arts with money, they're willing to fund something that is more like them. So they made it more like them. And because of them, the institution survives. Because it was not going to survive just on Puerto Ricans, it wasn't. We weren't going there! People forget that it was a good intention, but it has to—cash has to feed it."

But if the political loss over El Museo did not smart enough, there is the perceived cultural encroachment of Central Harlem into El Barrio. "Since the 1940s this has been Spanish and that has been black, and never shall the twain meet, culturally. We're different." José refers to the differences between Central and East Harlem, marked most clearly in the boundary of Fifth Avenue. But that boundary will be tested by plans for the new Museum of African Art, which will be built on a vacant lot at 110th Street and Fifth Avenue. "They got all of Harlem to do their thing. We're not biased, but why can't we have our own space, and within that space have our own thing? There's plenty of space, Harlem is a lot bigger than East Harlem."

The boundary of Fifth Avenue was tested once before, when the musician Bobby Short arranged for a memorial statue of Duke Ellington to be erected on the same intersection as the proposed Museum of African Art. The statue, dedicated in 1997, places Ellington high above the street and looking east down 110th Street into East Harlem.[30] "It needs to be moved," José says. "Don't be surprised someday if it's moved. You just melt the bottom with acid, you get a crane and quietly drop it in Harlem somewhere, maybe Morningside Park. It is an affront. They had their argument, that you have to be inclusive. But how come we always have to be inclusive? You don't see any Hispanic stuff over in Harlem. We wouldn't want it there anyway. We didn't grow up there."

Not to be outdone, Puerto Ricans in East Harlem arranged for 110th Street to be renamed shortly after the death of the local Puerto Rican music icon Tito Puente. Today, Tito Puente Way runs directly into the Duke Ellington statue, much to José's satisfaction. "And! There's hope that a Tito Puente statue could be on the opposite side. There are people trying to raise money for that. But that costs millions."

Like Pete, José can see the changes around him, but he sees them in a different light. Whereas Pete laments the rise of public housing as the death sentence to economic development in his neighborhood, José sees buildings like DeWitt Clinton as the only impediment to rampant escalations in the cost of living.

"106th Street will be like 86th Street. Not fast, because of the projects. There's too many people in the projects, so that kind of lowers other things like prices, or keeps them low." But not forever. José senses it is only a matter of time. "It's hard. People won't be able to stay, they'll have to go to the Bronx, and then keep moving until—I'm not sure where we can go. I think it will take a while for the neighborhood to change a lot, if it even changes."

Part of that shift, however, is the cyclical transformation of the neighborhood that José himself attempted to engage when he moved to Florida. As Puerto Ricans find a foothold in the changing economy, more and more find homes outside the cocoon of Spanish Harlem. "Many of them ended up in Florida. Another enclave! But a different place, with a home. East Harlem, with a home and grass and mosquitoes and hurricanes." It was a dream José allowed himself to pursue, if only for a few months.

But as the Puerto Ricans find their way to the Bronx or New Jersey or even Florida, who will be left to fill the void? José has a ready answer: "Mexicans."

He has noticed the rise in Mexican migration to the new Spanish Harlem; it is impossible to ignore. "116th Street used to be Puerto Rican, but that's more Mexican now. The good thing about the Mexicans coming in is that it will still be Spanish Harlem. A different type of Spanish, a different sense of Spanish, but it will still be Spanish. This to me is what makes it Spanish Harlem."

But José knows this, too, may be transitory. He has participated in the street life of the neighborhood too long to be fooled by the so-called permanence of an ethnic enclave. He sees the Mexicans, the West Africans, the Asians. "But in another fifty years, it might not be any of them. It's very dynamic. You can't expect the neighborhood to stay the same forever. The most we can call it is East Harlem, but we can't call it Spanish Harlem forever, or El Barrio forever. But historically for that time period, for a specific time period, it will be called that, and that's cool."

José's extended family spills out of the front doors of the DeWitt Clinton building, children revved up from ice-cream cake and adults weighed down by barbecue. José's brothers and sister pile into their cars, preparing for the drive north to the Bronx and beyond, where they have all scattered in their years since childhood. Only José remains, just a few blocks away, and after the late-night hugs and gentle teasing, he shepherds his kids across Lexington Avenue toward home.

"If it meant moving to the Bronx to have a house, I would move to the Bronx." José reflects on his long years in the neighborhood, his futile attempt to escape, and his prospects for the future. "I could always come back. I've done enough community work so no one can say, 'You just came and left.' What more can you ask of somebody? Now I want my own place, especially if it has some green that's mine. I would rather it be East Harlem, but I don't think that's going to happen. I would love for that bubble to burst in the real estate market. Burst good! Blow up! Implode! 'Cause maybe there would be a shot for people."

José hesitates, then adds, "It's not likely to happen."

FOUR 125th Street

Bare fluorescent bulbs cast a green pall over the lobby of UPACA Gardens, a low-rise public housing building tucked among tenements and vacant lots near 125th Street. The lobby, submerged in the algae light, feels like the bottom of a public pool with stark white tiles running from front door to back and up the few steps to the elevators and stairwells. The walls are covered in a thick fondant of paint, layer after layer of the same industrial yellow caking the thick columns and running over conduit, light switches, and electrical outlets.

Lucille and Ms. McQueen sit in the deep end of the lobby, twenty feet from the front door and fewer to the back, perched on two folding metal chairs. Between them waits the folding card table, with its peeling vinyl top and thin metal legs—waiting for visitors to sign its neatly printed log while Lucille and Ms. McQueen share a knowing look. For two hours each weeknight, visitors and residents wade through the empty lobby under the watchful eyes of the two-woman tenant patrol, cautiously grumbling about their overbearing rules and quietly thankful that some-one has an eye on the door.

Sounds ricochet off the bare walls—squealing children, gossiping adults, and the deep bass of neighboring apartment stereos—pierced every few minutes by the high tone of the two-inch-thick stainless steel security door opening and closing. Under the riot of noise, the occasional Metro North train rumbles over the trestle half a block away toward its stop two blocks north on 125th Street.

"I need to show you something in my apartment."

A neighbor on the second floor has shuffled into view and stands bashfully by the steps leading out of the lobby. She is dressed in fuzzy slippers, shorts, and a bra, her hair in oversized curlers.

Lucille, approaching middle age, with dark skin and shoulder-length, iron-straight hair, is the president of the tenants' association. Her thin, almost frail-looking frame hides a hair-trigger temper and fearless indig-nation about disorder and disrespect. When she speaks it is in the low tones of the soft-spoken, until a neighbor's music deafens the conversa-tion or a child who should know better tests her authority.

Lucille looks at the woman half-dressed in her lobby and waits for the story.

"You know how they fixed that lady's washing machine upstairs and there was that leak? And remember they came and fixed my whole ceil-ing? Now my paint is peeling."

Lucille lets exasperation contort her face but remains silent. The woman, staring down at the bright pink toenails peeking out of her slip-pers, giggles.

"See, I'm laughin' but it's not funny."

"No, it's not funny," Lucille finally replies.

"I'm laughing because me and her had an argument two days ago. We was in the hallway on the second floor. And then it happened again today . . ." The woman launches into another in a string of dramas played out in the hallways of UPACA Gardens, all of which eventually make their way to Lucille on her folding metal chair. "I can't do this anymore," the woman concludes. "I wanted to put carpet down, but I can't now, the water came through my living room."

"No, you can't put no carpet down." Lucille settles the matter, and the fuzzy slippers retreat to the second floor.

Ms. McQueen looks up from the glossy circular from one of the local stores, and the two share another look. Ms. McQueen, older and even more soft-spoken, likes to read the promotional circulars with a ballpoint pen and a ready pack of mints, lozenges, and hard candy. Neither woman needs many words in the execution of her duty; a quick glance or a subtle move of the eyebrow as a newcomer signs the log is all that is needed to communicate suspicion over what goes on in 2G, 4B, or 3C.

Around 8:00 P.M. Joyce shuffles into the lobby and takes a seat a few feet from the tenant patrol. Several years older than Lucille or Ms. McQueen, Joyce still has the slow drawl of the South but doesn't speak often enough for the casual observer to notice. She nods hello to the two women and settles into her role as innocent bystander to the drama of the UPACA Gardens lobby.

.   .   .   .   .

"I was born in 1948. Right on the spot." Lucille jabs a finger down on the table and offers a firm nod of affirmation. She was the second child of a single mother living with her parents in a tenement building on 117th Street. Lucille would eventually share the four-room railroad apartment with two sisters, two brothers, her mother, and two grandparents.

In the years after the Civil War, African Americans began a long transition from agricultural to industrial laborers. Factory jobs, which paid higher wages and were better insulated from the fluctuating market for agricultural products, were mostly in the North, and that's where African Americans headed. From 1890 to 1910 the African American population in New York alone almost tripled. In just two decades roughly 200,000 African Americans emigrated from the South to the manufacturing centers of the Northeast and the West Coast. By 1910 there were more than 91,000 African Americans in New York City, and of the 60,534 who called Manhattan home, only 14,309 were born in New York State.[1]

In the decades that followed, world wars and tighter immigration laws created an ever-widening space for African Americans eager to leave behind the tenuousness of southern agricultural labor. But the economic pull factors paled in comparison to the push factors of segregation and white supremacist terrorism. Between 1910 and 1930 New York City's African American population tripled again, to more than 300,000.

Many of those making the journey north in the first decades of the twentieth century settled in Harlem, and those who didn't had at least heard of the area above 110th Street as the capital of Black America. And though the community east of Fifth Avenue had always been distinct from Central Harlem—culturally more diverse and economically more depressed—African Americans tended to take Harlem with them wherever they settled. As the novelist Ralph Ellison described it, "Harlem has a way of expanding. It goes where Negroes go, or where we go in certain numbers."[2] By 1940 African Americans made up 20 percent of East Harlem's population. By the time Lucille was born in 1948, almost one-third of East Harlem residents were African American. Indeed, despite the perception of a Puerto Rican majority, at least in terms of outnumbering African Americans, in East Harlem the two groups were dead even at 30 percent of the population in 1950—two years after Lucille was born and five years before José's birth.[3]

Lucille's mother traveled north from Georgia with her parents sometime in the early forties—in the waning years of the Great Migration. By the time they settled into East Harlem, African Americans had long laid claim to upper Manhattan. Jobs were plentiful in the absence of the young men shipped off to fight World War II, and after the lean years of the 1930s cities like New York were preparing for a long cycle of prosperity. Lucille's grandmother, like many African American women, had little trouble finding work as a domestic employee, and her grandfather secured a position as a Pullman porter on the Penn Central Line, which ran over the elevated trestle along Park Avenue half a block away.

Lucille's mother was just seventeen when she had her first daughter and nineteen when she gave birth to Lucille. In the ensuing years, she would have three more children, the last daughter in 1965, just ten months before her death at the age of thirty-seven. Lucille remembers her mother as the quintessential young Harlem socialite—member of several social clubs and always out on the town: "She was an Elk, she was an Eastern Star, and she was a Royal Deluxe Girl. They were social clubs, they gave dances and things like that." Nights out were usually spent west of Fifth Avenue in the legendary dance halls of Harlem in the early 1950s. "You had different places you could go: the Renaissance Ballroom, and you had the Savoy, and I remember Small's Paradise, Wilt Chamberlain's place." Lucille's mother spent time in all the clubs, listening to Duke Ellington's big band sound slowly become the bebop jazz of Miles Davis and Jimmy Smith.

Lucille's father was a mystery, a void in the family history that was filled to the extent it could be by her grandfather and family friends. "I met my father after my mother died. I met him one time. Next thing I knew my aunt called and said he'd passed. Maybe I had bitterness in me, but I wasn't going to go to the funeral. I regret that now, but, you know, I didn't know him." Her elder sister's father remained close to the family and looked after Lucille as his own, though he never married Lucille's mother or lived in their apartment.

Lucille peers over the top of her glasses in the direction of three children stumbling and laughing from one end of the lobby to the other. "We were blessed. I don't know how we did it, but we were blessed. We had clothes on our back, and we were a family." She leans in closer and raises her voice to compete with the squeals of the children who have disappeared around a corner and let their voices careen through the halls. "You didn't disrespect nobody. You were taught to respect. I had a childhood—" Lucille stops midsentence, rises from her chair, and takes a step toward the hallway.

"HEY!"

Lucille's voice bellows through the lobby, smothering the tinny voices of the children. The echoes drift back to relative silence.

Ms. McQueen shakes her head, lamenting the future and remembering her childhood past. "When I was coming up we had different things for activities. We had hopscotch, we played double Dutch. You don't see too much of that anymore."

"M-hm," Joyce responds in the deep-throated affirmation that only older and wiser women can muster. "Children aren't children anymore. Children enjoyed themselves."

"Red Light, Green Light, One, Two, Three," "Red Devil," and "Hot Peas and Butter." The three women toss out games and memories like cards on the table, laughing at themselves and the innocence of their remembered youth.

Lucille lets a restrained chuckle escape and leans over the vinyl table-top to say, "It didn't matter what side of the track you were on, each block was a family, regardless of who you were. You know that saying, 'It takes a village to raise a child'? I don't care what block you lived in, that block was your village." Despite a father unknown and a mother untethered, Lucille's childhood was centered on a stable and dependable kinship. Due in large measure to the strength of her grandmother, it was also a by-product of the communal life of the street.

When Lucille was still a girl playing on the sidewalks of 117th Street, Jane Jacobs published her landmark book *The Death and Life of Great American Cities*. In it, Jacobs captures much of what Lucille describes as her home on the street, with the public characters of store owners, stoop dwellers, and even drug addicts maintaining a sense of continuity and security in an otherwise insecure time. As Jacobs argues, "Lowly, unpurposeful and random as they may appear, sidewalk contacts are the small change from which a city's wealth of public life may grow."[4] Lucille's wealth was measured in the social connections that spilled out of the overcrowded third-floor apartment and into the public life of her narrow patch of asphalt.

One block over, however, was foreign territory. "And you know it was vibrant, the families and the blocks," Lucille says, "but you couldn't go in nobody else's block 'cause then you was fightin'." The same crumbling asphalt, the same red brick tenements, and the same struggling street-bound entrepreneurs, but crossing streets was like crossing the threshold of another family's home. "Each block you went in it was a different atmosphere, 'cause each block was a family. Each block you went in to visit it was a family unit, you knew you were an outsider. You might know the kids or you might know the parents, but you were still an outsider. When you move in, you are accepted into a family, but if you didn't live there—"

These street-level boundaries were no doubt invisible to the uninitiated, but the larger boundaries of community were evident, especially during Lucille's childhood: 117th Street, between Park and Madison Avenues, was as unique and generic as any East Harlem street in the early 1950s when Lucille was playing Hot Peas and Butter with her friends. A few avenue blocks to the east, things were changing rapidly for the Italians as tenements were razed for low-rise public housing. And across Fifth Avenue to the west, the rumblings of a different sort of change were beginning to take shape in Central Harlem.

"It was different. I had friends who lived uptown on the West Side. It was a whole different scenario up there," Lucille remembers.

Harlem in the 1950s was caught in an awkward historical moment. For most of the early twentieth century, it was the center of African American cultural attention. The Harlem Renaissance had produced some of the most notable writers and artists in contemporary American history, not to mention some of the first African American millionaires. But by the 1950s postwar economic prosperity had accelerated the emigration of middle-class residents, and the businesses and adequate housing that remained were often owned by nonblack outsiders. Perhaps most paradoxically disheartening, the attention Harlem relished had shifted south, exposing the courage of leaders like Martin Luther King Jr. in their struggle against American apartheid and leaving Harlem in a long moment of collective uncertainty.

Out of that history came some of the most forceful and memorable figures of the African American community. In 1952 Ralph Ellison published *Invisible Man,* a compelling chronicle of one man's odyssey during the Great Migration from the South to Harlem. Adam Clayton Powell Jr., former minister of the famous Abyssinian Baptist Church, became the first African American congressman from the Northeast in 1944 and served the cause of the Civil Rights movement throughout the 1950s and 1960s. And in 1954, two years after his release from prison, Malcolm X became the minister of Temple Number 7 in Harlem.

For all its economic and cultural despair, Central Harlem continued to dominate the public imagination concerning upper Manhattan. In a long tradition of racializing geography and essentializing race, New Yorkers knew, for all intents and purposes, that Manhattan stopped where Harlem began—96th Street, river to river. But for insiders, those essentialisms could not erase the power of Fifth Avenue to divide the urban streetscape. East Harlem was never considered an extension of its better-known neighbor, at least not by those who grew up on its streets. Not even by African Americans who knew something changed once you passed Fifth Avenue.

"We know that this is the line," Lucille explains. "Once you cross over Fifth Avenue, you know you are on the West Side."

Fifth Avenue marked the boundary between Central Harlem and East Harlem, but the internal boundaries of ethnic turf were often harder to pinpoint. "El Barrio" and "Italian Harlem" were labels tossed around from time to time but they did not register as discrete geographic locations. They were diffused references to the way languages, music, and food seemed to change the farther south or east Lucille walked from her block on 117th Street.

These changes were most apparent on days Lucille and her friends visited the public pool at Jefferson Park. Walking down the wide thoroughfare of 116th Street past Park, Lexington, Third, and Second Avenues, Lucille could see the storefronts and skin tones change with each passing intersection. By the time she turned right on First Avenue, she was in the heart of what remained of Italian Harlem. By the mid-1950s, when Lucille would take this long walk to the pool, many of the Italian residents were on the way out. Pete had settled into 114th Street between First and Pleasant Avenues, with a second-story view of Jefferson Park. His father, perpetually poised at the window of their apartment, would have seen Lucille and her friends pass by and turn into the park for a swim.

"Jefferson pool was a great pool," Lucille remembers. "We would go over there and have cookouts. Basically, when we went, the Italians didn't bother us. Now, maybe the boys had a problem, and they'd have to run through because some people want to get edgy. We didn't have to run through, because basically we just walk straight across." But Italian Harlem was not just a turf to avoid or pass through undetected, for

Lucille remembers its place in the joy of a day at the pool. "And they used to have a little stand on First Avenue that they used to sell the zeppoli. They used to fry them right then and there, and you'd come out the pool and buy them."

Lucille's interactions with Puerto Ricans were only marginally more intimate. By the time of her youth, Italians were rapidly becoming a less dominant presence in the neighborhood. As she explains, "The Spanish they kept to themselves, but you know, we played together. One of my best friends was Hispanic. We lived in the same building together. But they're spread out more now."

Lucille would have been a head taller than José as they might have passed each other under the steel girders of the Park Avenue elevated train tracks, accompanying their mothers as they strolled past the vendors of the Market. "116th Street and Park Avenue used to be all stalls," Lucille says. "It was the shopping center for everybody." Many of the vendors were Jewish, the last holdouts from their East Harlem community that had long since moved on and left the synagogues to be proselytized by architects and converted to churches. "You had the fish market, you had the chicken part of it, in the next stall was the vegetables and a little pharmacy. Each shop had its own purpose all the way down to 112th Street."

In later years the Market became known as La Marqueta, a touchstone for Puerto Rican settlement and local identity. Then, slowly, it drifted into disuse—a vacant patch of poured concrete under the train tracks that reminds each resident of some different overlapping and competing East Harlem. "Jewish people owned the stores. Spanish people worked there, black people worked there, but it was the Market, the Park Avenue Market. They named it La Marqueta some years afterward, but I knew it as the Market."

·   ·   ·   ·   ·

"You know how you hear the comedians talk about Big Mama?" Lucille peers over the top of her reading glasses and lets her *Daily News* rest on her lap. Ms. McQueen looks up from her circular, and Joyce returns Lucille's questioning look.

"Who was it? What's his name?" Lucille asks. "He's the comedian now. He was one of the Kings of Comedy. He had a show on TV, too."

"Steve Harvey?" offers Ms. McQueen.

Lucille bites her lip and searches the tiles on the floor for the answer. "No, not Steve Harvey," she replies.

"Wait a minute, wait a minute . . . Cedric?" Ms. McQueen asks.

"No, no, not Cedric."

"Oh, um, um," Ms. McQueen taps the table trying to beat the answer out of the vinyl top. "What's the one with Regina?" she asks, and then suggests, "Martin Lawrence?"

"No, not Martin Lawrence. He had a TV show."

"On Channel 5, right?" clarifies Ms. McQueen.

"Not Hughley, the other one."

"I thought you were talking about the one on Channel 5."

Lucille settles back into her chair, dropping the memory quiz and returning to her point. "The one that was saying how, you know, you go to Big Mama's house on Sundays. Everybody met at grandmother's and great-grandmother's houses on Sundays, and you had a family dinner. It wasn't fast food. You had a dinner. We all had that. Every evening we had to sit down at the dinner table. It wasn't have dinner and watch TV, no. You sit down at the dinner table."

When Lucille graduated from elementary school in 1959, life seemed set at a different pace for her and the streets around her. The nostalgic images of family unity she now gleans from the sort of television sitcoms she was prohibited from viewing as a child remind her of a life not exactly gilded but longed for nonetheless. She can still remember playing in Central Park or the much smaller Mount Morris Park after dark with no fear. And the railroad apartment she knew as home until her mother passed away—four rooms connected front to back by a central open hall-way—stirs mixed emotions: "It was a rat-infested place. When we went into the bathroom, we had to hit the bathroom door and the steam pipes to scare away the rats. But even though it was raggedy, we were a family. I always will remember that building."

Lucille's image of life before the 1960s was one of tight-knit communities and supportive neighbors, "even down to the drug addicts." As she explains: "We had drugs around there, but the drug addicts, they'll come and say, 'Ma'am, can I take your bags upstairs?' Like for my grandma, and anybody else." There is a gleam in her eye as she describes the gallantry of heroin addicts. "And they'll take you to your door. And will not take anything out that bag, and didn't want you to give them anything. Regardless of their situation, they were brought up to respect their elders. It was a whole generation. They was taught to respect, regardless of what they did. They didn't disrespect nobody, not children, nobody."

Joyce suddenly bolts upright, turns to Lucille, and exclaims, "Bernie Mac!"

A smile spreads across Lucille's face, and with a nod, she agrees, "Bernie Mac."

"I graduated out of Cooper in 1962," Lucille recalls. What was once James Fennimore Cooper Junior High School on Mount Morris Park is now Bethel Gospel Assembly on Marcus Garvey Park. The same building, the same park, but new iterations in the narrative of the community. Still one of the last regal structures on the park, it stands on 120th Street between Madison and Fifth Avenues. The brick has been repointed and the gardens tended, but instead of thirteen-year-old schoolchildren, the building welcomes a transplanted congregation of African American evangelical Christians who outgrew their Central Harlem location.

Back in the 1950s, James Fennimore Cooper Junior High School swallowed up the tenements along 120th Street between Madison and Fifth Avenues and, after its dedication, swallowed up many of the area schoolchildren as well. "I had to go to P.S. 45, but then in the second year, they did another rezoning, and they sent me over to Cooper."

In 1960, when Lucille was rezoned to Cooper Junior High School, New York was in the middle of a public education crisis that centered on communities such as East Harlem. Since the 1954 Supreme Court decision *Brown* v. *Board of Education,* New York City had struggled to come to terms with a system of de facto educational segregation that had gone uncriticized until it was deemed unconstitutional. It was Kenneth Clark, the first African American professor at a New York City public university, who first charged that the city school system was maintaining segregated schools in the weeks after the Supreme Court decision.[5] What followed was a decade of recriminations and stopgap measures to conform to a new policy of proactive school integration.

It would take five years for the first real attempt to integrate New York City schools in what then superintendent of schools John Theobald described as "permissive zoning." In 1959 more than three hundred elementary school children from the predominantly African American neighborhood of Bedford-Stuyvesant in Brooklyn were rezoned and bused to all-white schools in Queens. The plan met with strong resistance from white parents concerned about property values and their right to circumscribe their own sense of community.[6] But when Theobald implemented the same plan in Manhattan six months later, there were few complaints from the Yorkville schools on the Upper East Side that welcomed a few hundred new students from East Harlem.[7] In 1960, the year Lucille was rezoned from one segregated East Harlem school to another, 40 percent of New York City public school students were black or Puerto Rican, but that figure climbed to 75 percent for elementary school children.[8] The 1960s saw a contentious struggle between communities and the board of education, resulting in a number of boycotts, the most famous in 1964 when well-organized protesters managed to convince 44.8 percent of New York City schoolchildren to stay at home.[9]

Lucille remembers those years of transition as a study in contradiction and confusion. The overarching message from the board of education was one of inclusive, open education for all children, but Lucille's own educational experience was relatively narrow and largely segregated. "If you went to school in New York, you went with whites and blacks and Hispanics, all nationalities. But if you went to school in the community, it was basically black and Hispanic."

For all of the changes of that era, Lucille remained disconnected from the events swirling around her and her community. The Civil Rights movement seemed to her a rumbling in the South that made little impact on her street. "It wasn't noticeable. We couldn't see it," she remembers now. "I had a friend, she used to go down South and come back, and I had a neighbor from Alabama, so they knew more about that than I did. But it didn't affect us. Being that we were all friends, we didn't talk about it. I was New York born, so I was afraid to go down South."

It wasn't until Lucille was in high school that the movement rolled northward, carried by the assassination of a president and, later, that of the iconic leader of the movement, Martin Luther King Jr. In those years, veterans of the war for equal rights, black and white, filtered into northern urban communities, like East Harlem, to effect similar changes. Eventually, groups like the Young Lords would take the message to the streets of El Barrio, but for Lucille, these were forces beyond the boundaries of her block, her world.

"I remember that era, with Martin Luther King marching on Selma," she explains. And then, with a glimmer of regret, "But like news events."

Lucille was busy with her own private social movement: high school. In 1962, after leaving the junior high school around the corner, Lucille was faced with a choice. Permissive zoning remained controversial, and the construction of new schools in communities such as East Harlem led to further protests when white parents faced the possibility of their children being bused to poorer neighborhoods.[10] Two years earlier, under threats of a citywide boycott, Superintendent Theobald implemented an open enrollment plan whereby students in certain districts could choose which schools they wished to attend.[11] Most of her friends were signing up for Commerce High School on the West Side. But Lucille wanted a change, a radical break from the path of her friends, some of whom were already slipping into destructive patterns. "You have to break the chain, and I did. And I am happy I did," she says.

Just one year after José's sister graduated from the same institution, Lucille enrolled in Julia Richman High School. "When you graduated out of junior high school, you picked certain schools you wanted to go to. I picked Julia Richman." It was an all-girl high school on the Upper East Side, and Lucille still remembers the intimidation of the older, larger girls.[12]

Though she credits the school with "saving" her from the fate of her friends at Commerce, she dropped out of Julia Richman six months before she would have graduated in 1965. "I had a stubborn streak in me at that time. I was so adamant to get out of there. My mother was very upset, but she wasn't going to push it." Lucille took jobs caring for neighborhood children and working at neighborhood summer camps. Mostly, she "ran the streets, had fun." "I have no regrets about that," she adds.

Lucille's mother counseled her with a philosophical fatalism: "She always told me, 'The streetlights are gonna be here when you're gone, they'll come on regardless if you're here or not.' "

In 1966 Lucille's mother died.

"It was a hot, hot summer day. She was in a club, helping prepare a dinner. She felt faint, laid down in my godmother's house, and she passed." Her sister, the youngest, was just ten months old. Her grandmother, who had long since moved back to the West Side, agreed to take care of Lucille's infant sister. Lucille and the rest of her siblings moved one block over to 118th Street.

With her mother gone, "everything fell apart." The fledgling family entered the welfare system, a new and demoralizing experience. Lucille soon gave birth to her only daughter at the age of twenty, and conflict between Lucille and her older sister made it increasingly difficult to live together. "We got into a fight, and she put me out. But it helped me. I've been on my own ever since."

Lucille moved down the block, still on 118th Street but on the east side of the elevated train tracks. "My brothers came with me. We were always together." But caring for two younger brothers and her own newborn daughter was more than she could manage. "I had to stay on welfare. I didn't know anything about welfare until my mother died. We were never on public assistance."

For Lucille, 117th Street would remain iconic, a stretch of city that had its own problems but domestic, inward-focused problems—like any home. East Harlem, for Lucille, was reduced to one city block between Madison and Park Avenues, and the elevated train marked a boundary she was reluctant to cross. But as the death of her mother and the birth of her daughter thrust her from childhood, she crossed that boundary into uncharted territory. Street life has never felt as secure since.

Not long after, Lucille would move into a new building a few blocks north, a building that would become the center of her social and political world.

·   ·   ·   ·   ·

Lucille stands in the cool night air, just outside the metal security door, the smoke from her lit Newport drifting into the sky toward the towering high-rise apartment building behind UPACA Gardens.

"That's 1990," she says and flicks some ash to the concrete of the paved-over courtyard. "That's a UPACA building, and you just have a conglomerate of all different types of people. You just have all walks of life, and some of them are wild. I remember when they built that building."

It was 1974, five years after Lucille moved into her fifth-floor apartment with her daughter, that a small gathering of housing officials, reporters, and local residents dedicated the 32-story, 341-unit buildings known officially as Upper Park Avenue Community Association (UPACA) Sites 1 and 2 and locally as "1990" from its address on Lexington Avenue. S. William Green, regional administrator for the Federal Department of Housing and Urban Development, made sure the reporters had plenty of time to scribble in their notepads his thoughts on the new towers: "The UPACA Towers will surely have a tonic effect on the development of East Harlem and make a significant contribution to the national campaign against urban blight."[13]

Standing somewhere nearby, but doubtless in the shadow of Mr. Green, were two women, Mary Iemma and Margaret Jenkins. A decade earlier they were mothers and wives and had little interest in "other people's causes." But a young white woman named Jo Adler, fresh from the waning years of the Civil Rights movement in the South, inspired a renewed commitment to their community. It started with tending to the trash-filled lots that marred the grid of streets in that northeast corner of East Harlem and soon became a campaign for improved housing. In just a few years, Iemma and Jenkins had incorporated the Upper Park Avenue Community Association and established a network of financial support.[14]

By 1970 they had renovated or built 147 housing units in the area between 111th and 125th Streets, Park and Lexington Avenues,[15] and by 1972 they had received more than $25 million in mortgage loans from various New York financial institutions.[16] Their vision was myopic and effective, providing comfortable housing for their neighbors and avoiding the typical association of urban renewal and "black removal." The tower dedicated in 1974 was more than a brilliant example of city planning; it redefined what was possible for the community. Even the architect, Robert Glasgow, was an African American.

As Mr. Green climbed back into his car to be driven back downtown and the residents celebrated the smell of fresh paint and breathtaking views, the towers faced an uncertain future. Many of UPACA's developments would dissolve into the bureaucracy of NYCHA, the New York City Housing Authority. Known as turnkey developments, they were designed and built to be sold to NYCHA according to a prearranged contract. UPACA Towers avoided this fate, but private management fared little better than NYCHA in handling what was still heavily subsidized housing. A year later President Ford infamously told the city to "drop dead" in the wake of its debilitating financial crisis. By 1976 Iemma and Jenkins were no longer on speaking terms, and UPACA, having lost most of its financial support, would dissolve.[17] The building known as "1990," still privately managed, would slowly, surely shuffle into disrepair and social dysfunction.

Thirty years later Lucille stands in the shadow of the pale brick tower and grimaces. Not long ago her daughter was struck by one of the many bits of debris—soda bottles, batteries, soiled diapers—that rain down from the sky around 1990 Lexington Avenue. These days Lucille won't even cross in front of the "brilliant example of city planning" dedicated that December day. Before retreating to tenant patrol in the lobby of UPACA Gardens, Lucille looks up and says, "You have some decent people in there, but you have too many wild people in there, too."

"I moved into this building in 1969," explains Lucille with a wave of her hand around the lobby of her building. Lucille is quick to point out that official records show that UPACA Gardens opened in 1970, but as one of the first tenants, she moved in in August 1969. It was the same month that the Young Lords dumped garbage on Park Avenue to protest the lack of city services in East Harlem.

"I had my own place, it was my own place. My mother had passed, and I was taking care of my daughter. We were taught back then to be able to take care of yourself. I had my family, you know. That was my independence." Independent, perhaps, but not alone. Lucille's two brothers remained residents in her apartment on and off for decades. And even her sister moved down the hall a short time later.

By the time Lucille moved into UPACA Gardens, NYCHA had presided over more than thirty years of public housing construction and administration. In that time, new housing stock had provided homes to tens of thousands of New York City residents through federal, state, and city subsidies. But the single most important force for change in the urban streetscape was the Committee on Slum Clearance, formed by Robert Moses in response to the Federal Housing Act of 1949.[18] The Housing Act included the new law known as Title I that subsidized the acquisition and disposal of sites considered "blighted." Just what qualified as urban blight would supposedly be left to the city planning commission and local communities, but Moses and his master plan for slum clearance circumnavigated public input and eviscerated working-class and immigrant communities throughout the city. Combined with banking policies that precluded investment in these same communities, which was a practice known as "red-lining" and made illegal in the late 1970s, Title I enabled Moses to engineer complete control over the development of new housing in neighborhoods such as East Harlem. The result was high-density public buildings built in already overcrowded and underdeveloped communities.[19]

The bitter irony of Moses's slum clearance committee creating the very slums they claimed to be clearing was not lost on neighborhood women like Mary Iemma and Margaret Jenkins. Grassroots tenant movements and the miraculous appearance of local development corporations such as UPACA in the 1960s were bolstered by the political momentum of the Civil Rights movement, but they achieved their modest collective strength too late. Public housing in the United States had already fallen from the pedestal of prewar idealism, and initiatives like UPACA were only adding to the long list of high-density housing detached from the communal life of the street Lucille knew as a child.

But even as public housing was descending into one of the single most identifiable symbols of the modern urban slum, Lucille saw the move from the 118th Street tenement to UPACA Gardens through the same filter that colored José's experience of Jefferson or DeWitt Clinton Houses. "From where I came from, this was a nice, decent building. I lived in a sixth-floor walkup in my first apartment by myself, and I had my daughter. I don't know how I did it then. You know, groceries and strollers. There wasn't an elevator. People get accustomed to elevators and things of luxury."

UPACA Gardens was a turnkey development. "Once they were built, they turned them over to the Housing Authority and we were hand-picked to move into this building. The people who ran UPACA, Ms. Iemma and Ms. Jenkins, came to our apartment and interviewed us. They hand-picked us. We had a balance. You had working people, you had people on public assistance. You had half black and half Hispanic. And we knew one another. Some of us came from the same places, so we knew one another."

But as tenants of NYCHA, residents of UPACA Gardens had little in common with the rest of the block. Lucille could sense this closing off from the surrounding community, and the descriptions she once reserved for public characters on the block at 117th Street turned inward to refer to those in the elevators and corridors of UPACA Gardens. "In this building, we were a family. We were all family. We were neighbors; in every sense of the word, we were neighbors. We stuck together for the betterment." Eventually, their insulation from the communal life of the street would destroy her early enthusiasm for her new home: "The other people on the street treated us like outsiders."

.   .   .   .   .

"This block here—this is the block that Jack built." Who's Jack? Lucille just shakes her head and says, "The devil."

By the mid-1970s Lucille's sister had given birth to a second child and moved out of UPACA Gardens. The sense of community was sagging under the weight of economic hardship and overcrowding. "They didn't want to leave me here, none of my family wanted me to stay here." Lucille crosses her arms with a look of determination. "I can't let people walk over me."

While José was away in Albany, Lucille was setting her jaw against the rapid descent of East Harlem into social and economic chaos. Crime rates were soaring throughout the 1980s, and though there had always been tumble-down buildings, substandard housing, corner stores, and drug addicts, the quality of it all seemed somehow altered. "Now, they sell drugs, they'll kill you for a dollar," complains Lucille. "Back then when I was growing up, they weren't killing people for a dollar. You know, it was different. Everything was different."

With a subtle shake of her head, Lucille adds, "But this block here was always off the hook. This block was wild."

Crack cocaine. A cheap new drug introduced in the 1980s, crack was largely responsible for the devaluation of human life in East Harlem: it radically affected the economy of violence in relation to the illegal drug trade. Crack is a dried solution of powder cocaine and baking soda that produces an addictive high when smoked. The chemical combination provides an intense but short-lived euphoria, and it is much cheaper than pure powder cocaine and therefore more accessible in poorer communities.

Crack's explosion on the underground drug market in the 1980s was due in part to the Reagan administration's war on drugs, which emphasized the repression of the international drug trade and forced smugglers to find cheaper, more efficient products to move across national borders. Cocaine took up much less space and was worth much more on the street than marijuana, creating a glut in the market that reduced the price and inspired some creative chemistry to keep the profit margin high. By the late 1980s crack users could buy $5 and $10 vials of crack cocaine on the streets of East Harlem and smoke it in a glass crack pipe purchased at the corner bodega. East Harlem quickly became one of the centers of the crack cocaine epidemic, with the intersection of 110th Street and Lexington Avenue receiving the lion's share of media attention for its infamous volume of illicit business.[20]

Lucille's brother, like José's uncle, became one of the many casualties of the crack cocaine phenomenon. "My baby brother waited until he was thirty-five years old to start getting locked up. You see, that crack took over. He's almost forty-seven now, but that taste for crack never leaves your mouth. It's an uphill battle every day once they got that taste for that crack." Since the early 1990s Lucille's brother has been in and out of prison but never far from the streets that sell his addiction. "He comes to me, and if he's hungry, I'll feed him. I make sure he has clean clothes. I leave him alone and he leaves me alone. You know, he's grown, I can't control his life." As far as Lucille is concerned, her brother is a ward of the state; prison seems to be the only place he can stay clean. "He's in jail now, so he's okay. When he comes out, I say he's on vacation. When he goes back, I say he's at home."

According to Lucille, the crack cocaine scourge of the 1980s and 1990s was not the beginning of East Harlem's decline: "No, it was before crack." Almost from the moment she moved into UPACA Gardens, Lucille noticed life on the street changing. "I remember one time we were sitting out there. And families that lived across the street started grabbing their kids and taking them in. And I said, 'Something ain't right.' Before we could even get into the building, they opened fire like the OK Corral. That's the type of stuff that happened. That's why I say, 'If you haven't lived here—nobody knows unless you lived here.' This is back in 1978."

In fact, when asked to describe the worst of times at UPACA Gardens, Lucille reaches back long before crack cocaine appeared in the neighborhood. In the half decade after the watershed year of 1975, when gun battles scattered social life from the streets of the neighborhood to the corridors of high-rise buildings, youth gangs became the clearest and most intimidating symbol of community dysfunction. "When we had the gangs here, in this building, residents were petrified. This was late seventies. They hung out right next door, in the apartment next door to me. They had these people here scared."

Lucille's outrage at the invasion of youth gangs strengthened her resolve to protect her new home. The interlopers had entered the building and taken over the corridors like strangers on a new block, but few of her neighbors seemed ready to meet the challenge. "They didn't even live here. They would stand in the hallway and try to intimidate me, and I said, 'Oh, no, no, no.' You know, I had to be a gangster just like they were. It wasn't that I was bad or whatever, it's just that you cannot come in here and control things. We had a resident at the time, and she was supposed to be their queen. She got involved with them. I'd knock on her door and tell her, 'You get them out of here or I am calling the police.'"

The gangs were a catalyst for Lucille's renewed commitment to protect her turf. UPACA Gardens was her home, her daughter's home, and she met the challenges of the decade to come with steely determination. "If you didn't stand your ground, you lose. You would have been a hostage in your own house. You can't be a hostage where you live. That was my philosophy. And it works, 'cause all of them respected me. All of those boys respected me. I am not a bad person. I just try to stand my ground."

"When I moved here, I knew my neighbors. But then when it started changing, I started getting involved." Getting involved meant putting her own life in order. She fell ill in 1971 and was in and out of hospitals until 1975 struggling with gastritis, the same disease that presumably took her mother at roughly the same age. Once out of the hospital, she was determined to complete her education, find steady employment, and get off public assistance. She took classes at the Education Opportunity Center on 125th Street and was the only one in her class to pass the GED, or high school equivalency exam. "When I graduated, my grandmother was there, and she said, 'Your mother would be real proud of you, because she sees that you're doing what you're supposed to be doing.'"

Back at UPACA Gardens, however, Lucille could see the first casualties in the fiscal crisis that cut social services and degraded her beloved public housing—the children. With a daughter not quite ten years old, Lucille took it upon herself to provide direction for the other kids left to their own devices on the front stoop of her building. "These same bad kids that was out here, they helped me set up a community center downstairs in the basement. I ran it by myself. And I told them I wouldn't take no stuff from them. They knew it, and they didn't like it, but they didn't disrespect me."

The initiative Lucille demonstrated in establishing the youth center was quickly tapped by tenant leaders in upper Manhattan public housing. "They started the tenant patrol the same year they formed the tenant association in the late 1970s. And we had a president, but I worked with her, and then I ended up becoming the interim president for the time when we were consolidated."

Public housing consolidation was an attempt by NYCHA to more efficiently manage the growing number of housing units under their control. This was especially important as the fiscal policies of President Ronald

Reagan slashed funding for public housing by 75 percent throughout the 1980s.[21] UPACA Gardens joined Jackie Robinson Houses and three other sites to form the Jackie Robinson consolidation. According to Lucille, "The consolidation of the developments allowed modernizations of the buildings, 'cause we were missing out on a lot. The residents back then made suggestions, and we had a majority."

Lucille claims, "In the beginning I was just on the tenant patrol, and I was happy." But throughout the past two decades, Lucille has served as the president of her tenant association. She says that no else will do the job. And despite their grumbling, her neighbors continue to vote for her strict rules and firm discipline.

·   ·   ·   ·   ·

Another piercing wail from the front door, and a couple saunters into the lobby. Turning toward the elevators, they are brought up short by Lucille's surprisingly loud voice.

"Excuse me!"

The two turn, notice the table and its clipboard, and move shyly toward Lucille and Ms. McQueen. Lucille turns to Ms. McQueen and says not too quietly, "I'm about tired of her coming in here and not signing in."

The woman stooping over to sign in giggles and says, "I forgot which apartment number."

Lucille holds her stare a beat past awkward and replies, "I'll tell you which apartment number. You going to see Jeanine. It's 2C."

Ms. McQueen gives Lucille one of those exasperated looks and shakes her head. She's seen Lucille's small frame stand up to just about anyone who passes through the lobby. But even with her steely gaze and intimidating bark, according to Ms. McQueen, "she's changed a whole lot from what she used to be."

"Don't do that no more!" Lucille bellows across the lobby at a young girl repeatedly beating the front door window with her fist. She turns back to the table and in a low growl explains, "I had to calm down." After more than thirty-five years at UPACA Gardens, Lucille continues to struggle with gastritis, which in recent years has reached the point of physical debilitation. "I didn't let people walk all over me, and I don't let people walk over me now. I just don't get so upset now. I don't want to have a heart attack. That's why I had to calm myself down. I believe in what I am doing, but I'm not going to let nobody kill me either."

Lucille's infrequent but effective outbursts of reprimand, usually for unsupervised children in the lobby, contrast starkly with the soft-spoken, gravelly whisper of her conversational tone. "Most people come in here and take advantage, or try to take advantage," she explains. But not because of her deceptive vocal range. "They see a woman, and they feel they can just come in here and say what they want, and do what they want and how they want to do it. So I had to stand my ground. I'm not going to take that stuff. You can't come in here and walk over me."

Public housing was never an institution of last resort for Lucille. It was a first taste of independence—not too far from the street where she grew up—a taste that never left her mouth. "A lot of people live in public housing, especially here in Manhattan, and they don't know what they have. It's like you own gold, only thing is you can't dig it out of the ground. This is precious property. You know, take care of what you have." It is a motto she has adhered to assiduously, at the cost, perhaps, of closer friends in the building. "They say I'm the meanest person in the world, they call me the wicked witch of the west. I don't let the kids run wild, like that little girl banging on that door. 'Cause if you damage that, and it breaks down, then what? You fight for things to make it livable. It might not be the best conditions, but it could be a lot worse."

Lucille's reputation in the building has developed with each wave of new tenants, like so many coats of paint that smear the walls of the lobby. She can count the few apartments on every floor that still house original tenants from the early 1970s, only about one-third of the residents in all. Echoing José's lament, Lucille claims NYCHA has lowered standards and corrupted the dream of affordable, subsidized housing in the city. "What the city has done, they eliminated the rules and regulations. They were more stringent, and people had to qualify. The rules started changing, but it doesn't seem to be changing to the betterment of the decent people who live in public housing. They're putting homeless people in public housing. A lot of people burnt out their apartments to go into shelters and move into public housing. Public housing is a dumping ground right now."

A dumping ground, like the dozens of vacant, rubble-strewn lots that dot East Harlem, is an easy target for "urban renewal." The specter of Robert Moses and his slum clearance committee looms in the not-so-distant past; bulldozers have been replaced by another coat of paint, a doorman, and market rents. "This is not a state building, it is a federally subsidized building," explains Lucille. And with a note of dread, she adds, "But if the government stops the funding for federal housing, what happens to all the people that live in public housing, not only the people here, but in the entire city?"

But Lucille has faced down more formidable challenges to her sense of place. Her connection to the community may have exchanged a front stoop for a vinyl-topped card table, but East Harlem is all she has ever known. "I'm not going. I will stay here as long as I possibly can. This is public housing, and that's fine." Leaning forward and making sure her words are not lost in the scattered noise of the lobby, Lucille says, "They use that word *project*, and I say, 'Excuse me, I am not an experiment.' I am not an experiment, I am a person. Regardless of where you live, you make your way as best as possible. And that's what a project is, an experiment. And I am not a part of it. I am not an experiment, and I refuse to be an experiment. I don't live in a project. I live in an apartment in a development."

Semantics, maybe. But the difference between a project and a development may be the difference between a tenement and a townhouse. Pete and José are both convinced that public housing stopped the floodtide of economic development. Both assumed 96th Street proved impervious to the effects of renewed investment and real estate speculation. But Lucille has seen it happen just a few streets over in Central Harlem and wonders how long it will take for the new frontier of gentrification to shift from 96th Street to Fifth Avenue. "That's a big problem right now with Harlem, period. You got housing developments around co-ops and condominiums, and they're going to try and upgrade their situations, and some people can afford it and some people can't."

Signaling a curious turn in the economic fortunes of upper Manhattan, the clearest evidence that renewed investment is filtering in from Central Harlem and not from the Upper East Side is the townhouses swallowing up the streets of Lucille's youth. Where once tenements lined the streets from 116th to 125th Street between Fifth and Park Avenues, now there are rows of identical pale brick townhouses. The redundant roof lines, forest green trim, street after street—a Levittown in East Harlem, a suburb in the city. The loss for Lucille is palpable.

"No," Lucille says, "my building no longer stands—it was a tenement. Basically they built townhouses in that block now. I walk through that block and I feel like I'm in a strange place. You know where certain build-ings were, you know what was here and how it was situated, and now you have a row of townhouses. My godmother lived at number 58, my mother died in that building. I can go to that block, and I can see the buildings that were there. I can see the people that were there. It was vibrant, and it was good."

Like José, who was cut off from his past by the changes in public hous-ing tenancy, Lucille yearns for a permanent connection to the neighbor-hood. And even in the meticulous erasure of 117th Street, Lucille still finds reminders, bits and pieces of the physical space that formed her. One building, number 61, still stands on 117th Street, wedged among the new townhouses like a bad tooth. "They have built all them townhouses over there, but that little raggedy building is still right there. But at least there is something there from the original block. I am not going to say it's a landmark, but something there to say this block existed and the people. It was a block, it was a community." Another reminder was carted away by old neighbors when developers literally blew away a granite out-cropping that threatened the plumb rooflines of their new houses. "We had a mountain behind, between 118th Street and 119th Street. They blew that up to build the townhouses. Some friends of mine still have a piece of the rock. You know, it's history."

History—blown away by developers' dynamite and carted off piece by piece by tenants of the streetscape—the same history that was appro-priated and settled into by each new immigrant wave, German, Irish, Russian Jew, Italian, Puerto Rican, and African American. Each planted shallow roots in the city block, the turf, home. "It was a family in that block. There are a lot of memories, good memories there. Even though the buildings are not there anymore, it brings back good memories, because I remember what was there. Regardless of what happens, that is always going to be home. That's my home, you know. My mother passed over in that block, that's home."

It's late now. There are no clocks on the yellow walls of the lobby, but Lucille keeps an eye on the time displayed on her mobile phone. Half past nine. Time to fold up the wobbly card table, the few metal chairs, and stow them in the utility closet down the hall. Most of the younger children, the loudest children, have gone upstairs. All that remain are Lucille, Ms. McQueen, and a few young men from the street on the stoop out front.

"I give respect and I expect it," says Lucille at the end of another long night. "A lot of people don't like me. Ms. McQueen can tell you."

"They sure don't," Ms. McQueen confirms, deadpan as always. Then a slight smile and a chuckle.

"She knows," Lucille laughs. "She knows. But that's fine. I know I can't live in the world by myself, but those who are negative, I don't have time for them. I know I was young at one point in time, but I respected my elders. We're not on the same page. We're not on the same level. It's not about being better than anyone, it's about a mentality and how you respond."

Lucille stands, stretches, and grabs the pack of Newports from the table for one more smoke outside. Before she heads for the door, before she takes her last cigarette in the company of young men most outsiders would avoid at midday, Lucille turns and says, "We try to make a difference. I'm not going to say that it is all going to work out, but just by a little strength, something will come from it. That's what life is about, if you can do one little thing. I believe in that."

FIGURE 1. Housing, old and new

FIGURE 2. At play in the shadow of public housing

FIGURE 3. Bodega at night

FIGURE 4. Jefferson Pool

FIGURE 5. Our Lady of Mt. Carmel, Pleasant Avenue

FIGURE 6. Puerto Rican Day festival

FIGURE 7. St. Cecilia's Church

FIGURE 8. Cinco de Mayo on 116th Street

FIGURE 9. 99 cents

FIGURE 10. New housing, old sidewalks

FIVE 116th Street

Maria squats at the bottom of a graffiti-covered metal gate and slips a key into a padlock as big as her fist. It's 7:30 in the morning on a side street just off Third Avenue and not far from 116th Street. A few schoolchildren and their parents dot the sidewalks, but for the most part it is quiet in the early morning sunlight. The streets are quiet as well, disrupted at regular intervals by the cars headed north on the avenue, neatly grouped by the timing of the traffic lights.

With some effort, Maria heaves the heavy gate up from the pavement to reveal the painted window of the Augustín Unisex Barbershop. A broom handle from inside helps push the metal gate out of view above the glass facade. It's early fall, but the residual heat of summer still clings to the city, and the morning mist will soon give way to a hot and humid afternoon. Wiping some of the moisture from her brow, Maria uses the same broom handle to flick on the air conditioner over the front door.

As she makes her way around the shop, arranging bottles of hair spray, gel, shaving cream, and comb sanitizer, Maria slips on her black vinyl smock and occasionally checks her hair in the mirrors that line both walls of the long, narrow space. She stands a little over five feet tall, average for the mostly female Mexican clientele who trundle their children in for $10 haircuts each day. But unlike most of her customers, Maria does not wear the weary look of motherhood, and her slim, confident frame does not show the fatigue of many other Mexican immigrant women under thirty. Her black shoulder-length hair is usually pulled back to reveal a round, caramel face, with a subtle but effective amount of makeup highlighting bright eyes and pouty lips.

Maria turns on the tired and beaten television and plays with the antennas until Univision can be seen through a bearable amount of static. She takes a seat in her own barber's chair, crosses her legs, and waits as the chatter of a morning news program fills the shop.

A young man pushes open the front door. "Vic here yet?" he asks. His oversized white T-shirt hangs down around his knees, and his eyebrows arch beneath the perfectly flat brim of his all-black Chicago White Sox cap. Maria shakes her head, and the young man sits down in one of the garish red metal chairs to wait.

In a few minutes, Maria will be joined by Victor, a Puerto Rican barber who shares the space. They both pay the owner, a local Puerto Rican, a percentage of their earnings to use the shop. The young man will wait for Victor, who will trim his quarter inch of hair and meticulously sculpt his pencil-thin beard, all while comparing notes on music, movies, and women. A small crowd will gather around Vic, their voices rising, their language becoming more coarse. Maria will try not to hear.

In the chaos, she will have her customers, mostly Mexican, mostly unauthorized, undocumented migrants. A few will have just arrived, full of stories about the crossing, the load houses, the long car trip to New York, or maybe even landing at JFK. Maria will offer advice, share her stories, and wish them luck. Vic will put some salsa music on the stereo that will drown out Univision, but Maria will be too busy to mind.

For now, though, it is just Maria, her television, and the young man sulking by the front door. For now, she is alone.

.   .   .   .   .

"I was born in 1975," says Maria. "In Cuautla, the state of Morelos."

A century ago, Cuautla, a town the size of East Harlem not far from Mexico City, was the center of a revolution that pitted the landless poor against the landed elite. It was a conflict exacerbated by the regime of Porfirio Díaz, the dictator whose economic reforms created a nation of landless poor farmers—a mobile population ready to seek opportunity elsewhere.[1]

From the humble farmlands around Cuautla, a peasant revolutionary named Emiliano Zapata emerged to challenge the consolidation of wealth and power in Mexico City. Zapata's plan focused on agrarian reform and sought to redress Díaz's emphasis on rapid industrialization, land consolidation, and, ultimately, the export of labor from low-yielding agricultural sectors to the booming industrial economy of the United States. In 1917 Zapata's ideas took form in Article 27 of a new constitution that made land available to Mexico's largely landless peasantry. The *ejido* land grants constituted the most important agrarian reform in Latin America, distributing over the course of several decades more than 1.5 million parcels from fallow government land and haciendas that exceeded the legal limit of private landownership.[2]

Two years later, on April 10, Zapata was assassinated by one of several factions connected to the seat of power in Mexico City. He was buried in Cuautla.

Perhaps it is fitting, then, that growing up in Cuautla, the town most closely linked to the martyr of the rural poor,[3] Maria started working at an early age to help support her family. "My father died when I was seven years old," she explains. "That's when my older sister took over the home. My mother and I, we went to work."

The predicament of Maria's family, four children and a single mother, was not uncommon in rural Mexico, but it was usually the result of labor migration. Since the beginning of Mexico's industrial awakening after

World War II, hundreds of thousands of men and women, sons and daughters, husbands and wives have left behind those they loved in search of wage labor. At first it was to the urban centers of southern Mexico, then it was to the industrializing north with its now infamous *maquiladoras,* or factories. Migration to the United States had always been a factor, a constant amid the waxing and waning of the local economy. But it was not the only force that left families fractured—spread thin across the hardscrabble economic landscape.

Like many young men and women forced to add to the income of their families, Maria was a pragmatist when it came to education. "I never went to high school," she says. "Maybe because I saw my mother having more kids, and I saw my friends buying clothes and shoes. I wanted to work."

While her sister, Aracely, stayed home to care for their younger brothers, José Luis and Armando, Maria and her mother picked up work where they could. Eventually, Maria's mother remarried in a vain attempt to bring some stability to their lives. "I was ten or eleven when my mother got married again. I fought with him a lot." By the time she was a teenager, Maria had left home to live with an aunt. She visited on weekends but spent the rest of her time working to pay for beauty school. "I needed money to study to be a beautician. I was fourteen when I entered beautician school."

Three years later, in her first year as a beautician, Maria earned 50 pesos, or about $5, per week. "At that time, it was good, because things were not very expensive. And I learned a lot in that year, permanents, colors, everything." She was still living a day's journey from her mother, working for a woman she met through beauty school, but most of her earnings were sent back home. "After one year, I said, 'I need a salary because the money is not good enough for me. I need money for my mother and my brothers.' The next week, she gave me $10."

On January 1, 1994, less than a year after Maria's raise to $10 a week, the Ejército Zapatista de Liberación Nacional (EZLN) seized the municipal palace in the small highland town of San Cristóbal de las Casas.[4] Two years earlier the Mexican government had amended Article 27, not only ending its obligation to distribute land through the ejido system but also allowing for the privatization of ejido land grants and extending the right to own land to foreign interests.[5] It was a thinly veiled capitulation to foreign interests in preparation for passage of the North American Free Trade Agreement (NAFTA) in 1994, and, not coincidentally, the EZLN insurrection began on the same day NAFTA went into effect. The EZLN would come to be known as the Zapatistas, resurrecting the cause of the peasant revolutionary buried in Cuautla. Their message of agrarian reform and government accountability would reach as far as 117th Street in East Harlem, where a mural splashed across the wall of a Mexican dance hall commemorates their struggle.

By 1997 Maria had left her first job as a beautician to work in a friend's salon closer to home. The Zapatistas continued to capture the imaginations of many rural Mexicans, especially those disillusioned by the revisions of Article 27 and the free-falling prices for agricultural products in the wake of NAFTA. Thousands left their farms in search of wage labor in the factories springing up along the U.S. border to the north or to cross the border itself in search of higher wages. In 1997 alone, the Tucson sector of the U.S. Border Patrol apprehended more than a quarter million undocumented entrants, and more than 1.3 million immigrants were apprehended along the entire southwestern border between the United States and Mexico. In the same year, at least one hundred fifty lost their lives trying to cross La Frontera.[6]

"I never thought about coming to the United States. I told my mother that I would save money. All the time, we were saving money." But not fast enough. Since Maria left home, her mother had had two more children with her second husband. According to Maria, "That man never tried to help. He never worked. He'd work one month, and the other month would be drinking." At $10 a week, it would take years before Maria could provide money for a house on the little plot of land they purchased in Cuautla.

It was impossible to ignore the benefits of having family in the United States. While Maria struggled to save her meager earnings, neighbors were building and improving their homes all around her on the remittances sent from New York, Houston, and Los Angeles. Still, the decision to head north, alone, was not Maria's.

"My mother's best friend, Victoria, said to my mother, 'My friends will lend the money for your daughter to go to New York. Maybe you can save money faster and build a house.' "

The idea was initially rejected by Maria and her mother, but Victoria offered a peculiar and only mildly appealing compromise. In exchange for Maria's safe passage to New York and a prearranged job as a housekeeper, Victoria's friends would send their daughter to live in Cuautla with Maria's mother.

"You will exchange," Victoria persuaded her.

Maria still bristles at the arrangement: "The first time I came to the United States, it was a very problematic decision because I didn't really want to come. My mother said okay, but I didn't want to go." After five years of steady work as a beautician, the idea of a job cleaning someone else's house seemed several steps backward. "I knew I was going to take care of someone's house, but I preferred to have more control over my situation."

But after a few months of uncertainty, Maria made arrangements to make the trip north. Reluctantly, she crossed the Arizona border on September 11, 1997.

.   .   .   .   .

It's Christmas on 109th Street. Maria is busy preparing a feast of goat meat, chalupas, salad, and fruit punch in the kitchen of her three-room apartment on the second floor of an overcrowded and rapidly deteriorating tenement building. She shares the cramped space with her husband, Eduardo, two brothers, Armando and José Luis, and a cousin, Lalo. They all sit around the kitchen table on folding metal chairs watching an oversized television that sits precariously on a narrow chest of drawers. Through one door is the men's bedroom, three young men in an 8-by-10-foot room. Through another door is Maria and Eduardo's room, a slightly larger space with windows on the street.

The men in the room have all come across the same border since 1997, the year Maria made her journey through Sonora and Arizona. Her brothers waited for her to settle in and send money, then followed to find jobs in Manhattan and the Bronx. José Luis, twenty-one, left the Mexican army to immigrate to the United States, and Armando, twenty-five, has crossed back and forth a few times since he first arrived.

A knock on the door, and a few guests arrive—a couple from upstairs, both from Mexico, and their daughter, who was born in East Harlem the year before. Maria, godmother to their daughter, greets them with a warm smile and nudges her brothers to make room. The couple will return to Mexico within the year, tired of hard winters and the ambiguity of their lives as undocumented immigrants.

Eventually, the small kitchen is packed tightly with friends and family. Cousins from Queens, Ecuadoran friends from the neighborhood, even a couple of gringos from down the street. The television continues to flood the scene with a soccer match on Univision, but laughter and ranchero music drown out the sound.

Conversation, in Spanish with an occasional phrase or two in English, turns to the upstairs couple's thoughts of returning home. Stories are traded about La Frontera, their experiences with illegal alien smugglers, known as coyotes, and the Border Patrol.

"In Mexico, the problems of the Frontera are always on the TV. It is more dangerous. That is the reality. For some people it's just two or three days to cross, but for some people it's not easy," Maria explains. "They live on the Frontera for a month or two months. I know people who took three months to cross, they crossed eleven times."

Maria retreats to the stove, stirring her goat stew, perhaps thinking about her mother, whom she has not seen in six years.

"The lady told me it would just be like thirty minutes and then you're across." Maria makes a quick slice through the air with one hand, and adds, "You're in New York."

She laughs now, at her own naïveté. The lady was Delila, a woman who had worked as a housekeeper in New York for seven years before returning to Mexico. She advanced Maria $1,500 to cross the border and left her own daughter to live with Maria's mother. Then Delila accompanied Maria back across the border to return to consistent work in New York.

Maria awoke in the border town of Nogales, Sonora, on September 11, 1997. She and Delila had arrived the night before, failed to make contact with the coyote who would lead them across the border, and stayed in a hotel. Maria remembers being unable to sleep and peering out her hotel door late at night.

"I saw lots of people, a crowd, all hurrying out of their rooms and heading for the door," she explains.

Delila told her to shut the door. Their turn would come in the morning.

Nogales, Sonora, sits across a small stream from Nogales, Arizona, a relatively large border town sixty miles south of Tucson. Located in the Tucson sector of the Border Patrol, Nogales has become one of the most popular crossing points for undocumented migrants since the border regions of Southern California and Texas were tightened in the 1980s. Between the Immigration Reform and Control Act of 1986 (IRCA) and the passage of NAFTA in 1994, Nogales, Sonora, tripled in size to more than 350,000 inhabitants, dwarfing its sister city in Arizona, with only 20,000.[7]

But it wasn't the ebb and flow of unauthorized migration that inflated Nogales's population. Since 1965, when the U.S. government simultaneously liberalized immigration policies and ended the Bracero Program that imported Mexican laborers on a short-term basis, the Mexican government had worked to promote industrial development along the northern border. Known as the maquiladora program, it attracted foreign companies to set up factories along the border to take advantage of inexpensive Mexican labor. By the 1980s the idea had caught on, and by the time NAFTA went into effect there were more than four thousand maquiladoras in Mexico—almost one hundred in Nogales.[8]

The strain of such rapid urbanization was felt at all levels of the growing population. A woefully inadequate infrastructure left thousands homeless and almost everyone without clean water, law enforcement protection, and other basic services. Squatter settlements sprang up around the town center, creating makeshift communities as laborers flooded the region in search of the jobs advertised in newspapers throughout the nation.

Whereas Nogales boasted a relatively equal gender division in the newly arrived labor pool, most maquiladora centers were notable for the disproportionate number of women who filled the ranks of factory workers. In fact, until the 1980s, 80 percent to 90 percent of the maquiladora workforce were women.[9] Recruited by foreign management that had few reservations about hiring female labor, women flocked to the border region to compete for wage labor usually reserved for men in the nation's interior. Their mobility was in part a function of their disconnection from an already mobile male workforce that was persuaded by similar recruitment techniques to enter the U.S. labor market. The result was a high concentration of single women in underserved, overpopulated border towns.[10]

When Maria awoke the next morning, the idea of staying in Nogales and applying for a maquiladora job never crossed her mind. She, like thousands of Mexicans from the interior, was not simply looking for a job. She was looking for a standard of living, one attainable only across the small stream that divided the two Nogaleses. Most women who came to Nogales to work in the factories never intended to cross the border.[11] They came for the jobs.

Maria's coyote arrived. After a brief wait for the Border Patrol to leave a certain crossing point, Maria and Delila followed this stranger into the desert wilderness on the outskirts of Nogales. Delila and the coyote, both practiced in the art of crossing the border, were dressed in black—hoping to remain inconspicuous and unseen. Maria, thinking only of her new life in the United States, wore a bright green sweater and yellow pants, a fashion choice she laughs about now but regretted as they moved through the well-worn paths of unauthorized migrants.

"We started walking across at two o'clock in the afternoon," Maria remembers. "We walked for two hours, then Delila saw someone." It was a Border Patrol agent. Their coyote encouraged them to continue, but they were easily caught. "The immigration man said to stop and showed us his gun. I had my little bag of money in one hand, and I was so scared I dropped my money."

By five o'clock they had been fingerprinted, processed, and sent back to Nogales, Sonora. By eight o'clock that evening they were crossing the border again.[12]

Since the current border with Mexico was established in the mid-nineteenth century, attempts to control the flow of migration into the

United States have produced mixed results.[13] A series of shifts in U.S. policy on Mexican immigration created boom and bust years for migrant laborers. One year, they would be courted by U.S. employers. The next, they would be deported en masse. In 1942, when the United States was plunged into world war and industry lost thousands of workers, the Bracero Program instituted renewable six-month work visas to Mexican men, marking one of the first, fully regulated policies of labor migration between the two nations. Despite the end of World War II, the Bracero Program continued to import close to five million Mexican workers until 1964. Even after the Bracero Program officially ended in 1964, legal immigration from Mexico increased to more than 680,000 in the 1970s.[14]

In 1986 under the Reagan administration, when border security was equated with national security, Congress passed the Immigration Reform and Control Act. The IRCA both tightened border control and offered amnesty to undocumented migrants already settled inside the United States. In the next five years, almost two million undocumented noncitizens became legal residents.[15] But the IRCA also implemented new strategies to end unauthorized border crossings, effectively militarizing the southwestern border region. These strategies included augmenting the resources of the Border Patrol with fixed-wing aircraft and other tactical equipment and constructing controversial barriers along certain stretches of the international border. This militarization was in part a response to drug interdiction efforts along the southwestern border, including the reassignment of the newly formed Border Patrol Tactical Team (BORTAC), which was given paramilitary training similar to that of U.S. marshals and SWAT teams.[16]

With the start of NAFTA in 1994, fears that increased foreign investment would lead to increased migration inspired another massive buildup of border control. Between 1994 and 1997 the Immigration and Naturalization Service (INS) increased Border Patrol agents by 76 percent, to nearly six thousand, and spent more than $2 billion on border enforcement.[17] In 1996 the U.S. government passed the Illegal Immigrant Reform and Immigrant Responsibility Act, which redoubled the enforcement efforts of the Border Patrol and the INS along the U.S.-Mexico border. In that year, an estimated 5.0 million undocumented immigrants were living in the United States, up from 3.5 million in 1990, with 2.7 million of them from Mexico.[18] The new measures invested heavily in the Border Patrol, which targeted traditional points of entry such as Southern California and Texas. The result was a shift in the routes for unauthorized immigration to the remoter and more inhospitable sections of the Arizona border, like Nogales. Between 1993 and 1996 as many as sixteen hundred migrants died crossing the southwestern border.[19]

"I did not trust that man after we were caught the first time," Maria says now. Although he promised to take them a different way through the desert hills surrounding Nogales, Maria came across the little bundle of money she had dropped several hours earlier. "Delila asked me, 'What are you doing?' I showed her the money and said, 'It's my money, I dropped it here before. He is a liar.'"

In the next several days, Maria and Delila traveled from Tucson to Phoenix, from Phoenix to Los Angeles, and finally took a flight to New York. Maria arrived at JFK airport on September 22, eleven days after starting out from Nogales.

"As we left the plane, Delila told me to walk behind her and blend in with the crowd. I remember a man came from behind Delila and touched her on the shoulder and said, 'Where are you going?' Delila froze. She thought it was Immigration. The man said, 'Because I have a taxi if you want to go into the city.' Delila laughed and said, 'You know I am illegal, I thought you were Immigration.' They both laughed, but I didn't. I was still scared."

·   ·   ·   ·   ·

Maria sits in her barber's chair during a midafternoon lull in the flow of customers. She has little to do but read magazines and wait. Vic sits near the painted front window.

"Hey, Maria, you gonna come in on Monday?" Vic asks. He swivels around to face Maria, a mobile phone in one hand.

"Yes, of course."

Vic thinks for a moment, starts to dial his wife's number, then stops. "I could come in for the morning."

Maria looks up from her magazine, and says, "You don't have to come. It's okay."

"You know that's a holiday, right?"

"Yes, I know, but I need the money."

Victor, in his midthirties, with three kids and a wife of fifteen years, needs the money, too. He has been cutting hair for as long as he has been a father, honing a skill highly prized by young men in the neighborhood. Like most men who run a chair in a local barbershop, Vic is known for precision details in the short-cropped layer of hair most men prefer. He is also known for his easy wit and disarming charm, which puts customers at ease and attracts small crowds as interested in the conversation as they are in the latest hairstyle.

In contrast, Maria is quiet. Her English, much improved after seven years in East Harlem, still escapes in mumbled insecurity when confronted with a non–Spanish speaker. Fortunately, most of her clients are Mexican. Puerto Ricans, even those who have managed to retain or rediscover Spanish, prefer Vic's gregarious chair-side manner.

Vic is still thinking about Monday. Maria returns to her magazine, knowing that Vic finds it difficult to take a day off if Maria is cutting hair.

"If any of my customers come in on Monday, you could call me and I could come in."

"Okay," Maria replies without looking up from her magazine. "Yeah, I'll do that." Vic starts to dial his wife's number.

Vic's dilemma amuses Maria. She does not take holidays. Since she arrived in New York, she has struggled with single-minded intensity to earn money for her mother's house and perhaps a future for herself. Now that she has her own barber's chair, life in East Harlem has already improved from her first few months in the city.

"For five months, I lived with Delila, but it was very difficult for me," Maria explains. She arrived in New York with no family, no friends, only Delila, and had already been contracted to work as a housekeeper for a family in New Jersey. She would live with Delila and her partner, Oralia, in Harlem on weekends.

Delila and Oralia shared their room with Maria in a small apartment on 125th Street and Broadway. An aunt of Delila's lived in the next room and lent Maria clothes for the coming winter. But her relationship with her roommates was somewhat more strained.

"I said, 'Okay. I need to build a house for my mother. I don't know what the job is like, but . . .' My weeks were good when I stayed with the family in New Jersey. But on the weekends, I had problems. These two women lived together. They were lesbians. I couldn't sleep because they drink too much, they smoke, they kiss in front of me. One of them, Oralia, she would buy me things, but Delila would get jealous. I said, 'No, no, no, I like men, I don't like women. I don't want any problems.' Weekends were always like that.

"When I was working in the home in New Jersey, the family was very good to me. They had three girls and one boy. When he saw me, he would say, 'I love Maria!' He always played with me, and he would teach me English. He was seven years old."

But even the warmth she received from her employers in New Jersey could not lessen her sense of disconnection from family and familiarity. "The lady noticed I was always crying," Maria explains. She hesitates, not sure how to refer to her employer, then continues, "She asked, 'What is wrong? You are always crying.' I told her I missed my family. I had never been in another country. It was not easy because when I had weekends off it was not with them."

Her employer suggested Maria stay through the weekend, but Maria refused. As uncomfortable as her living arrangement was in Harlem, she feared being trapped in an even less familiar environment. "I would never be off from work," she explains.

Maria's early experience in New York fits many of the stereotypes constructed around undocumented Mexican women. Working as a housekeeper in a private home, she received her pay in cash and undetected by the U.S. government. But according to a study of undocumented Mexican women in the 1980s, Maria's experience may be more rare than is commonly assumed. In a survey of 562 undocumented women in Los Angeles County, almost 75 percent reported that income tax and social security were deducted from their pay—though few of them would ever see any benefits from those contributions. Only 7 percent of undocumented women said they attended school in the United States, and only

10 percent received vocational training. Moreover, half of all undocumented women worked in factories, and only 10 percent worked, like
Maria, in private homes.[20]

Maria's job as a housekeeper in New Jersey is just one example of the
segmented labor market in the United States. The economic changes that
transformed a largely industrial economy into a rapidly expanding service economy not only affected U.S. citizens, such as the Puerto Ricans of
East Harlem, but also created a seldom acknowledged but indispensable
category of employment for undocumented immigrants. This is true
because native-born beneficiaries of the new U.S. economy refuse to take
jobs as housekeepers, janitors, or menial day-laborers and also because if
they did, minimum wage guarantees would inflate wages at all sectors of
the economy. Such a shift would deflate profits and undermine the pro-
ductive expansion that enables high employment rates.[21]

In other words, employing unauthorized migrants at below-market
wages helps to create jobs in the legitimate wage-earning economy by
keeping the costs of doing business relatively low. Unfortunately, it
seems the response to this predicament is to vilify the workers rather
than the employers who take advantage of their illegal status. Despite
studies that demonstrate the minimal impact of illegal immigration on
U.S. wages,[22] the reality of the segmented labor market continues to be
reduced to the oversimplified political rhetoric of "stealing jobs."[23]

Three months after Maria started working as a housekeeper in New Jersey, her employers gave her two weeks paid vacation. It was an unexpected generosity that quickly embittered her roommates. "They said,
'You are lucky. Nobody gets paid for two weeks off.' They were jealous.
When I was on vacation, one of them said, 'You're sending your mother
money and she is probably not building her house.' "

In fact, Maria had already sent her mother more money in three
months than she would have made in three years cutting hair in Cuautla.
She was earning $250 a week cleaning the house in New Jersey, com-
pared to $10 in the salon back home. A portion of the money went to her
mother in Cuautla, and the rest went to repay the $1,500 advanced by
Delila to bring Maria to New York.

This was exactly the kind of earning power Maria and millions of other Mexican nationals assume is available in the United States. In 2003 Mexicans sent an estimated $14 billion in remittances to their communities in Mexico. Overall, Latin American migrants sent home approximately $30 billion in remittances to Latin America and the Caribbean in 2003, making it the largest single remittance channel in the world.[24] Compare that to the $772 million in foreign aid offered to the same region by the U.S. State Department in 2000, or even the $13 billion in combined aid from the Inter-American Development Bank and the World Bank, most of which was in the form of interest-bearing loans that can drive developing nations further in debt.[25] The few hundred dollars a month individuals like Maria send to their families in towns such as Cuautla add up to almost double the amount of international aid.

Delila understood the economies of scale that set so many men and women like her and Maria on the journey north. But Maria's early fortune impressed even her. According to Maria, "Delila sent $200 a month to my mother to take care of her daughter, but when she saw I had vacation, she said, 'Oh, well, maybe you have more money than me. Maybe $200 is too much money for your mother.'" It was the kind of veiled threat that scared Maria. She was convinced she needed a new place to stay.

"I said, 'You found a job for me, thank you. You lent the money for me to come, thank you. But if we are going to have these problems, I don't want to stay with you on weekends.'"

Maria called family and friends in Cuautla, looking for any way out of her living situation. Finally, a friend from beauty school there told Maria about some of her brothers and a cousin named Eduardo who lived on 110th Street and Second Avenue.

On New Year's Day, 1998, Maria stepped out of the subway at 110th Street and Lexington Avenue. On the other side of the turnstile stood Eduardo, cousin of Maria's friend back in Cuautla. He was tall, with an easy smile but quiet at first.

Maria explains, "Eduardo and I were very close from the beginning. I don't know why. I didn't know him, and he didn't know me. But he was very close to me. When I came to them, I told them I didn't have much. Most of what I had, I borrowed from these women. Eduardo said, 'When you talk to this woman, have your things ready. I will come and pick you up in Harlem.' "

Maria headed back to 125th Street, ready to start over in East Harlem. "So I talked to them, and said, 'I have friends, I am leaving. I paid your money. I tried living with you, but I don't like it." It was a difficult moment, but Maria was prepared. Her mother had already made arrangements for Delila's daughter to live elsewhere. As Maria describes it, "The contract was terminated."

The capital investment required to make the journey across the border is often supplied by family members already settled in the United States who are eager to reunite their families. With no family or friends in New York, Maria pursued a less conventional route to U.S. migration by contracting with a more experienced migrant to advance the funds needed to cross the border. Without that support, families like Maria's become indebted to strangers who establish their own, informal social network of contracted labor. Fortunately, Maria was able to buy her way out quickly and simultaneously tap into a nonfamily social network willing to help.

Delila's anger at Maria's ability to extricate herself from the arrangement puzzled Maria. "I am very thankful that she brought me here, but I already paid her the money. I will never be able to thank her for her help, but the fact that she lent the money doesn't mean she owns my life."

Maria left the apartment in Harlem with little more than the clothes on her back. The winter coats had all been lent by Delila, and she demanded their return. "I had my whole life in two plastic shopping bags on the street," Maria says. Stepping out into the January cold with only two shopping bags, she felt good but also alone. Eduardo was on his way to meet her, but despite their initial connection, she felt she was moving from one house of strangers to another.

Standing on a corner on 125th Street, Maria remembered the long talks she had with her mother before she left Cuautla. They agreed her sojourn in New York would last no more than two years.

"My mother said, 'But if you don't feel good about it, you should come back.' My mother and I are very close. My mother said, 'I don't want a house, I want you.' "

It had only been four months. Although Maria had already begun sending money to build her mother's house, she still needed much more.

"I knew I couldn't go back to Mexico. I had to keep fighting to make it."

Eduardo arrived, took her bags, and listened to Maria's fears and frustrations. As they walked toward East Harlem, Eduardo could tell she was despairing of her new and uncertain life. He stopped, turned to Maria, and said, "You are not alone. You have friends."

"He hugged me. I felt strange, but I also felt good. That's why I love my husband. He was the first person who said those words to me, 'You are not alone. You have friends.' "

When Eduardo walked Maria down the crowded sidewalk of 116th Street toward her new home, she joined thousands of other Mexicans who had turned the 1990s into the Mexican decade in East Harlem. In 1990 there were less than 3,000 Mexicans settled in East Harlem—according to census records notorious for undercounting Latinos, Mexicans in particular. That was just 6 percent of the Latino population in East Harlem and only 3 percent of the total population of the neighborhood.

Ten years later, there were more than 10,000 Mexicans in "Spanish" Harlem, 10 percent of the total population and 17 percent of Latinos. More than 8,000 of those counted were born in Mexico, like Maria. Over the same period, Puerto Ricans actually lost more than 7,000 residents and slipped to an increasingly shrinking majority among Latinos in East Harlem.

This was a trend felt throughout New York City and, certainly, throughout the United States. Of the more than 20.0 million Mexicans and Mexican Americans residing in the United States in 2000, an estimated 4.8 million were undocumented migrants, an increase of almost 2.0 million in just four years.[26] In New York, ranked third behind California and Texas as the destination of undocumented migrants, the number of Mexicans went from less than 50,000 inhabitants in 1980 to 100,000 a decade later and more than a quarter million by 2000.[27] As in East Harlem, the number of Puerto Ricans has decreased throughout the city while the number of Mexicans has increased.

That shift was perhaps most noticeable along 116th Street, the wide two-way street that, along with 106th Street, slices the neighborhood into thirds. "116th, from Third, Second, First Avenues, is like a Mexican community," Maria explains. Grocery stores, vegetable markets, record stores, restaurants—every facade was a blitz of green and red, eagle and serpent, all images of Mexican nationalism. By the time Maria arrived, more than thirty new Mexican businesses had opened on the East Harlem stretch of 116th Street in the previous five years.[28] One of the most important new arrivals was the travel agency, one-stop shopping for placing long distance calls to Oaxaca, Mexico City, or Cuautla, arranging a trip home, or, most likely, wiring cash back to family.

Whereas for Pete, José, and Lucille, 116th Street was the most visible tributary from Pleasant Avenue and Italian Harlem, it is now the boulevard of Mexican Harlem. After decades of Italian and then Puerto Rican dominance, Maria could move into the new Mexico of 116th Street and feel like she was coming home—if still thousands of miles away. "116th is very Mexican. Everyone says, 'I'm going to 116th.' Because you can find anything you want."

Maria settled into her new home on 110th Street, sharing a small apartment with Eduardo, a few of his cousins, and the wife of one of the cousins. She continued to commute to New Jersey to work as a housekeeper for the first few months. Eduardo remained just one of the men with whom she shared an apartment, at first.

On December 23, 1998, Eduardo handed Maria a thin gold ring. No attendants, no priest, no church—just a subtle shift in sleeping arrangements that made Eduardo Maria's husband.

"It's very common, even in Mexico, for this to happen. People will have a big wedding and a big party, or they will have nothing at all. It's not important."[29]

There were a few months of hand-wringing as Maria tried to convince her mother from thousands of miles away that Eduardo was worthy of her and that she did not need a big wedding or big party. It had taken Eduardo almost as long to convince Maria herself. Maria explains, "I came here to make money for my mother's home. I listen to people all day tell me about coming here, meeting someone, getting pregnant, having a husband that drinks too much or even hits them. I did not want that." Maria finally agreed to marry Eduardo on one condition. No children—at least not yet.

Within a few months, Maria found a new apartment for her new life with Eduardo and invited her brothers to join her from Cuautla.

"Now I live with Eduardo," Maria says. "I've made my life with him."

One of the first of Maria's siblings to brave the crossing to join her in New York was her elder, unmarried sister, Aracely. "She crossed the border alone. No friends or family. My cousin paid for the coyote. But she didn't like it. She was only in the United States eight months."

After Aracely returned to Mexico, Maria's brothers, Armando and José Luis, journeyed to New York. Another of Eduardo's long list of cousins, also from Cuautla, soon joined the household, sharing the small three-room apartment. The men all found work at dry cleaning establishments, Eduardo in lower Manhattan, Armando in the Bronx, and José Luis just a few blocks away on 106th Street.

Graciela, a friend from Mexico, arranged for Maria to work with her in an East Harlem barbershop. After two other employees left the small shop, Graciela married, became pregnant, and quit. "So then I worked at the barbershop by myself." Each morning she raised the metal gate, prepared the narrow space for the day, and waited for customers at $10 a haircut to walk through the door. Five years earlier, she barely earned $10 a week cutting hair in Mexico.

The owner of the space, a local Puerto Rican entrepreneur, charged Maria $450 per month or 30 percent of her earnings, whichever was higher. According to Maria, "He rents the space, but he doesn't know anything about haircuts." After almost three years of this arrangement, the owner came to Maria with a proposition: if she paid the rent and overhead for the shop, she could keep every dollar she made. "I said, 'I'll try it, and see if I have money for the rent and bills.' That's why I worked seven days a week. I didn't have any time." In less than four years in the United States, Maria effectively ran her own business.

"So I paid everything for one year," Maria says. It moved her financially closer to finishing her mother's house in Cuautla, but her two-year experiment of living in the United States now ran close to five years, and the extra effort of running her own business wore her down. In 2003 she hired Victor and renegotiated the situation.

"When Victor came to the shop, we said, 'No more. I will pay the same as him.' We went back to the old arrangement."

.   .   .   .   .

"Why are they speaking Spanish?" Victoria, Vic's seven-year-old daughter, is exasperated with the conversation. Maria agreed to watch her at her apartment while Vic took care of some business. A second-generation Nuyorican, Victoria knows only a few greetings in Spanish. Her only surviving grandparent has long since moved back to Puerto Rico, and her parents speak English.

Maria's small kitchen is more crowded than usual, with a dozen well-wishers celebrating Eduardo's twenty-ninth birthday. Half-empty Corona bottles litter the table, and the remains of a taco dinner lie about the room. Maria chuckles at Victoria's frustration and tries to shoo her into her bedroom to watch television.

Arturo, one of Eduardo's cousins visiting from Queens, speaks to Victoria in English. "You don't understand?" he asks. His thick accent undermines his ad hoc English, but Victoria latches on to anyone who can speak her language.

"No," replies Victoria, "my grandma talks like that, but I don't understand her either."

"Do you know the word *citizen?*" Arturo asks.

"Yes," Victoria responds precociously, "but I don't know what it means."

Arturo tries to explain the difference between her grandparents' coming from Puerto Rico and his own arrival from Mexico. Language and experience push the two farther apart, until Maria interjects in Spanish, "She's too young."

Arturo gives up with a sigh and a laugh, "It's the same at work, the Koreans say they are better than me because they have a green card. We do the same work, and they get paid more than me. For what?"

"She doesn't understand that."

Arturo isn't speaking to Maria now, or Victoria. He has turned to Eduardo, José Luis, and Armando. "They think we want to come here to be 'American.' It's not patriotism. I'm here to make money, that's it. Why shouldn't I earn what they do? Then I could go home sooner."

"Maria," complains Victoria, "he's speaking Spanish again."

Maria guides Victoria into the bedroom and sits her down next to two shy Mexican girls, both of them younger than Victoria and neither fluent in English. Victoria rolls her eyes and slumps to the floor. Maria returns to the kitchen.

Arturo's frustration was born in part out of his most recent experience crossing the border with Maria. In December 2003, after the unexpected death of her stepfather, Maria could not bear the separation from her mother any longer. Despite the tightened security after September 11, 2001, Maria wanted to return for a visit.

As Maria boarded a flight from JFK to Mexico City, Eduardo stood by anxiously, concerned about her ability to return to New York. At the gate Maria showed her picture ID from the Mexican consulate in New York, stating her hometown of Cuautla just above her address on 109th Street in East Harlem. She waved to Eduardo and was back in Mexico by that afternoon.

She surprised her mother in Cuautla on her fiftieth birthday. The joyful homecoming held all the tears and laughter one would expect. Victoria, her mother's best friend who had arranged for Maria's trip to New York, apologized for the trouble she had caused.

"She gave me a big hug and cried and said, 'You are a good daughter. A lot of people go to the United States. They promise a lot of things, but they don't do them. But you've done it. You are a woman, a woman that is moving forward.' "

Maria enjoyed a few months in Cuautla, including her first-ever trip to the beach, then turned her attention to the return. Her husband and brothers awaited her in East Harlem; this meant another treacherous border crossing. This time Eduardo's cousin Arturo, who had also returned for a visit, would accompany her.

Arturo and Maria left Cuautla on February 26, 2004, and headed for Nogales, Sonora. After one night in one of the hundreds of hotels that dot the border region and serve as way stations for migrants, they boarded a van with thirty others. The van, overloaded and driving too fast, took them deep into the desert. Maria helped the only child, a five-year-old girl, get near a window to breathe.

Just after dark, the passengers were let out and told to run quickly into the night. Spurred on by the panic in the coyote's voice, they ran as fast as they could for over an hour. The group eventually slowed to a single-file march in the darkness. "I could not see anything, nothing, not even the person in front of me," Maria remembers. She and Arturo had two gallons of water, some cookies, and a can of tuna.

"Everyone stop!" cried the coyote at the front of the line.

The group crouched low, wary of the ever-vigilant Border Patrol. It would take some time before Maria discovered the reason for their delay—a dead and decaying body on the path. "Everyone was very scared and walked much more quickly than normal. It was cold, but I could not feel it."[30]

They arrived at their rendezvous point at 9:00 A.M., two hours early, and had to split into two groups. Maria agreed to go with the little girl and her father. Arturo was placed in the other group.

The morning sun began to scorch the Arizona desert, replacing the chill of the previous night with a dangerous heat. As Maria started off in her group, their coyote once again sounded an alarm. Three strangers approached, beckoning them to come out of hiding.

"It was two women and a man, all American. They called out that they were not Immigration but were there to help." The frightened and fatigued migrants came out of hiding to find food, water, and clothing. One of the women, a nurse, tended to a broken foot and other less serious ailments. Maria recognized one of the women from a news report about U.S. residents helping migrants crossing the desert.

The coyote had long since vanished, and as the strangers left the group to carry on, one of the migrants spotted Border Patrol agents on the horizon. "We all tried to run, but with the little girl, we could not get away." After more than twelve hours on the run in the desert, they were caught, processed, and sent back to Nogales.

Meanwhile, Arturo learned Maria had been caught. Not wanting to return to New York without her, he began the unthinkable: he started looking for Immigration officers to turn himself in and reunite with Maria in Mexico. "He was walking along the freeway, toward Mexico, and people would stop and tell him he was going the wrong way. He told them, 'No, I am going back to Mexico. Can you tell me how to find the Immigration office?'" It took Arturo an hour to get himself captured.

"I called Eduardo, and I explained everything. I told him about the dead man, everything. And he was scared. I said, 'I am going to stay with the man and his daughter and two other women. We found a hotel." At the hotel, Maria, Arturo, and their small group of desert-weary travelers arranged another crossing with a new coyote. She remembers with disgust the coyotes competing for the frightened migrants huddled in the overcrowded border hotels. One seemed especially dishonest. According to Maria, "He said everything is nice, everything is beautiful. But nothing is beautiful."

Maria and Arturo negotiated $1,800 per person to cross with the new coyote, $1,000 when they reached Phoenix and the rest when they reached New York City.

"We crossed at night, until six o'clock in the afternoon the next day. We crossed at Naco, Sonora, in the desert. We walked too much, with no sleep. We had to hide in the mountains, among the rocks, and it was cold. Everyone was shaking. My cousin hugged me, everyone hugged. And the little girl, everyone hugged her because I think she was the coldest, she was so small. For two or three hours everyone was shaking."

Early the next morning, Maria's group met at a rendezvous point to pick up a car that would take them on to Phoenix. Fifteen migrants climbed into a single sedan, but before they could begin the second leg of their journey, the colored lights of a patrol car forced them out of the car.

"They said, 'Don't move, we are the police.' And the coyotes ran back to the border. Then they asked a lot of questions. I was scared and nervous and crying, because I could not do it again. It was the second time. I give up. It's too much for me. Other ladies were crying."

They were narcotics officers looking for drug smugglers. The bleary-eyed migrants, including a young child, did not fall under their job description. Maria recalls that one officer was a Mexican American who said his parents had crossed the border many years before.

"He said, 'I called Immigration, and they said it was too far, that they wouldn't come here. That I should take you to the station and they would pick you up there. But it's not my business. I don't know whose car this is, but when I close my eyes, everyone run.' So everyone ran like cock-roaches. Without the car, without anything."

The coyotes waited for the officers to leave, picked up the car, and rounded up the scattered migrants. By 11:00 P.M. they were in an apartment in Phoenix.

Maria's trek across the desert marked, in thousands of paces, her devotion to her family, in both Cuautla and East Harlem. The return to Mexico, albeit temporary, shored up ties stretched thin over the length of a continent. But with half the family now in East Harlem, the meaning of "home" and where one "returned" grew harder and harder to define.

Transnationalism has become convenient shorthand for this dual existence. The concept is certainly not new, as many European migrants of the past century came as temporary laborers and maintained close ties to home communities in Russia, Germany, or Italy.[31] But as the technologies of communication and transportation increase abilities to maintain connections, transnationalism has received substantial attention from scholars and migrants alike.[32]

One obvious form this transnational identity takes is financial. The remittances from the United States to Mexico are not only remarkable additions to the Mexican economy but capital investments in fractured families—maintaining connections through wire transfers and bank accounts.

Maria enacts this monetary kinship ritual every couple of weeks at a Mexican travel agency on 116th Street. For a 5 percent commission, Maria can send any amount of cash to an office in Cuautla for her mother to pick up the next day. After seven years Maria has learned the power of that monetary link between the two countries and uses her earning power to influence domestic life back in Cuautla. "When I came here I talked to my mother, 'You know, I don't want your husband at home. I made the house for you, not for him. I send the money for you, not for everybody.'"

When Maria's stepsister decided to marry at eighteen, without going on to a university, Maria scolded her, "You want that life? Why did I spend all this money for everything?" Her brother José Luis, also speaking with the authority of a transnational breadwinner, advised, "You opened the bank account, so now you close the bank account. No more money for her. When you have the money, you give it to Mother. That's it."

Transnationalism is marked most notably by a divided self—torn between two "homes." Maria questioned the initial motivation for migrating to the United States, but the two-year experiment has lasted more than seven years. Now, even a few months in Cuautla could not stop her from braving the border crossing again to return to Eduardo, her brothers, and her barbershop.

Back in East Harlem, Eduardo's birthday party winds down. Arturo still has a long commute back to Queens, and some friends are saying good-night. Maria, finished entertaining, fumbles under the television in the kitchen and retrieves an unmarked videotape. She slides it into the VCR, and after a few moments of static, the screen comes to life.

A short, round, and much older version of Maria—Maria's mother—stands in the middle of a simple but immaculate living room weeping. She sheds tears of joy as she greets her daughter all the way from New York who came for her fiftieth birthday. The scenes dissolve into the loud frivolity of a middle-aged birthday party—a sharp contrast to the staid celebration petering out in Maria and Eduardo's East Harlem kitchen. The New York contingent had wired money for an impressive event, complete with professional deejay and colored lights that swirled to the beat of salsa, meringue, and even New York hip-hop music. After the party there are the long, unedited scenes of household chores, inside jokes—daily life in Cuautla with Maria and her mother.

Maria smiles a courageous but thinly drawn smile and says, "I like watching my mother, but it makes me more sad."

.   .   .   .   .

Es el señor, nos acompaña al caminar,
Con su ternura a nuestro lado siempre va.
Si los peligros nos acechan por doquier,
Nuestro amigo Jesús nos salvará.[33]

The voices of a few hundred parishioners rise up from the pews of St. Cecilia's Church one midsummer Sunday. The grand red brick church occupies most of the block of 106th Street between Lexington Avenue and the elevated Metro North railway. Inside it is a cavernous two-tiered space, whitewashed to emphasize the shrines adorning the altar and the corners of the sanctuary.

It's the second Spanish mass of the day at St. Cecilia's, and many of the mostly Mexican congregants at this service crowd around a faux grotto near the entrance to celebrate an infant baptism. Maria stands nearby, along with Eduardo and Armando, singing along softly as they witness their friend's first child inducted into the church.

From a nearby corner, Our Lady of Guadalupe, patroness of Mexico, watches over them. The shrine is a recent addition to St. Cecilia's, providing a specifically Mexican vision of the Virgin Mary. Long the spiritual center for the Puerto Ricans of Spanish Harlem, St. Cecilia's has embraced the new influx of Mexican, Ecuadoran, and Filipino faithful, providing new shrines to match the new nationalisms that have in some ways competed for sacred space in the church. Not unlike the growing pains of a Catholic parish on Pleasant Avenue a century ago, when Italian and Irish Catholics found it difficult to share an altar, St. Cecilia's has experienced a milder but no less significant adjustment.[34] The same church that guided José's formative years now guides those of his children alongside the ever-diversifying population of Latinos.

The inclusion of Mexicans and other new Latinos at St. Cecilia's has not always sat well with many of East Harlem's older, more settled residents. Maria has experienced resistance to the rapid influx of Mexicans, not only at church, but at the barbershop as well. As she explains, "Some people don't like to sit for me because they don't want a Mexican." Maria can recall a time when other Latinos would refuse to sit in her chair if Vic was too busy. As she has improved, that resistance has weakened—though Vic, like many Puerto Ricans in East Harlem, is still wary of her adaptability. According to Maria, "Now, I have Mexican and black and American customers. They see me, my work. Sometimes it makes Victor angry. A lot of customers wait for him, but if the customer is new, they will come to me. He has a lot of customers, but, a lot of times, he wants to have all the customers. He gets jealous."

Victor's alleged jealousy is not unique. As Mexican groceries, record stores, and travel agencies supplant those of Puerto Ricans along 116th

Street, Puerto Ricans grow increasingly outspoken about their fears of this changing character of "Spanish" Harlem.[35] Despite their common language, the tensions between Puerto Ricans and Mexicans are no different from those between Italians and Puerto Ricans a generation earlier. Indeed, with second- and third-generation Puerto Ricans, such as Vic's daughter Victoria, even language provides little common ground.

At worst, these tensions turn violent, and the turf wars of Italians around Pleasant Avenue are revisited on the side streets near 106th Street. Maria remembers, "Once, I couldn't sleep, because there were people fighting in front of my building. I looked out the curtain a little bit, and there were a lot of Puerto Ricans fighting one Mexican guy with a baseball bat. But the Mexican guy ran to the car wash, because there are a lot of Mexicans who work at the car wash. They defended the Mexican. If he hadn't run to the car wash, he would be dead."

The tensions, however, like those interethnic conflicts of the past, are not one-sided. Maria and her siblings harbor their own misgivings about their multicultural neighbors, often lumping ethnicities together into one amorphous force with which they must contend. "José Luis doesn't like to speak with Puerto Rican people. When he worked on 106th Street, he worked with black people, but my brother did everything for them. He said, 'They work, but they don't do anything.'"

For Maria, easy stereotypes are never comfortable. As more Mexicans crowd the tenements, her fears turn as much to them as to ethnic outsiders. "There are a lot more Mexican people here. Sometimes I trust them, and sometimes I don't. Sometimes on the weekends, late at night, I am scared to walk through the streets. With more Mexicans there are more conflicts, with other races or even among themselves. Because there are a lot of Mexicans who fight other Mexicans."

Intraethnic conflict, especially among immigrant youth, has long marked the streets of East Harlem. Back in Pete's day, Leonard Covello knew the Italians would fight other Italians from different blocks as quickly as they would fight Puerto Ricans or African Americans. Today, it's young Mexicans, either the children of immigrants or the veterans of solitary crossings in search of the new gringo El Dorado—promising streets paved with gold.

"There are a lot of gangs now," explains Maria. "On 116th, when you are walking in the middle of the night, there are a lot of Mexicans there waiting for other Mexican people. They fight because they are different gangs."[36] Maria, always focused on the business of transnationalism, is at a loss trying to explain the phenomenon. "Sometimes I think, 'Who is sending these young people? Who lent the money to come here and cause problems?' They don't work. They sell drugs. They cause problems with other Mexicans, with Puerto Ricans, always fighting."

After the baptism, Maria heads to the Julia de Burgos Cultural Center ready for a party. The renovated public school serves as a gallery space, theater, and artist workshop for a group of local artists-activists in East Harlem. The cultural center, named for the Puerto Rican poet Julia de Burgos, who died in East Harlem, stands next to St. Cecilia's Church. Together they anchor 106th Street and Lexington Avenue, the community board's "Cultural Crossroads."

In a large hall, often used for Puerto Rican music and poetry events, rows of tables with white tablecloths and flower arrangements line the walls. An open space in the center of the room is reserved for dancing, complete with a light show and a professional deejay. Most of the guests won't show up for a few hours, and the dancing will go on into the night. For now, the dance floor is the playscape of toddlers and their balloons. The newly christened infant is already fast asleep.

Eduardo and Armando stake out a table and make room for a few more friends. Maria holds the sleeping baby, laughing at her own awkwardness with the child and fending off inquiries from the women at the table about her plans for a family. Soon food and drinks arrive, pulled pork and beer. Men fall into a gustatory silence, as the few women discuss the details of the event.

"The room cost $800," says one woman. The night before, a close friend asked Eduardo and Maria to serve as godparents to his first child. An honor and a burden: godparents help to pay for the party. "The dress, just by itself, costs $200," says Maria with a subtle roll of her eyes.

The proud godfather of the guest of honor stops by the table and promises to return with more beer. Talk turns to Mexico, border crossing anniversaries, return plans, and new rumors of elusive visas. The men slouch into a shy silence. The women attempt to talk over the blaring cumbia music that now fills the room.

As Maria made her way to New York with Delila in 1997, she went against a century of male-dominated migration from Mexico to the United States. Statistics on unauthorized migration consistently demonstrate a 3:1 ratio of men to women making the journey north. But Maria, like many Mexican women who find themselves in the United States, is not interested in gender conformity. She finds this aspect of her existence at the barbershop almost humorous.

"Sometimes, men won't sit in my chair. Not because of my country, it's because I am a woman. They think, 'I don't want a woman to touch my face.' But a lot of people now think I do a good job, even though I am a woman." She has even noted an ethnic distinction in customer responses to her gender. "A Mexican, or any Spanish person, will think it strange for a woman to trim their beard or their mustache. They don't like it. It's like the machismo of these people. It's different for the black people, they come and say, 'Shave and everything.'"

Maria does not laugh as easily about other gender implications in East Harlem, especially within her community of Mexican immigrants. "On 110th and Lexington there is a Mexican restaurant, they have women for dancing. You pay $2 if you want to dance with one of the girls. Not more than dancing. It's for men only. If the ladies speak with the men, they get more tips. That's their job."

After the baptism, after the party, there is nothing to do but return to her apartment. Maria climbs the worn plywood stairs that wait in vain for new linoleum and pushes through the thick metal door to her apartment at the end of the hallway. She walks past the bunk beds shared by her brothers, through the small kitchen, and into her bedroom. She turns on the television and waits for Eduardo, José Luis, Armando, or Lalo to invade the small space.

"One day I would like my own house," she says. "I would like some privacy. Not have to share the bathroom. But I feel okay, because I am with my brothers. I talk to them and give them advice, that they can move forward."

Maria is torn between two homes, neither entirely her own. She sent the last payment for her mother's house a few months earlier. Though stretched out and evolved, the plan is still to return, someday. She sends money now to be deposited into her own account, for her own house and her own barbershop. After fulfilling the dream of a house for her mother, Maria began to dream her own dreams.

"I told my mother, 'I need to make my life, my home. There are a lot of things I want.' Sometimes I think people look at me like a gold mine. But I feel content now. As a daughter and wife, I feel content. At times, it is hard to live your life for others, but I think there is some compensation. I tell my brothers that if you want to get ahead, you can. You can reach your dreams. You can make them a reality."

"Now," she says, "I only send money to my mother when she needs something." She hesitates, then adds, "Now it's different because I have Eduardo."

As if waiting for permission, Maria has arranged her affairs to leave at a moment's notice. "I don't like to save my money in the bank here. Some people say that if you leave for any reason, they don't give you your money fast." And yet life with Eduardo in East Harlem has slowly shifted allegiances, blurred boundaries, altered plans. "We are thinking about maybe having a baby. We have to plan. I think we will have a baby here. I think in maybe three more years, we will return to Mexico. But some people say, 'Once you have a baby here, it is better for its development. There are more possibilities.' But I also want to be with my mother," Maria says as she slips an unmarked tape into the VCR. "It's not easy."

six Third Avenue

THE WEST AFRICANS

Spring Clip Mop Handle, 65 cents.
AA Batteries, 16-pack, 65 cents.
Sponge Dish Brush, 65 cents.

Mohamed circles items on the glossy pages of a wholesale catalog with a red pen. It's Friday, and he's standing behind the counter of his 99-cent store on Third Avenue.

11 Piece Kitchen Set, 65 cents.
8″ Wide Lens Flashlight, 65 cents.
Water Guns, two-pack, 65 cents.

"Where's the paper towels?" a middle-aged Puerto Rican woman asks.

Mohamed looks up from his catalog, his eyes white against his dark skin, and motions to the back of the store. "In the back, ma'am," he answers, his voice coming high-pitched but casual. It's a slightly labored English filtered through French and the rather more obscure Susu of Guinea and Sierra Leone. The customer shuffles past the counter, down the narrow aisles of glassware, dishes, pots, and pans, to the back elevated nook of the store that is bedecked with paper goods.

Mohamed returns to his work, silently figuring the current state of his inventory, the time of year, and what combination of inexpensive, mostly Asian manufactured goods will move quickly among his clientele. Behind him, the shelves are lined with batteries, cassette tapes, and individual packs of various over-the-counter drugs—the impulse commodities of customers usually picking up a month's supply of 69-cent toilet paper or 99-cent shampoo. To his left, the front door and glass facade are stacked to the ceiling with plastic toys, action figures, novelty games—the impulse commodities of passing children and their beleaguered parents.

Outside, on Third Avenue, from 96th Street to 125th Street, the sidewalks are punctuated with the folding tables of West African vendors. Tube socks and T-shirts, backpacks and cassette tapes. Some of the more industrious have rented space in the entryways of residential buildings from the superintendents, but all of them pay rent to someone—buying their time in the path of the heavy foot traffic.

Mohamed has taken the street sale inside; he rents a 500-square-foot space on the first floor of a tenement building. Next door, a twenty-four-hour laundry keeps customers coming in for detergent and other household goods. Across the street, a twenty-four-hour bodega, a new beauty supply store, a pharmacy, and, the most successful business on the block, a liquor store, all keep the foot traffic moving.

Another middle-aged woman pushes through the front door, its cracking glass held in place with duct tape. "¿Disculpe, papi, pero no tiene papel hygenico?" she asks in staccato Spanish.

Mohamed smiles and calls out toward the back of the store: "Alex!"

Alex, a Mexican employee in his midtwenties, wearing a white baseball cap and a sleeveless shirt, bounds toward the front of the store to intercept the monolingual customer. A few words are exchanged, and Alex leads the woman to the 69-cent toilet paper.

"If I had to do it over again, I would not open a store here," Mohamed states flatly, closing his catalog and folding his arms. "Maybe not even a store at all."

.   .   .   .   .

"I was born in Guinea, 1964, but I grew up in Sierra Leone." Nationality is a fluid concept for Mohamed, as it is for many living in postcolonial West Africa. "Half of the family was in Sierra Leone, and half of the family was in Guinea. My parents had a house in Guinea, but the main house was in Sierra Leone."

Mohamed's ancestors, like so many in Africa, were subdivided by the imposition of national boundaries linked to European colonizers. The boundaries were the subject of centuries of dispute among most of the European powers, including the Portuguese—who claimed and named Sierra Leone in the fifteenth century—the French, and the British. In international conferences, like that in Berlin in 1884–85, and bilateral treaties, like those between France and Britain in the 1890s, the African continent, West Africa in particular, was partitioned into neat commercial sectors organized around so-called free trade and the humanitarian enlightenment of its inhabitants.[1] With the stroke of a pen, half of Mohamed's ancestors were French and half British.

But the particularities of local culture proved resilient under the assimilationist pressure of colonization. Language, like religion, was well suited to subversive conformity. It took on the mantle of colonial expectations without sacrificing precolonial practice.

"We were all the same people," Mohamed explains, "but when they divided the country, they drew a line—some spoke French and some English. But people in the boundary between Sierra Leone and Guinea, they speak a local language, Susu. I speak French, English, and Susu."

Susu, a language spoken by a relative minority of Guineans and even fewer Sierra Leoneans, is one of dozens of languages that straddle the colonial borders of West Africa. Only 800,000 Guineans, or 10.0 percent, speak Susu; only 120,000 Sierra Leoneans, or 3.1 percent.[2]

"In the 1950s there were certain tribes from Guinea who came over to Sierra Leone to look for diamonds," Mohamed says. "My parents immigrated there during the early fifties." Thousands of would-be miners converged on Sierra Leone during the so-called diamond rush of the period. Since a British geologist discovered the first gem-quality diamonds in Sierra Leone in 1930, the small British colony–turned–independent nation has boasted one of the largest and most valuable diamond deposits in the world.

Attempts by the British government, which exercised colonial rule over Sierra Leone until 1961, to monopolize control over the deposit proved futile as independent miners flocked to the riverbeds and dense jungle. By 1954 there were an estimated thirty thousand illegal miners digging out diamonds and selling them, primarily to Lebanese middlemen, effectively ending the London-based monopoly on regional mining, the Sierra Leone Selection Trust. By 1955 the powerless monopoly on mining rights was dissolved, and individual miners, like Mohamed's father, were issued licenses in the hope of regulating the trade.[3] On April 27, 1961, Sierra Leone celebrated its first day of self-rule, inheriting a poorly managed, multinational system of diamond mining and trading that would ultimately bloody the mud paths of the Sierra Leone hinterlands in one of the most horrific conflicts of the late twentieth century.[4]

But it would be some time before the corrupting influence of the diamond trade undermined the stability of the Sierra Leonean government. According to Mohamed, "Diamond mining was easy then in the 1950s. Eighty percent of them were right there on the surface, you don't have to dig. Now to get to the diamonds, you have to go further, and people are digging all those years in the same pit. But at the time of my parents, it was not too hard."

It did not take long for Mohamed's father to work his way out of the digging and into the trading of precious stones to Europe. "My father was working for himself, he had like thirty people working for him. They would collect them and he would go to Europe to sell. At that time, you could travel easily. The economy in Africa was just like the economy in Europe. The exchange rate was good. There was not a lot of corruption, the country had a lot of reserve. It was just at the end of colonialism, you could go to London without a visa, and the banks were directly linked to the English banks."

Thanks to his father's success in the diamond trade, Mohamed came of age in Freetown, the capital of Sierra Leone. As the name might suggest, Freetown was founded—by British philanthropists in the late eighteenth century—as a refuge for freed slaves. Former slaves, most of them from North America, who had agreed to fight for the British during the Revolutionary War in exchange for freedom, settled in what would become the capital of a British colony in 1808. By 1842, when the crew of the now famously commandeered slave ship *Amistad* were finally returned to their home country of Sierra Leone, Freetown boasted between 10,000 and 20,000 inhabitants. The year Mohamed was born, Freetown was a bustling city of more than 100,000. Twenty years later, the population was half a million.[5]

By the time Mohamed reached high school, his father had died, leaving three wives and several children. His father's success as a diamond trader permitted many of Mohamed's elder siblings to be educated in England, but after his mother remarried, Mohamed was forced to attend high school in Freetown. "It was tough then, for my mother, financially. My stepfather was not as well off, and he had other family already. The resources were divided."

"I never wanted to work with diamonds," he says of his early aspirations. "When my father passed, my mother was in the city, and there was no way to do that anymore." Though his siblings in England were building professional careers, Mohamed focused on the unstable but sometimes lucrative market economy of Sierra Leone. "When I was in high school, I would go to Guinea and buy stuff there to sell in my school. So I used [to] sell T-shirts and women's shoes when I was in high school. It was an instinct. I just liked it, I knew I could do it."

The business of buying and selling for a local market proved more attractive than higher education. After receiving his high school diploma, Mohamed devoted himself to his growing enterprise. "I would go to Guinea for a few months, because there was so much merchandise you could get there at a reasonable price. And I was selling wholesale to stores in Freetown. I accumulated a little bit of capital." Eventually, Mohamed bought a boat to ferry merchandise between Guinea and Sierra Leone. "Then," he explains, "I started to go to Nigeria. That was a little bit farther out. I had to use an airplane. I started doing that in about 1985."

The same year Mohamed was expanding his small international business Sierra Leone was at a critical point of economic and political contraction. In 1985 Siaka Stevens, the autocratic ruler of Sierra Leone since 1968, transferred power to the head of his military, General Joseph Momoh. Stevens had presided over two decades of economic decline, including the nationalization of diamond mining, which put most of the proceeds of diamond trading into his own pocket.

Momoh continued Stevens's misrule, as official diamond exports continued to decline, along with state spending on health, education, and the country's debt.[6] Seven years later, when Mohamed was settling into an overcrowded Harlem apartment, Momoh would be forced out by his own military in the wake of an invasion from Liberia by the Revolutionary United Front (RUF). It was the start of a near-decade-long conflict that would leave thousands dead and many more terrorized.

War was still several years in the future, and Mohamed continued to move merchandise between Guinea, Sierra Leone, and Nigeria until 1986. But, he remembers, "I got bored." Always looking to expand, Mohamed set his sights on Europe. "I said, 'I have some money, let me go to England and see if I can buy some goods there and come back.'" Looking back on the experience now, Mohamed laughs. "Oh, that was funny! I think I had like $600 or $700, that was my whole capital. It seemed like a lot of money, but when I went to England I found out that was not a lot of money!"

Mohamed arrived in London and sought out a sister who had stayed on after completing her education to work in finance. "I had my sister there, she was working for some company. I told her I was trying to look for goods with $600. She laughed. I spent a week there, and I realized that there was no way I could go back with $600 in goods." Rather than return to Sierra Leone, Mohamed decided to stay on himself, trying to earn extra capital in England's considerably stronger wage-labor market.

Through contacts with other West Africans in England, Mohamed found work in a warehouse. However, despite Sierra Leone's long history of colonial subjugation, Sierra Leoneans were no longer British;

Mohamed did not enjoy the privileges of British citizenship. He was an undocumented immigrant working illegally, like many other West Africans at the time.

"You just apply to work with someone else's name, you would borrow somebody's papers. There are a lot of Africans there, and there is a kind of network. They know the system. Employers know, but they turn the other way. The way it works there, they don't check if you don't get into trouble. So you just don't get yourself into trouble."

But work in a warehouse, tied to the demands of unskilled labor, did not suit Mohamed. "I worked there for more than a year," he says, "and it wasn't in me just to work. I didn't feel happy." After eighteen months he quit, took his $4,000 in savings, and headed back to Sierra Leone.

With a broad smile, Mohamed explains, "Then I started to be a used car salesman." He purchased two used cars in Amsterdam and shipped them to Freetown, where he sold them for a small profit. With the proceeds from the first two cars, he returned to Amsterdam and purchased three more. "I did that for another two years, from Holland and back to Sierra Leone. There was not a whole lot of profit in the cars, maybe $600, and it took about fifteen months to sell them. But it was enough in Africa, because you don't have that many expenses. I liked it better than living in England, than going to work. So I didn't complain. I was happy."

But by 1990 the economy of Sierra Leone approached the bottom of its prewar downward spiral. General Momoh continued to profit from the illegal diamond trade. Inflation reached into the triple digits. Civil war was under way in neighboring Liberia.[7] Mohamed, demonstrating an impressive cultural dexterity, remained remarkably detached from these portents. "I did not think much of it at the time," he says now. "The war really happened after I left."

Mohamed, after all, was a man of relative privilege. The son of a diamond trader with well-educated siblings living in Europe, he spoke several languages and claimed at least two nationalities. But for all of his cultural capital, he had little access to commensurate financial resources. Mohamed had to hustle, employing a geographic flexibility that kept him politically and socially disengaged but materially well connected. It was a practical philosophy that served him well in high school as an adolescent transnational trader, and it would serve him well years later in East Harlem as a small business owner.

In 1990, when politics threatened profits, Mohamed took advantage of his loose social moorings once again. "The economy was really depressed, and every time the currency devalued, it cut into my profit," he explains. "So I packed up from there and went to Guinea to sell cars. I did that for almost a year."

It did not take long for Mohamed to tire of buying and selling used cars. Restless in Guinea, he began to cast about for a new venture. "At the end of 1991, during the Gulf War, I said, 'Maybe I want to start to go to Asia.' Because the market was starting to change, people were bringing goods from China, reasonable goods, cheaper goods. I thought I would try that, something that people can afford instead of a car."

But Mohamed would not go to Asia. He applied for a business visa to the United States. When asked, "Why the United States?" Mohamed says simply, "Somebody told me I could get cheaper cars here."

.   .   .   .   .

Mohamed stands at the curb on Third Avenue in front of his store feeding quarters into a meter. His maroon Mercedes SUV waits to carry him back to Queens before the evening rush.

"I just lease it," he explains, unprompted. "I don't own it, you know."

Two doors down, Kaba, another West African from Guinea, busily unloads milk cartons from a delivery truck in front of the Extra Savings Meat Market. Kaba was the manager of the 99-cent store before Mohamed bought the business. He didn't last long as an employee, and after bouncing from store to store up and down Third Avenue, he settled into his job at the Puerto Rican–owned supermarket. The two exchange a friendly wave but otherwise ignore each other.

Mohamed leans against the front fender of his Mercedes and dials a number on his mobile phone. Soon he is barking orders about an important shipment for a new business venture. The shipment is late, and Mohamed is anxious.

He holds the phone away from his mouth and laughs, "It's funny how I end up in places I never planned to end up." He waits, apparently on hold. "It's funny," he continues, "I was just coming to buy some cars. I was coming for a month."

Mohamed flew into JFK in 1991. Also in 1991 a relatively small band of RUF rebels invaded the diamond-rich eastern province of Sierra Leone from neighboring Liberia. Within a year General Momoh was removed from power and the nation was thrust into a decade of brutality. The war between the RUF, a West African "peacekeeping" force known as ECOMOG, and the national army terrorized the countryside as each competed for control of the still-lucrative diamond trade. The death toll and mounting human misery associated with diamond exports from Sierra Leone during the 1990s garnered international attention but little intervention—except for an uneven boycott against "conflict diamonds." A fragile peace was negotiated in 2001 with help from the United Nations but not before thousands had been raped, tortured, maimed, and murdered.[8]

Mohamed's business visa allowed a short-term stay in New York to purchase merchandise, specifically, used cars, to sell in Guinea. After a few weeks he decided to overstay his visa, violating the terms of his agreement and becoming one of the thousands of undocumented immigrants in New York. From 1990 to 1996 the estimated number of sub-Saharan Africans living in New York nearly doubled, from 44,000 to 84,000—many fleeing the violence erupting throughout the region.[9] Official records show that an average 1,500 sub-Saharan Africans were legally admitted to New York City each year throughout the early 1990s, though the number of undocumented immigrants was obviously much higher.[10]

Mohamed's story is not unlike many other West Africans' stories—a short-term trip that proved more permanent than intended. But the war in Sierra Leone was not what kept him in New York. "Like I said, I didn't think much about what was going on there," Mohamed explains.

Most of his family had retreated to the relative safety of Guinea, and Mohamed turned his attention to making a fresh start. "I was staying on Staten Island, I had a friend there, and I was looking for cars," Mohamed recalls. His friend was a messenger, ferrying documents from businesses in lower Manhattan to New Jersey with his own van. At first glance the $200 to $300 a week the job paid seemed more than his profit on used cars in Guinea. "So I thought, 'Let me work two or three months and make enough money, add more to my capital, and get more cars.' So I started doing that for two or three months, and after two or three months, I started liking it."

If the war in Sierra Leone was a factor in Mohamed's decision to stay in New York, it was not the overriding concern. Whether it was currency devaluations cutting into used car sales in West Africa or welfare reform turning away customers in East Harlem, politics was only as important as its effect on his profits. According to Mohamed, "The main reason that you decide to stay, you just don't realize that the job you are getting that you just can't save money. But then you start to like New York. You start meeting people. You start dating. For some reason, you just put away the plans you had before. I put away my plans. I said, 'Let me just stay here awhile.' "

While Sierra Leone spiraled into civil war, Mohamed adapted quickly to the social climate of the city. For Mohamed, however, Staten Island, the remotest island in the New York archipelago, was too far removed from the city's social center. "For three months I lived in Staten Island, but I didn't like it there," he remembers. Mohamed was drawn northward, to the capital of Black America. "I moved to Harlem, on the West Side."

West Africans had made their presence felt in Harlem for some time before Mohamed found an apartment with fellow Sierra Leoneans on 116th Street and Lenox Avenue. According to Mohamed, being black in Harlem was more democratic than it had been in England. He sensed a dignified defiance of the mainstream in Harlem—a tradition that stretched back a century.

"You know, really, I didn't have any problem when I moved to Harlem, because I think that blacks here are more tolerant than blacks in England. Blacks in England, they try to be more like English than like black people, but blacks here, they really want to be black."

It was a liberating denationalization—a blackness that trumped origin, citizenship, language, all the trappings of his past he was ready to shake loose. "The more time that you spend there, I don't care if you are from wherever, you start to do stuff differently. You start to see things differently." Mohamed downplayed his command of several languages, preferring instead to fit in as an English speaker, and he dated black American women. "So I think they are accepting, they didn't worry about it."

Although Mohamed's experience in Harlem was not unlike that of other West African immigrants, generalizations prove futile with such a diverse population. Most of the sub-Saharan immigrants of the 1990s were Francophone, mostly from Niger and Ghana but also from Senegal, Guinea, and Mali. Most of these new immigrants were men like Mohamed who sought to expand international trade businesses they already maintained in their home countries, which kept them in New York much longer than they intended. But unlike Mohamed, many of them left behind wives and children. The most devout Muslims among them remained faithful to their faraway spouses.

Few West Africans actually settled down in Manhattan, making good on their intentions to remain physically as well as economically mobile, but some, like Mohamed, found private housing with several other single men hoping to make fast money on the streets of New York. Others, like Kaba, who would briefly work for Mohamed, found public housing recipients willing to illegally sublet their apartments in East Harlem housing developments such as Johnson and Jefferson Houses. And still others found themselves in the Park View Hotel, a notorious single-room-occupancy establishment overlooking the north end of Central Park. Known as the "cent-dix" by French-speaking West Africans, the two-hundred-room hotel was a rude introduction to the worst stereotypes of living on the urban margins in the United States.[11]

And, of course, many of the West Africans living in Harlem were street vendors, selling what they could. Since the 1980s thousands of West African street vendors have crowded the sidewalks of Manhattan. As early as 1982 Senegalese traders orchestrated a monopoly on street vending in midtown Manhattan, selling everything from Afrocentric craftwork made in New Jersey to "I Love New York" T-shirts made in China. With the expansion of immigration from sub-Saharan Africa in the early 1990s, thousands of would-be traders were forced to the margins of the already informal economy—namely, 125th Street in Central Harlem.[12]

Indeed, by 1994 West African trading on Central Harlem's famed boulevard had become so crowded that Mayor Rudy Giuliani declared street vending illegal on 125th Street. It was not the first time the city tried to dismantle the network of West African street vendors in Manhattan. Mayor Ed Koch had successfully removed the pioneering Senegalese traders from Fifth Avenue in the 1980s. Mayor David Dinkins had attempted the same on 125th Street in 1993, but the newly formed 125th Street Vendors Association staged a well-organized demonstration that delayed the ordinance Giuliani enforced the following year. After Giuliani shut down their operation along 125th Street, many of the traders moved their businesses to an open-air, city-sanctioned market on 116th Street owned by the Malcolm Shabazz mosque. Others preferred to keep their folding table enterprises, like themselves, on the move.[13]

Mohamed, born in Guinea but raised in Sierra Leone—a man who packed for Asia but left for New York—also preferred to remain on the move. Still, he refused to join his countrymen as a street vendor. "I never sell on the street, never," Mohamed asserts. "That does not interest me. I get bored doing the same thing." But a deeper motivation, beyond boredom, explains his reluctance to follow the street-vending path.

"There are some Africans, if they are Fula from Guinea, this might be a businessperson," Mohamed says in the measured tones of a lecturer. "If he is Susu, he might be an intellectual. The people that sell in the street, they come from Senegal and Guinea. It's rare to see people from Sierra Leone, because they go to school, get a profession, they are not business oriented."

Though most of his elder Sierra Leonean siblings followed that path, receiving their education and pursuing their professional careers in England, Mohamed considers himself somewhere in between these two stereotypes of Guinea and Sierra Leone. "I could say 60 percent of me is from Guinea," he says, explaining his passion for business. "I have the blood of Guinea." The other 40 percent of Mohamed, the part from Sierra Leone that resists hustling odds and ends on the street, drove him to professionalize his passion.

While other West Africans sold wholesale from sidewalk folding tables, Mohamed drove a van for his friend's messenger company, hoping to earn investment capital. "Most of the companies were financial companies downtown, down in Wall Street. These companies have offices in Jersey and have a trading office down in Wall Street. And I would just move documents back and forth." For four years, Mohamed saved his money and waited for an opportunity.

It was during those early years that Mohamed met his wife, a naturalized immigrant from Haiti. "There was a place called Kilimanjaro on 43d Street, between Seventh and Sixth Avenues. They played African music there, and all Africans went there. People from the Caribbean, Africa, and African Americans. So you party and meet a lot of people."

A Haitian woman caught his eye.

"She was from Haiti, but she was a citizen here. She was here since she was eleven years old." They married in 1994, moved to Queens in 1995, and bought a house in 1996. Mohamed left the ranks of the undocumented. "She applied for me. That's the way I got my green card."

Soon after he married, Mohamed began searching for new ways to maximize his capital. "I started to talk to the clients of the messenger service directly," he explains. "My employers did not like that too much. I went to the customers and gave them a better rate." Undercutting his employer's prices, Mohamed earned enough money to buy a van and start a document delivery service. "So the last four years I was driving for myself. It was a good job, I made good money. I saved money there to open my business."

"That still was really the goal," Mohamed says now. "I didn't really like working, I wanted my own business."

·   ·   ·   ·   ·

"I was looking to rent a store," Mohamed says, his long legs improbably crossed in the cramped office. "But it was very difficult to get a store. Whenever you call the real estate offices on the phone, they want to give you a headache, 'Have you ever owned a store or a business before?' This and that."

Mohamed sits in his office, a space in the rear of the store no larger than a closet and filled with unsold merchandise. Alex works the cash register, and Mohamed's cousin Barry, a recent immigrant from Guinea, restocks the shelves. Mohamed is left with a few minutes to himself and his ideas on expanding his business.

In 1999, when Mohamed was casting about for a new venture and an end to his messenger business, the thought of opening a store in Manhattan was especially appealing. Unfortunately, despite his legal status and owning a home and a business, finding real estate for such an enterprise proved daunting. So Mohamed did what most entrepreneurs in the urban margins would do: he went to get a haircut.

"Barbers in Harlem have a lot of information," he explains, "because when people go to get a haircut, they always pass along information." Mohamed's barber, on 106th Street in East Harlem, proved a savvy businessman with an ear for opportunities. "My barber told me that this guy from Egypt was ready to sell this store here."

Mohamed offered the owner $100,000 for his business, $50,000 up front and the rest spread over monthly payments. By January 2000 he had dissolved his messenger business and opened his store on Third Avenue.

Mohamed's success, ten years in the making, should come as no surprise. For decades, new immigrants like Mohamed have outpaced the native born when it comes to self-employment and small businesses, especially in communities such as East Harlem.[14] Often the hardest hit in periods of economic decline, marginal urban communities depend on local formal and informal entrepreneurs to provide goods, services, and jobs.

East Harlem was hit especially hard by the fiscal crisis of the 1970s that precipitated the massive economic restructuring of the 1980s. Thousands of unskilled laborers were left jobless, with little prospects for employment in the emerging service and information-based economy. While crack cocaine was one of the more notorious entrepreneurial activities that filled the vacuum in the 1980s, it was the bodegas, groceries, and 99-cent stores that anchored the economic life of the neighborhood. Most of these businesses were founded by immigrants, many of them recent and not all of them documented.

Lack of outside investment is one glaring reason that immigrant entrepreneurs are able to fill the vacuum in an underserved and unstable local marketplace. Immigrant social networks also provide a ready source of flexible, cheap labor, keeping costs low and economic efficiency high. It is not unusual to find high employee turnover at East Harlem bodegas, many of them operated by Yemeni families, as distant kin are brought to New York and put to work behind the counter. In addition, the ability to target goods and services to specific concentrations of ethnic groups helps to maintain stability—thus the proliferation of Mexican groceries, record stores, and travel agencies in the past decade.[15]

In this context Mohamed's 99-cent store fit the emergent pattern of West African trading along Third Avenue. The store simply enclosed and legitimized what his countrymen were doing all along the sidewalk and enabled a wider assortment of merchandise for a community lacking any of the mass-market corporate stores that serve suburban and middle-class urban neighborhoods. As Mohamed describes it, "It's a step up from selling outside." His was certainly not the first 99-cent store on the avenue, but it was one of the first owned and operated by an African.

Since his early days trading Guinean goods to Sierra Leonean school-mates, Mohamed has had a keen sense of what people want. Like any small business tied to a local community, it is that ability to meet local demand that allows him to continue in operation. "I choose my products based on the location, what your customers ask for. You have a sense of what they need." It is the same sensitivity that keeps his compatriots in business on the street outside his store and ensures that his already narrow profit margin does not shrink as the cost of doing business increases.

"People that only sell one thing, they are going to go out of business," explains Mohamed. "In a 99-cent store, you sell a lot of different stuff, you are not going to go out of business easily." Since Mohamed opened his store in 2000, he has seen several small businesses on his block close almost as quickly as they opened. The most recent casualty was a large beauty supply store across the street. Its closeout sale drew crowds of shoppers only a few weeks after a sparsely attended grand opening.

"If they had asked me," Mohamed advises, "I would have told them, 'Don't open.' Because I sell the stuff, I have a section of it, and people here don't buy it. Good beauty supplies cost like $3, good hair gel, but these people don't want to spend that, they want the 99-cent gel. Sometimes I

150   THIRD AVENUE

want to buy expensive stuff, but I don't even bother with it anymore because it is going to sit on my shelf for nothing. My money is going to sit there for nothing."

Mohamed's profits, like the items in his store, are measured in cents, leaving little room for error in calculations of supply and demand or responses to competition. This was made clear early on when a fellow Guinean set up a folding table on the sidewalk next door to Mohamed's store. Aki, as his customers knew him, sold an odd assortment of tube socks, T-shirts, and hats culled from the same suppliers Mohamed contracted used.

But Mohamed was not angry at Aki, a recent immigrant conforming to a well-worn entrepreneurial pattern; he was angry at the owner of the laundromat next door who "rented" Aki the space. "My argument was with the owner of the store. He is from Israel, and he owns two laundromats and the building upstairs. And he rents this place to Aki for $200 a month to sell the same merchandise that I sell. I mean, please, how can you do this? You are a millionaire, you own the building, and you are going to destroy my business for $200?"

Mohamed is still visibly upset by the confrontation, long since resolved. "I had a big, big fight with him."

Aki was one of dozens of West African traders who set up shop along Third Avenue after being displaced from 125th Street by Mayor Giuliani in 1994. In exchange for the freedom to sell their wares on the sidewalk in front of a particular store, or in the entryway to a particular building, the vendors paid an average of $200 a month to store owners or building superintendents. Ideally, the store owner would defend the vendor should the police attempt to issue fines for selling on the street without a license—arguing that the vendor was an extension of the store.

"Everyone who has a table on Third Avenue is paying someone," Mohamed says. "If I want to rent that space out there to someone, they are going to pay me, then I can cover for them when they come to me. If they pay you $200 or $300, you've got to back them up."

In East Harlem the informal renting of sidewalk space along Third Avenue makes for a congested but vibrant stroll on a weekday afternoon. But by the time one reaches the imposing mosque at 96th Street, the southern gateway to East Harlem on Third Avenue, the folding tables are gone, the sidewalks clear. Mohamed explains the shift: "The customers up here are tolerant, but the stores down there are paying like $20,000 in rent, and most of the stores are owned by big corporations. They don't need your $200, because the manager is not the owner of the place. He can't rent you space, because it's a corporation. And the private businesses, the landlord is not going to allow him to put people in front of the walkway."

As Mohamed says, "Small businesses want to increase their profit any way they can." The result is a reinforcement of the 96th Street border—homogenized corporate businesses that keep sidewalks clean and clear south and diversified independent businesses that enable the informal street commerce to flourish north. The socioeconomic forces that starkly define the differences between East Harlem and the Upper East Side are manifest in the aesthetic of street commerce.

Mohamed, however, resists the temptation to rent out the space in front of his store, not just because of competition. As he explains, "I won't rent the space because I just don't want to deal with the cops every day, you know, giving tickets out, I just don't want to."

Mohamed rightly points out that a laundromat provided little protection for Aki as it would be difficult to prove that Aki's business was an extension of their service. "That was the problem," Mohamed laughs. "It was weird. It was really weird why that guy want to rent that space for $200 when he didn't even need the money."

Eventually, it was the lack of protection from the laundromat that drove Aki away from Mohamed's store. "Every time the police came they gave him a ticket. So the tickets start piling up, and I didn't have to do anything. All the guys selling out there get tickets, and most of them they just ignore them." In the end, Mohamed felt sorry for Aki, preferring to direct his animus against the owner of the laundromat. "It was not a big, big inconvenience, but you know, that's the way it's supposed to be. This is a free country. If I were in Aki's position, I would do the same thing."

As for Aki, Mohamed says, "He is driving a gypsy cab now, so this was just a stepping-stone for him."

After leaving the laundromat, Aki moved his table to 116th Street and rented sidewalk space from a Mexican grocery. Like many West African vendors, Aki was not attached to a particular patch of concrete or any particular selection of merchandise. Some, like Aki, are even willing to cash in the tenuous business for a chance at driving a gypsy cab, if the opportunity allows. In the mid-1990s there were as many as eighteen thousand gypsy cabs on the streets of New York City, and their drivers were twice as likely to be killed on the job.[16]

"About 70 percent of the gypsy cabs are African," Mohamed estimates. "A lot of Africans follow a path. They come here and other Africans tell them, 'Go do this, then go do that.' Most of them are followers." Mohamed, never one to follow, sees himself as a pioneer opening new economic territory. "I remember when I opened my 99-cent store, I think maybe two or three Africans had one," he says. "I think a lot of Africans want to have a 99-cent store now."

"Change, boss?" Alex stands in the doorway to Mohamed's office holding a $100 bill.

"You don't have any change up there?" Mohamed asks incredulously.

"No, no, I need twenties."

Mohamed unfolds himself from his metal chair and pulls a wad of bills from his front pocket. As he peels off five twenties, he asks, "Who is up front now?"

Alex glances back toward the front of the store. "Barry is there."

Barry has been working part-time in the store since he arrived from Guinea a couple of weeks earlier. Alex exchanges the $100 bill for the five twenties and hurries back to the register. Mohamed carefully folds the single bill and slides it into his pocket.

"I have one Spanish employee," Mohamed says as he returns to his seat. "You have to have one to speak Spanish here. About 50 percent of my customers don't speak any English. Some people, even when they speak English, they speak Spanish."

With Latinos still in the slim majority of East Harlem residents and with Puerto Ricans still suffering a disproportionate economic burden in the new economy, it is not surprising that many of the customers at Mohamed's discount 99-cent store speak Spanish. Though Mohamed can hire a Spanish-speaking employee to overcome the language barrier, there is no easy solution to the economic barriers that seem to hold back native-born East Harlemites, the majority of whom are Puerto Rican. The frustrations of remaining profitable in an uncertain economy have led to strong convictions about his clientele: "If it weren't for immigrants, for Mexicans, Dominicans, there would be no business up here."

Though newer immigrants such as Mexicans enter Mohamed's store more and more often, Puerto Ricans remain his most frequent customers—a fact he begrudges. In a subtle double insult, Mohamed argues, "I even think that black Americans have better purchasing power than the Puerto Ricans. I don't see Puerto Ricans going to school. I don't see them having good jobs. It's really frustrating." That frustration is only one small part of an economic chain reaction three decades in the making that has left urban minorities at distinct disadvantages.

About the time Mohamed was looking to open his store in East Harlem, in 1998, more Latinos received public assistance in New York City than in Los Angeles, Miami, or the entire state of Texas. While thousands of white and black single mothers had dropped off the welfare roles in the wake of reforms passed in 1996, the majority of single mothers on welfare were still Latina.[17]

Newcomers may find creative ways to adapt to an already transformed economy (especially since most of them are ineligible for public assistance), but even they cannot completely escape the shock waves that continue to rattle the New York wage-labor market. This reality is not lost on Mohamed.

"Before, the Mexicans used to have two or three jobs in restaurants, they used to make money, but now restaurants are not doing as well as they were before 9/11. So most of them have few jobs. Every day they come here looking for jobs. So when the economy is not good, these people don't make money, the foreigners. You know, the people that really want to do odd jobs."

Doing "odd jobs" has long been the mainstay of immigrants laborers, but hope of finding living-wage work in the formal economy of New York City has proven more and more difficult for most of the residents of East Harlem. Despite an overall improvement in the city's economy since the 1980s, at the turn of the millennium twice as many East Harlemites were unemployed compared to New Yorkers as a whole, and 36.7 percent of neighborhood residents were on some kind of public assistance, compared to 19.3 percent for the city.[18]

Public assistance in East Harlem was largely invisible when Mohamed first opened his store in 2000. "When I was opening the business, the economy was booming, but you don't realize that there are things beyond your control. At the time, people would be on welfare for a year or more until they found a job, or just give them an extension forever." It was only as welfare reform began to restrict payments and then end them altogether that Mohamed began to see how such changes can have wide-reaching consequences. "Now I see a customer who has stopped coming, and I ask, 'What's happened?' And they say, 'Oh, well, they stopped my checks.' Every week you have some customers who used to get assistance, and then they drop them off. So that's one customer that's gone. Gone."

The timing of Mohamed's entry into the retail market catering to the urban poor could not have been worse. Four years before his store opened, President Bill Clinton signed into law sweeping welfare reforms that ended monthly cash benefits to more than 12 million people, including 8 million children. The cash benefits were replaced with block grants to states and employment requirements for aid—dubbed "workfare." The reforms also cut $24 billion in food stamp benefits over six years and effectively ended all benefits to even legal immigrants.[19] It was an evisceration of a welfare system that had saved millions from abject poverty since the 1930s.

The one adjustment in the new law that most directly affected Mohamed was a five-year lifetime maximum for receiving federal benefits. The clock began ticking when the law was passed in 1996, and in 2001, one year after Mohamed opened his store and the same year as the September 11 terrorist attack on the World Trade Center, 59,000 New York City families were faced with losing federal public assistance.[20] Under the reforms, New York State would take over payments at drastically reduced rates that in many cases would only be paid out if recipients were enrolled in Mayor Giuliani's controversial workfare program.[21] Most devastating for Mohamed and other small business owners in neighborhoods like East Harlem that have high concentrations of welfare recipients, the bulk of public assistance payments would be made through a new debit card system. Mohamed's store, like most in the community, accepts only cash.

For those still on public assistance, the shrinking monthly payouts stretch only so far, a fact that affects their consumption patterns and therefore the stability of local small businesses.[22] Complaining about the consistent pattern of high volume at the first of the month before welfare benefits run out and then three weeks of creeping sales as residents wait for the next check, Mohamed argues, "I would rather my customers spend $10 a week than spend $60 a month. I would rather my customers had jobs and spend $10 every week than sit down and wait for the first of the month. It's just a big drag to the business. It's tiring. I really don't like it."

Mohamed has received a crash course in U.S. welfare policy and its impact not only on the urban poor but also on the viability of small businesses, the so-called engine of the U.S. economy. As he remarks, "I remember when I came to this country, when it comes to jobs and such, I was more like a Republican. You know, everyone should stand on their own. But when I started my own business, that's when I realized that it's not going to work in this country. Some people just need help." But Mohamed, the businessman, is not talking about a moral obligation. For him, it's about the health of the economy. "I think if some people don't have help, the economy is really going to stink. Because these people are never going to have a job. There is no way they are capable of having a job."

With a shake of his head, Mohamed says, "Government assistance is really necessary." After a weary, contrite sigh, he adds, "My God, I really do believe that now."

.   .   .   .   .

"How much do you think this costs?" asks Mohamed, holding up a bundle of paper plates. He is standing near the front counter, watching as Alex and Barry handle the latest shipment of merchandise. With a weary smirk, he answers himself: "Seventy-two cents, and I sell it for 99 cents.

And I have $5,000 in rent. This is not enough. I can't survive on just this stuff. The profit margin is too small."

Evening is approaching, and outside the sidewalks are becoming full again after a midday lull. Mohamed steps to the front door, hands on hips, to check on his neighbors. Across the street, the liquor store is filling with an after-work crowd—half of them lining up to purchase lottery tickets, the other half waiting while the owner, safe behind bulletproof Plexiglas, retrieves bottles of rum, wine, and cognac. Mohamed's store is still nearly empty, as it has been all day.

He points across the street and without turning, states flatly, "There are two businesses that will always do well—the liquor store and the cigarette business." Never especially religious, Mohamed dismisses the Muslim prohibition against alcohol, jealous of the brisk business across the street. "It's not that the profit margin is that high," he continues, "it's that people buy it no matter how broke they are. They don't have to have government checks or this that or the other. They will find money to get that, some way. They will find money to get that."

Like his position on welfare, Mohamed's attitude toward the ubiquity of liquor stores in the neighborhood is founded on the economic bottom line, not moral absolutes. As far as he is concerned, the liquor store meets a need created by others.

"The owner of that store doesn't have control over it, because it is an addictive commodity. The company already did the job for him. The distributors did the job for the people that are in that business."

It is the same logic that has always justified Mohamed's "other businesses," including importing and exporting among the United States, Guinea, and Sierra Leone. His newest venture is the wholesale distribution of blank CDs and DVDs. Like the liquor stores, Mohamed wants to meet a need in the community that he believes will be filled one way or another.

"A lot of Africans are into that business of selling CDs and DVDs," he explains. "About 80 percent are from Guinea. I know a lot of these guys, and that's what has inspired me to get into this business. I am going to have some partners. The idea is to supply the raw materials. That's why I don't judge these African guys that are in this business; they are making good money. Better than me."

The business of music and film piracy has indeed become quite lucrative for street traders and the producers who supply them. Often recorded with handheld cameras in theaters, the poor-quality video counterfeits require little overhead and can generate as much as $500,000 in revenue each week. Despite frequent police raids throughout the 1990s, video counterfeiting operations in the New York area often produced more than two thousand counterfeit videos or DVDs a day, getting them to street vendors who could sell them within a week of a film's theatrical release. Many of these vendors and an increasing number of the producers are West African.[23]

Mohamed, who refuses to participate in any illegal activity, hopes to capitalize on the West African dominance in the illicit industry by supplanting the mostly Asian suppliers of blank media required for the operation. "I have some qualms with it, but I am a businessman and the market right now is dominated by the Koreans and Chinese. I am hoping if the business really kicks in, I could have 20 to 30 percent of that market from the African side." That market share in a growing industry, though illicit, is too lucrative to pass up, especially after the exhausting experience of selling retail merchandise to an inconsistent clientele. "I don't watch the videos, they don't even work on my DVD player, but it's a really big business." Supplying blank media is perfectly legal in Mohamed's view, and, more important, it fills a need in the local market.

This perspective has kept Mohamed busy and on the move since high school in Freetown. "That's how I survive," he explains. "Never do one thing. I won't do anything illegal, but I always sit down and see where there is a market and what you can do and what you cannot do to survive. Because there is one thing I have learned in business—if you do one thing, you are going to go down."

Mohamed glances at his watch. Afternoon services have ended at the mosque on 96th Street, a dozen blocks south on Third Avenue. The gypsy cabs that usually crowd the avenue in the way yellow cabs do downtown are beginning to reappear—their pious drivers steeled against another few hours on the streets through communal prayer. Despite his namesake, Mohamed is not religious, but most of the vendors and gypsy cab drivers who work the avenue will have done their duty. During the fast of Ramadan, they will continue their trades decked out in colorful robes and satin shoes—transforming Third Avenue with splashes of color behind folding tables of white socks, plastic watches, and backpacks. Mohamed will wear his knit shirt and jeans, taking his lunch as usual.

"I am not religious. I don't go to mosque," Mohamed says simply. "The last time I went was maybe two years ago, but sometimes if I feel like it I go. If I just have nothing to do, I will go. Sometimes you just say, 'Oh, I don't have anything to do, let me go say hi to God.' "

The Islamic Cultural Center dominates the entire block on Third Avenue between 96th and 97th Streets. Though Friday services witness gypsy cabs three deep along the avenue around the site, the mosque actually predates the recent wave of Muslim immigrants from West Africa: plans for an Islamic cultural center that would "soften the edge" of East Harlem were announced as early as 1966. Construction on the $20 million building did not begin until the late 1970s.[24] In the following years, the mosque veered away from the expectations of developers who could not have anticipated the influx of West Africans in the 1980s and 1990s.

"I believe that I am a Muslim. There is Allah, there is Muhammad. I just don't practice," Mohamed says now. "I do have a faith, it's just that I don't practice."

Since he left his family in West Africa, Mohamed has "practiced" less and less of the standard expectations of West African men. "I like to throw back the bottle," he says with a conspiratorial smile. "In Africa, you go to hell if you drink. That is crap. It's really crazy how some people take religion so seriously. It's unbelievable. I can't stand it, it's just nonsense."

Mohamed also broke with tradition in marrying a Haitian, a Catholic, from whom he recently separated. "Getting married is not easy," he says, the smile fading. "Nine years was a good run. Sometimes it works, sometimes it doesn't work."

He is dating a Sierra Leonean now, though he is still not divorced from his wife. His new girlfriend has a story similar to his. "She came here, she got married, and she applied for citizenship. Same thing as me." Like Mohamed, she is separated from her husband, not divorced. The two relish their private rebellion against expectations. "We both married Caribbeans. A lot of Africans wouldn't marry a non-African, but she is not religious." With a laugh, he adds, "She pops the wine, just like me."

The United States has offered a level of comfort apparently unattainable in West Africa or even Europe, as Mohamed learned in his first foray out of Freetown. "I remember when I was in Europe, I always wanted to leave. But it's different when you come to the United States. I think you feel it. You think that you can expand, your goals can be whatever you want to." It is an image of America, particularly New York, that has defied economic downturns and draconian immigration laws. "The thing that makes you really, really want to stay here is the political and economic problems back in Guinea, back in Sierra Leone—they are not stable. That stability, that's what starts to dawn on you." That, and the inevitable attachments that hold even the most transient migrants: "Then you meet someone you love, too, you know. It makes you just forget about home."

Since receiving legal status in the United States, Mohamed has returned occasionally to Guinea (war in Sierra Leone throughout the 1990s drove most of his family back across the border). His success in New York is not lost on those he left behind. "People think that you did well for yourself, you made your family proud. That feels good, really. It really feels good. They know I am a store owner in New York. They know that I live a nice life here." But, despite his attempts to maintain some sense of connection to Africa (reluctant as he is to put down roots too deeply in any one place), returning to Guinea has become less desirable as he has become more comfortable in the United States. "It's so expensive to travel back," Mohamed complains. "And not only the ticket, because you know you have forty family members. Sneakers for each, two shirts for each. So to travel, you have to have money to go back."

Mohamed has drifted far from his own expectations on landing at JFK in 1991. A short trip to acquire inventory became a long-term investment in the life of New York and eventually East Harlem. Guinea and Sierra Leone seem farther away with each passing year.

"I was not thinking about going back to Guinea anymore," Mohamed admits. "I say, 'I'll go visit,' but that is one thing about living in America, you just get comfortable."

Mohamed is standing by his Mercedes again, scanning the avenue, gauging the traffic. Alex and Barry can close up later, long after he has crossed the Triboro Bridge and headed out to his house in Queens. He lives not far from the airport that welcomed him almost fifteen years ago. He is restless, as usual. "I don't enjoy sitting thirteen hours in one place."

"I am looking to do something else," he says finally, not just in reference to the blank media business. "I don't like doing the same thing for too long. In a few years, I would like to move out from New York."

A plan is forming. The same logic that motivated the moves from Freetown to London, from London to Guinea, and from Guinea to New York spills out in fragments, builds momentum.

"Ten years from now."

"I am not going to be retired, I'll be doing business."

"Less stress, maybe buy a fishing boat."

He is forty now and hoping for something "easy" in his fifties. "I have been doing business for so long, I don't think I can go more than ten more years. And I'm not thinking of going back to Sierra Leone or Guinea when I am in my fifties. I'm going to go where I think that I will relax and find that economically I don't have to do much and still survive."

Thinking out loud, Mohamed says, "If I had a choice, I would go to Las Vegas. I've been there, I like it there." With typical foresight, he is already outlining a plan for the theoretical move. "I would spend a month there. Not on the strip, but where people really live to see what is really needed."

"That's what I would do," he agrees, convincing himself and affirming a philosophy that has carried him around the world. "I think anything that you do, you have to find out first if there is a need for it."

With a wave to his two employees standing bored in an empty store, Mohamed climbs behind the wheel of his pristine Mercedes. Edging into the flow of gypsy cabs, public buses, and the luxury cars of fellow commuters, Mohamed heads north on Third Avenue.

Past the sulking housing projects.

Past the folding tables of West African vendors.

Past the bodegas, Chinese takeouts, and liquor stores.

As he turns right on 125th Street, the towering scaffold of the Triboro Bridge beckons—drawing him up, over, and out of East Harlem, for now.

SEVEN Second Avenue

The setting sun on 112th Street casts long shadows from St. John the Divine Cathedral two miles to the west. In East Harlem it reflects off the shear face of a wall of public housing—Taft, Johnson, and Jefferson Houses. Set back from the wide one-way street, the geographic center of East Harlem, is a short row of newly built townhouses, pale brick and green trim, built to evoke the tenements they replaced without all the history. Each sectioned off by a green-gated paddock, garage door, and concrete staircase to the second-floor entrance, the houses give pause to a few passersby in the twilight wondering who might be lucky enough, or rich enough, to afford the elusive urban splendor of a new home.

Behind the chest-high green wrought iron that separates each house from the sidewalk and the several thousand neighbors who live in Jefferson Houses across the street, a minivan waits—its engine humming, its bumper announcing the proud parent of a West Point cadet. Si Zhi, a thin, athletic Chinese man in his late forties steps out onto the concrete stoop and squints into the evening sun. His close-cropped hair, intense eyes, and expressionless mouth communicate little as he swings open the gate, careful to avoid anyone passing too close on the sidewalk. Behind the wheel of his minivan, a touch of a button lowers his garage door, sealing away his meticulously organized workshop—homespun homage to the nearest home improvement superstore. Si Zhi pulls his van into the street, locks the gate behind him, and waves good-bye to Sharon, his wife, standing in the window.

It is 7:15 P.M., exactly, and Si Zhi is on his way to work. Easing the minivan south on Second Avenue, Si Zhi motors past the red brick towers of 1199 Plaza, a housing development that was once his home, and the much larger Franklin Plaza at 106th Street, where Si Zhi's in-laws have lived since the 1960s. At 97th Street, he takes a right, past Metropolitan Hospital, the mosque at Third Avenue, and Mt. Sinai Hospital at Madison Avenue, until he enters Central Park, leaving East Harlem.

"When I first came here, I had a lot of problems," Si Zhi says. He heads south on Broadway now, East Harlem far behind him. "We lived with Sharon's family, my in-laws. Very, very difficult." It has been fifteen years since then, and Si Zhi's English has reached a conversational ease, though still filtered through the tonal peculiarities of Mandarin and the urban dialect of Shanghai.

Si Zhi parks the minivan on a side street not far from Times Square and walks the few blocks to the Paramount Hotel just off the Great White Way. Ducking into an unmarked doorway, he descends a black metal staircase into the belly of the building, offering a few pleasantries to day-shift workers as they head for the surface.

"At first, I feel bad having this job," Si Zhi says as he changes from his street clothes to the black T-shirt and black pants of his position: "Houseman, night shift." He steps out of the locker room and begins to make his rounds. "And Sharon's family, they make me feel bad." He deftly removes the bin liners from a few of the thirty-gallon trash cans in the employee lounge—a dank and poorly lit bunker with a microwave and a couple of tables—and just as deftly relines the bins without pause. After a few more stops in the fluorescent haze of the subbasement labyrinth, Si Zhi turns toward the stairs. "But this is a job, and I don't care anymore."

A few more twists and turns, and Si Zhi pushes through a shabby metal door. The lobby beyond is all gleam and polish, an improbably hip candlelit space teeming with well-heeled travelers and discerning celebrities. Si Zhi begins the painstaking process of checking each of the thousand or so votives that line the sweeping arch of a staircase, explaining that he added water to each glass container to make cleaning more efficient.

"This is just a job. That's it."

.   .   .   .   .

"I'm from Shanghai. It's a big city, like New York." On the second floor, Si Zhi straightens the hotel's small business center. He then quickly moves to an empty conference room. "Before my father, my family lived in the countryside. In Shanghai, it's just like America, there are no native people in that place—people come from all different places in China."

Si Zhi's youth was one of relative privilege. Born in 1956, he grew up in the age of Communism and Chairman Mao but before the infamous Cultural Revolution that began in 1966. "My grandfather was a very high-ranking politician in the city, sort of like the vice president of Shanghai, a second mayor," explains Si Zhi. "My parents were in business, like Wall Street. That's why I say, before the Cultural Revolution, my life was good."

The Communists took power in 1949. Mao Zedong supervised the reorganization of thousands of years of imperial rule—first linking with the Soviets in the period after World War II, then, when Si Zhi was just two years old, implementing the Great Leap Forward. The Great Leap Forward plunged millions of Chinese, primarily from the countryside, into abject poverty and starvation. From 1958 to the beginning of the Cultural Revolution in 1966, productivity targets for industrial output placed impossible strains on food production, creating one of the worst famines in the twentieth century.[1]

The tragic failure of the Great Leap Forward pushed Mao Zedong to the sidelines of Communist power in China throughout the early 1960s.

But by 1966 Mao had rallied enough grassroots support to effectively undermine the legitimacy of party leadership, restore his own position, and launch the Great Proletarian Cultural Revolution in May of that year.

Mao's famous Red Guard, mostly students, was sent throughout the country, implementing the "Sixteen Points" of the revolution and destroying the alleged symbols of capitalist culture—art, clothing, furniture, literature. Schools were shut down, and millions of urban secondary students were shipped off to isolated rural communes to be "reeducated" in the value of agricultural labor. Despite U.S. president Richard Nixon's historic trip to China in 1972, Chairman Mao continued to push the agenda of the Cultural Revolution until his death in 1976.[2]

Si Zhi remembers the day life in Shanghai changed forever. "I was sitting in the classroom. I heard something outside. We didn't know what was going on. Then the principal came and said, 'Okay, now we stop.' The teacher just said, 'Go home.' So we went home, and on the street you could see it was totally different. A lot of young people with the flag." The school was closed indefinitely and used as a detention center. "I didn't go to school again until four years later."

With parents and grandparents of position and privilege, it did not take long for the revolution to reach into Si Zhi's home life as well. "We were having dinner, my older brothers and my mother and father," Si Zhi recalls. "We were almost finished with dinner, and about ten kids came in and pointed to my father and told him to stand in the corner. Then they took a big sign with his name that said, 'You're against the revolution.' They put it on him and took the dining table out into the street and made him stand on it. He had to say, 'I am a bad person, I am against Mao Zedong, I am against the revolution.' Then they went inside and broke everything."

That same evening, Si Zhi, at ten years old of little concern to the political enthusiasms of the Red Guard, ran to his grandparents, hoping to find refuge there. "And when I entered the main door, I already saw my grandfather was standing on the table. Then my grandmother started crying, and they saw her crying, and they made her stand up on the table with him. I will never forget that day."

The humiliations continued throughout the first few years of the Cultural Revolution. A history of Shanghai written in careful calligraphy by his grandfather was burned, piece by piece, as he stood on the table in his courtyard. His grandfather refused to speak again and died three years later.

Si Zhi's immediate family fared little better. His father, sister, and brother were placed in the makeshift detention center that had been Si Zhi's school. There, a few months later, the brother was assaulted, stabbed, and left for dead. Si Zhi's sister, after weeks of separation from her infant daughter and the verbal, physical, and sexual assault of her captors, leaped to her death from the roof of the detention center. The rest of Si Zhi's few brothers were sent to work camps or farms in the Chinese hinterlands, forced to learn the value of manual labor under the doctrine of the Cultural Revolution.

It was all too much for Si Zhi's mother. "She became like a crazy person for about two years. She stayed home, didn't do anything but talk to the walls. She would not eat." Si Zhi, now only twelve years old, was left to care for his mother, grandmother, and orphaned niece. Each week he would bring provisions to his father at his old school, waiting in vain for his release and careful to hide as much of their misfortune as possible. "My brother just gave me a little money, and I had to figure out how to make the money last seven days. Each morning, I would wake up three or four o'clock and go to the market to pick out some things early because I don't want anyone to see me. If I see something good that someone threw away, I would hide and then go get it. I didn't let my father know, because if he knew, maybe he would commit suicide."

Eventually, Si Zhi's father came home. "He got a little money," Si Zhi recalls, "enough to survive. He worked in a factory, cleaning bathrooms or whatever they told him to do."

The schools reopened, and Si Zhi went on to finish high school. According to Si Zhi, "At that time, the number one choice was to work in a factory. Number two was a technical school, training, then go to factory. But the government knew that they needed smart people, so they opened colleges."

One of Si Zhi's teachers, recognizing his ability, encouraged him to apply to a new medical school in Shanghai, the first in more than a decade. Si Zhi agreed and gave up his place at a local factory. "But when

I went to apply, they did a background check and said, 'You can't be a doctor, your father is no good.' So I missed medical school and the factory job. I had no choice, I went to a metalworking school. I was seventeen or eighteen years old. My teacher was very sad."

By the time Si Zhi was in his early twenties, Mao Zedong had died, and his Cultural Revolution died with him. The reforms of Deng Xiaoping had completed the normalization of diplomatic relations with the United States, begun in 1972, and ushered in a new era of "openness" with the international community. But Deng's reforms would not undermine the continued authority of the Communist Party, as demonstrated in the Four Cardinal Principles he issued in 1979, which included strict adherence to "Marxism–Leninism–Mao Zedong Thought."[3] It was an intellectual and political lineage that would remain largely unchallenged until one historic day in June 1989.

This continuity with a more repressive past, even in the midst of Deng's reforms, was evident in Si Zhi's job as an engineer in a naval shipyard. His family blacklisted by the Communist Party, Si Zhi was not allowed on the boats he was helping to build for fear of sabotage.

"Everyone could go on the boats, except me, they didn't trust me, because of my father. In China, everyone had one file that followed you wherever you go. Anywhere you go. That's the Communist control. Every family has a book in the police station."

Despite his guarded status, Si Zhi distinguished himself at the shipyard, bringing to the construction process innovations that caught the attention of his managers. After a few years on the job, he was trusted enough to board some of the ships for small repairs, so long as he was shadowed by security personnel.

"The first time they called me, I felt good about that. I felt a little happier, that they trusted me, but the first day I went, two security people followed me. I helped them fix it, but the next time they called me, I said, 'Fuck you.' I don't care if they don't trust me."

By the early 1980s Si Zhi's father, no longer considered a threat to national security, was granted clemency and removed from the list of subversives. "Every factory had a security department, and it's these people that controlled everyone's background. Just like a policeman. Those people said my father was going back to normal status."

With the last obstacle to Si Zhi's advancement removed, his superiors encouraged him to join the Communist Party and become eligible for management. "I said, 'No, I don't want to.' My boss, he was a very good guy. He said, 'You should do it, forget all this past. If you join, you can move up. If you don't, you can't move up. This is the first step.' He really helped me, but I was still mad. I feel inside very hurt. He said, 'You have to go step by step, you have no choice, your life is here. You have to fol-low the steps, then you can change your life.' So I listened, I joined, and I moved up to manager."

Si Zhi was twenty-six years old, just two years away from eligibility as an adult member of the Communist Party. On his twenty-eighth birth-day, the day he was to advance in the party, Si Zhi renounced his mem-bership. His superiors, dismayed, tried in vain to persuade him, but Si Zhi would not change his mind.

"They said, 'Why? Give us a reason and we won't push.' "

Si Zhi kept quiet, then admitted, "I have to go to America. If I join this party, maybe they won't give me a visa."

"Why didn't you tell us?" they asked.

"My wife's family is over there," he replied.

Si Zhi says now, "At that time, a lot of people would brag they had American family to support them. No one says it, but after the Commu-nists and the Cultural Revolution, everything American was number one. But my wife is a very quiet person, so I didn't tell anyone."

Si Zhi had married Sharon in 1982, one year after her parents and two brothers left Shanghai to join her grandparents in New York City. Sharon, already over twenty-one, could not immigrate as easily as her younger brothers and would have to wait for her father to gain citizenship and sponsor her and her husband. When Sharon gave birth to Alison in 1983, she and Si Zhi began forming plans to join her family in New York.

"I wanted to leave the country," explains Si Zhi. "If I had a chance, I would go. If the door was open, I would go. I didn't want to stay there anymore. I trusted myself, I knew I could make a good life. I did not want to spend my life for the Communists. But I had no choice. Thank God my wife had family in America."

Sharon's grandfather had left China decades earlier, after spending several years working in American bars in and around Shanghai. In 1949, when the Communist Party seized power, he appealed to his American contacts and gained safe passage to Hong Kong, leaving part of his family behind. From Hong Kong, he arranged a job with an executive at R. J. Reynolds who sponsored his immigration to the United States. After a brief sojourn in Virginia, he left his employer and moved into the growing Chinese community of lower Manhattan. In 1961 he moved into the newly built Franklin Plaza on 106th Street and Second Avenue in East Harlem.

When Sharon's grandfather arrived in New York in the early 1950s, he was joining close to 20,000 other ethnic Chinese immigrants in a city not yet known for a large Asian population. Most of the 120,000 Chinese immigrants in the United States to that point had settled in California.[4] Indeed, their presence was so keenly felt in the West that anti-Chinese sentiment led to the passage of the Chinese Exclusion Act in 1882, barring any further Chinese immigration to the United States. The Immigration Act of 1924, aimed at stemming the tide of European immigration, only made matters worse by extending the exclusion to Japan. In 1943, in recognition of China's cooperation in World War II, Congress repealed the Chinese Exclusion Act but set the quota for new immigrants at a token 105 persons annually.[5] Sharon's grandfather was one of very few quota-based legal immigrants from China in the years after the Communist rise to power.

Sharon's parents followed in 1981, and Si Zhi waited for his father-in-law to gain the legal status necessary to sponsor their immigration. "A green card took five years, then he could apply for citizenship. But the first time he applied, he failed the test. Second time, he passed. So then the lawyer made the paperwork, we got the copy, and I went to the police station to apply for a passport. Eight months later I got the visa."

The year was 1989.

In the early morning hours of June 4, 1989, machine-gun fire rang out around the Forbidden City in Beijing. It came from Tiananmen Square, between the tomb of Chairman Mao and the Martyr's Monument. Since Mao Zedong's death, intellectuals and students had spearheaded a new democracy movement initially tolerated by Deng Xiaopeng. By the late 1980s Communist Party leaders were alarmed by the strength of the movement and began cracking down on its organizers. By May 1989 some students in Beijing had begun camping out in Tiananmen Square, declaring a hunger strike to achieve their goal of democratic socialism.

On the night of June 3, thousands of troops converged on Beijing. In the next twenty-four hours, they killed hundreds of the protesters.[6]

The most memorable image of the massacre was of a solitary young man standing in the middle of a wide avenue, holding back a line of tanks with nothing more than a couple of shopping bags. The image of one man holding back the advance of military might was an inspiring symbol of the democracy movement, but perhaps more powerful was the fact that the image was broadcast around the world, instantly. The "openness" encouraged by Deng Xiaopeng had undermined a half century of complete control over the media by the Communist Party. The repercussions would be felt throughout China, especially for those hoping to emigrate.

"Every day I listened to American radio," remembers Si Zhi. "If the Chinese government caught you, that was no good. That means you listen to an enemy country, that you are against us. They say, 'You don't love the country.' But I was scared they would close the border." Si Zhi had already filed the appropriate paperwork and was simply waiting for his interview at the American embassy when Tiananmen Square erupted in violence. "I was scared. I was really scared."

It did not help that his father, who had died three years earlier, had not wanted Si Zhi to leave China. Despite the decades of hardship and the public humiliation inflicted on him by the Communist Party, Si Zhi's father was a committed nationalist. "He didn't want me to go. They had a lot of problems with the Communists, but they loved the country." Si Zhi had known little of life in China before the Cultural Revolution and could not make so fine a distinction.

After several tense weeks huddled before a small radio, Si Zhi received good news: he was free to leave China for the United States. "We left on November 18, 1989. All three together. I was holding my daughter coming through the airport. I was lucky. After I left, the border was closed for about one year. I was the last one."

·   ·   ·   ·   ·

The wind plays gently with thin metal chimes on Si Zhi's backyard terrace. At ground-level below, an immaculate square of deep green is surrounded by a carefully laid brick path and a bed of blooming flowers and ripening vegetables. On all sides, the identically sized backyards of his neighbors in this small middle-income housing development are rambles of overgrown grass and mismatched outdoor furniture—throwing the precision of Si Zhi's labor into sharp relief.

Si Zhi sits overlooking his garden in the midafternoon, his morning, after returning from work around 4:00 A.M. and sleeping into the daylight hours. He points up to the green corrugated roof he built to shield his terrace from the sun, another innovation missing from his neighbors' properties.

"See that?" he asks proudly. "I made that for the sun. When the sun moves to the west, it's too much. And this middle piece, in the winter I take it out."

On a small, inlaid tile table he built from discarded furniture and a few trips to a hardware store, Si Zhi rests a porcelain-covered cup of fresh green tea. The steamy contents complement the rising humidity of the summer afternoon.

"I believe, when you are young, if you have a hard life experience, it's not a bad thing. If you can pass through it, it's not bad." Si Zhi takes a sip of tea, and Sharon appears behind the screen door inside. Behind her a large kitchen and dining room open into a sparse but spotless living room. Upstairs, three bedrooms are now mostly empty—their daughter, Alison, was away at West Point Academy. Above and below, two rental apartments provide a monthly income that covers their mortgage. Sharon slides back the screen and refills Si Zhi's cup with hot water. "Of course, a lot of people just lie down, they give up," continues Si Zhi. "If you can handle it. If someone help you go through it, I think that experience can help your life."

When Si Zhi, Sharon, and their six-year-old daughter passed through immigration security in San Francisco in 1989, on their way to JFK airport, they were leaving behind plenty of hard life experience. "They checked our passports, the Immigration asked us questions, they checked our fingerprints. For me, it was okay. I wasn't scared. Everything was legal, so I wasn't scared. What was a little tough was we didn't speak English. But the Immigration in the airport they did a good job, a few people spoke Chinese."

Like Maria and Mohamed, Si Zhi saw New York City for the first time through an airplane window as he landed at JFK. The Immigration Act of 1965 had long since transformed the patterns of immigration to the United States, not only with regard to transportation technology. After the repeal of the Chinese Exclusion Act in 1943, adjustments in U.S. policy on Asian immigration were made throughout the 1940s and 1950s, including admitting the Chinese wives of American citizens, many of them war brides, on a nonquota basis. But the overall restrictions would remain in place until the landmark legislation of the 1960s. The Immigration Act of 1965 abolished the ethnic discrimination of the national-origins quota system and opened legal immigration to the Eastern Hemisphere.

By 1989 Si Zhi was joining an unprecedented number of Asian immigrants to the United States. As Asian immigration climbed from 159,000 to 3 million between the 1950s and 1980s, European immigration declined from 1.5 million to 680,000.[7] Between 1970 and 1980 the Asian American population grew by 141 percent, compared to the national growth of only 11 percent. Between 1980 and 1990 the Asian American population grew by another, startling 99 percent. In 1989 alone 32,272 immigrants arrived in the United States from mainland China.[8]

In New York immigration from mainland China kept pace with these national trends. For the past three decades, Chinese immigrants have consistently ranked third in total legal immigration to the city. Between 1982 and 1989 some 53,000 immigrants arrived in New York City from mainland China. By 1996 another 71,500 ethnic Chinese arrived. By 2000 there were an estimated 500,000 ethnic Chinese living in New York.[9]

Many of these new arrivals were from regions in mainland China, such as Shanghai, that had not traditionally sent immigrants. As in Mexico, during the past century in China migration patterns have shifted from rural to urban. The earliest migrants to the United States from China were typically rural, mostly Cantonese from the southern areas of Guangdong province. But today many Chinese immigrants are departing from large cities such as Shanghai and Beijing, and Mandarin speakers are almost as common as Cantonese speakers.[10]

Like many of the new immigrants from mainland China, Si Zhi, Sharon, and Alison were greeted at JFK airport by family members who had sponsored their legal entry to the United States. Si Zhi's mother-in-law, father-in-law, and their two sons had been settled in East Harlem since 1981. The sons married and moved out of their parents' two-bedroom apartment in Franklin Plaza.

An unremarkable stand of high-rise brick housing projects arranged around 106th Street and Second Avenue, Franklin Plaza was Si Zhi's first home in New York. Si Zhi, like so many other sponsored family members, found in that first foothold in the city a connection to the community. Some of Si Zhi's in-laws estimate that about one-third of Franklin Plaza apartments are occupied by Chinese tenants—from a mere handful of original occupants in the 1960s. Even Pete, on Pleasant Avenue, had noticed the Chinese presence at Franklin Plaza.

Despite its commonplace design, Franklin Plaza is not like other housing projects in East Harlem. One of the last of the sprawling developments built in the community, Franklin Plaza was part of "the biggest single program of middle-income housing ever advanced at once in the city, state or nation," according to the chairman of the New York Housing and Redevelopment Board in 1961.[11] It was in 1961 that Franklin Plaza, originally designed for subsidized public housing, was converted by the New York City Housing Authority to cooperative ownership—1,635 cooperative apartments in fourteen twenty-story buildings in the heart of East Harlem. It was a visionary plan for home ownership in a low-income community, and at first it was a miserable failure.

By November 1961, one month before new tenants, including Sharon's grandfather, were to occupy the new cooperative, only 350 of the 1,635 apartments had been sold. It was not a great surprise. The city admitted that of the eight planned cooperative projects in the city, Franklin Plaza would be the toughest sell. East Harlem, they argued, "has the stigma of a slum."[12] Some two hundred merchants complained about their displacement from the site during construction and about the exorbitant rents charged by the development corporation to relocate in the new buildings.[13] To make matters worse, less than five years after the first tenants moved in, the state attorney general was investigating the board of directors for payroll fraud.[14]

By the time Si Zhi moved his family into his father-in-law's apartment in 1989, these problems had long since receded into the past. His wife's grandfather still lived across the courtyard, along with dozens of other ethnic Chinese residents who had followed parents and grandparents in the years since the project opened. Today, in the predawn hours, one can still find the aging pioneers of Chinese residency in Franklin Plaza gathering in the neatly kept courtyards of the fourteen high-rise buildings. "Very early in the morning," Si Zhi says. "They like it better when they have it to themselves." Though not the dominant presence in the development, Chinese settlement in Franklin Plaza, the first middle-income cooperative project in East Harlem, set a precedent for home ownership that Si Zhi would work toward from the moment he arrived.

Immediately after Si Zhi and his small family moved into his in-laws' apartment, their thoughts turned to earning enough money to strike out on their own. It did not help that Si Zhi knew no English and had none of the qualifications that would enable him to work as an engineer in the United States. "I have a very high professional license for welding in China, but not here. Nobody cares about that piece of paper here." Within two weeks he was commuting to Union City, New Jersey, with his father-in-law and brother-in-law to work for American Industrial Equipment Corporation, a manufacturer of industrial welding machines. Not as a welder but as a day laborer.

As he had at the shipyard in Shanghai, Si Zhi quickly distinguished himself for his skill and efficiency. "When I first got to the factory, I was shocked. I said, 'This is an American factory? Come on! In China, we've already thrown away this garbage, or maybe given it to the farmers.' " Si Zhi set about putting the factory and its warehouse in order, to the dismay of his father-in-law. "He is a very quiet person. Whatever the boss say, he say, 'Yes, yes, yes.' But I sometimes talk back to them. I say, 'You tell me to do it this way, but it's wrong.' And my father-in-law always complained, 'This is America, you don't know nothing. This is not China.' And I would say, 'Listen, I know this is wrong. When you make it, you are definitely going to have to do it over. Why say, 'Yes, boss'? I want to do it the right way, and save them money.' So I always talk to my manager."

Despite winning approval from his employers, Si Zhi still had an unskilled and entry-level job. "At the beginning, it was $5 an hour. Three months later, they gave me 25 cents more. When I left the job, they gave me $5.75. I worked nine hours a day, six days a week. Saturday, I worked six hours. Almost eleven hours for overtime pay."

Even before Si Zhi began working in New Jersey, Sharon found work in an industry known for absorbing immigrant women. "One week after we got here, my wife got work in a sweatshop making clothes."

Since the 1820s New York City, Manhattan specifically, has been the center of the U.S. ready-made clothing industry. By 1855 clothing production was the largest industry in the city, though concentrated primarily on men's clothing. By the early 1920s, when Pete's mother sewed gloves out of her apartment on 114th Street, New York produced 78 percent of the ready-made women's garments in the United States.[15] By the 1960s and 1970s the industry had experienced waves of growth and decline but continued to be a crucial economic engine for the urban economy, especially as an employer of immigrant women.

The New York garment industry has long been dominated by female workers if not female managers or owners. Cutthroat competition among small contractors eager to supply large manufacturers with the lowest-cost products enforced low overhead and even lower wages. Unsafe working conditions were rampant, resulting in widespread abuses of the largely female labor force. The most infamous result was the Triangle Shirtwaist Company fire of 1911, when 146 women died in a clothing factory in lower Manhattan.[16]

Since the tragedy of the Triangle fire, laws enforcing safer working conditions in the New York garment industry have made life easier for laborers but ultimately, by the 1980s, helped to uproot the industry. Competition from other states with lower costs of living and more room to produce higher volume, along with an expanding global factory, left the New York garment industry in a precarious position. It was Chinatown that would save the garment industry of New York City.

"In the beginning, she didn't know the job and was afraid she would not make any money," remembers Si Zhi. When Sharon began her job at what Si Zhi calls a "sweatshop" she joined more than twenty-five thousand Chinese garment workers in New York. "In one week, she made $80 or $90. So later on, she was working hard, and every day ten hours, six days a week, sometimes seven days a week. She worked very, very hard."

Sharon's job was in one of the many textile production facilities that sprang up in lower Manhattan after 1965. Changes in immigration laws helped to balance the gender gap in the Chinese population in New York City, which historically had been composed primarily of men. By the 1980s there was an almost 1:1 ratio of men to women among Chinese residents of New York, and there were as many as five hundred clothing factories in Chinatown alone.[17]

"Around there it was all this kind of job," explains Si Zhi. "It was very hard, and I would say it was 99 percent Chinese." An estimated three out of five women in Chinatown worked in the revitalized garment industry, which contributed $125 million annually to the city's economy.[18]

Although the rapidly expanding garment industry in Chinatown was well organized,[19] it followed a familiar manufacturing logic that often took advantage of new immigrants. New arrivals willingly endured poor working conditions, especially if their extended social network was already well entrenched in the industry or if they had entered the United States illegally.

As Si Zhi asserts, "Most people who worked in this place were illegal immigrants, that's why no one complained. So whatever they paid you, you took it. You don't want it, you go—a lot of people want to do it. It's very, very cheap labor."

After several years at the sewing machine, Sharon finally quit the factory. She suffered from chronic neck pain, and though she picked up some Cantonese, she could speak little or no English. "That's why I told her don't go anymore. We can't be rich, just relax," Si Zhi says.

Eighteen months after moving into Franklin Plaza, Si Zhi moved his family out of his in-laws' apartment and out of East Harlem. In the late 1980s and early 1990s, the same escalating crime that embattled Pete, José, and Lucille frightened Si Zhi: "When I lived at Franklin Plaza, I was scared. I told my brother-in-law, 'Maybe I need to carry a gun.' Because I could see it. Franklin Plaza was okay, but walking around the streets at nighttime, forget it. I saw people smoking drugs, I hear the gun shooting. When we were there, we never went past 107th Street. Farther up, it was worse."

Si Zhi's fear for his family on the streets of East Harlem at this time was only one reason for moving out. His relationship with his wife's fam-

ily was another. "They had been here already, and they had changed a little bit. So when I got here, it was tough thing to me, the family relationship. They were looking at me different. They see me like I am low class.
They looked at me like I don't know nothing. They want to act like they
are the boss." This conflict carried over to Si Zhi's job, with his father-in-
law's constant criticisms of Si Zhi's boldness with his employers. "I
couldn't say anything. I just held it inside. This is what pushed me to find
some other place."

Si Zhi moved his family downtown, to a small apartment on the second floor of a crumbling building on 28th Street and Second Avenue. It
was the same stretch of Second Avenue that Sharon's grandfather had
called home before moving uptown to Franklin Plaza in the 1960s.
Though some distance from Canal Street, the main thoroughfare of New
York City's Chinatown, even 28th Street felt the effects of an ever-
expanding Chinese immigrant population.

At that time Sharon still worked in the midtown sweatshop, and Si Zhi
sought a job closer to home so that he would be more available to his
daughter. "It was a hard time for my daughter. I put her in a summer
camp, but every day she was always alone waiting for me because I could
not get there in time. So I had to look for some job with a nighttime schedule." Si Zhi heard about a job at a Times Square hotel through one of his
many in-laws. "When I got over there, I didn't speak much English. I
didn't even know how to fill out a form. The department director, she did
it for me. I started with a lobby job, and I started working night shifts."

Si Zhi was joining thousands of other new immigrants in the service
economy of the city, a shift in the demographics of employment that
echoed similar shifts in times past. German and Irish laborers had been
supplanted by new Italian immigrants at the beginning of the twentieth
century, only to be displaced by Puerto Rican and African American
workers moving north a half century later. By the time Si Zhi punched his
timecard for his first night shift, Asians and new Latino immigrants had
replaced Puerto Ricans and African Americans as the new all-purpose
laborers. "In the beginning, Puerto Ricans and black people worked in
housekeeping," Si Zhi remembers. "Then Asian people took over. They
like Asian people, because Asian people don't complain. The language is

a problem, but they work hard because they are scared they will lose their job. Just like me."

Even with the new night schedule, Si Zhi found it difficult to balance life at work and at home. He can still remember standing on the corner of 28th Street and Second Avenue, scanning the horizon for Sharon to appear on her way home from the sweatshop while Alison sat alone in the apartment upstairs. "At that time, I started work at 6:00 P.M., and my wife would not be home yet. So when I see Sharon coming, I take the bicycle and go. We just switch to take care of my daughter. I only saw my wife on the one off day, and on the sidewalk," explains Si Zhi. "It was life. What could I do? I don't speak English. At least I had a job."

Like so many immigrant families, the sacrifices Si Zhi and Sharon made in their first few years of life in New York were centered on their daughter, Alison, and their hopes for her future. The sting of missed opportunity in Shanghai no doubt inspired Si Zhi's zeal to make Alison's education their highest priority.

"When I was in China, I already knew that the public schools in New York City were not too good. So when I got here, I put my daughter in a Catholic school at 106th Street. I paid the money, about $200 a month. For me it was big money. But I told my wife, 'This money, we have to pay. Otherwise, later on she will have a bad experience learning, and she won't want to go to school. Her whole life—gone.' "

Their move to lower Manhattan was motivated in part by a desire to enroll Alison in a better school. Si Zhi knew more affluent neighborhoods supported higher-quality public schools, but he quickly learned that the very best schools were much closer to East Harlem, on Manhattan's Upper East Side. Though residency in such a community was impossible financially, Si Zhi decided to enroll Alison in a public school on 78th Street and York Avenue.

"But we needed an address. So the sister-in-law of the lady that brought my wife to work in the sweatshop that first time lived on 78th Street. So we contacted them, used their address, and we got Alison into that York Avenue school. That school, when she got in, I was very, very happy."

Unfortunately, the commute from 28th Street to 78th Street was long and difficult for parents who rarely saw one another and had little time to take their daughter to school. Si Zhi remembers, "Every morning, I slept a couple of hours, then I had to take my daughter to the bus. Since we used someone else's address, we could not apply for the school bus." Occasionally, students had a half day of school, making it impractical for Si Zhi to return home. "So I would bring her in the morning, and I wouldn't go home. I would stay in the park. A lot of old people were there. I was the only young guy, the Chinese guy sitting over there sleeping."

Si Zhi and his family gained a measure of independence in the apartment in lower Manhattan, but they were soon disillusioned with life away from the only family they had in the city. "That apartment, very bad," Si Zhi says simply. "I could see that the landlord didn't care, but now, looking back on this, it was good for me. I became independent, I could do it my own way. I could take more responsibility for my family." That responsibility met with crisis less than a year into their independence.

"One night, it was heavy rain, and on the third floor somebody left the faucet on. For twenty-four hours, the water came into my home. The roof was falling in. So I put my daughter on the table and went to get police." Si Zhi could see a patrol car parked across the street and ran downstairs to appeal for help. "I told them, 'I need help. My baby is in danger.' This I can speak, I worked in a factory, and 'Dangerous' I know. Every sign says 'Dangerous.' I just speak out the word, not the sentence." The police officers sitting in their patrol car cracked their window and took one look at Si Zhi. "Then rolled up the window, drinking his coffee, and he shrugged. This was the police. If I knew then, I could have sued them. Maybe I could have gotten a couple of million. So I felt, this place, I can't stay."

Despite concerns about crime, East Harlem was at least familiar, and in-laws Si Zhi felt were too controlling were better than no family at all. He applied for an apartment in 1199 Plaza, a subsidized cooperative housing project along the East River and Jefferson Park, not far from Franklin Plaza. "A friend, he helped me fill out the application form. I didn't know how I could do it, but I had to do something."

Planned as "moderate and middle-income housing," 1199 Plaza was not unlike Franklin Plaza in its socioeconomic intentions. Dedicated in

1974, the cooperative housing project took eleven years to build, and the unconventional sponsorship of Local 1199 of the Drug and Hospital Workers Union gave the development its name.[20] Many assumed the sixteen hundred units of "moderate housing," along with the plans for a Second Avenue subway line, would finally breach the 96th Street boundary to economic development on the Upper East Side.[21] Indeed, the completed buildings earned the prestigious Bard Award from the City Club of New York; among the other winners that year was the reconstruction of the Avenue of the Americas.[22]

But the subway never materialized, and 1199 Plaza did not herald an economic revitalization of East Harlem. The development rises from the banks of the East River in a stair-step design before soaring into four U-shaped, thirty-one-story towers. As one of many high-density housing developments, it is unremarkable but for its height—matched by only two other projects in East Harlem built around the same period: Schomburg Towers due west on Fifth Avenue and Taino Towers due north at 122nd Street. The three developments form a perfect, skyscraping triangle over East Harlem, all of them attracting both controversy and accolades since their inception.[23] By the time Si Zhi moved into one of the high-rise towers in May 1992, almost twenty years later, the development had become as stigmatized as any other public housing project in the neighborhood.

Si Zhi moved his family into a small one-bedroom apartment, hoping that a two-bedroom unit would become available soon. Back in East Harlem, Si Zhi could see the subtle signs that life on the street was changing for the better. In the four years before Si Zhi's arrival there, crime had increased by 41 percent, but in the four years after he moved into 1199 Plaza, crime decreased by exactly the same amount. "When I moved in, I was a little scared. My friend, in the first few months, she was robbed twice in the elevator. I didn't have this problem. I'm lucky. But every year you could see it getting better."

Two months later Si Zhi received a call that woke him from his post-night-shift slumber. The manager at 1199 Plaza had something to show him. "So I went down and he said, 'This is a key. 2501. Go look at it.' " Si Zhi stood speechless in the two-bedroom apartment on the twenty-fifth floor. Floor-to-ceiling windows opened onto the East River and all of Manhattan. Standing in his new living room, alone with his command-ing view of a city that had not quite beaten him, Si Zhi wept.

"I'm telling you, that day, I was just crying. It was beautiful. I said, 'Thanks, God. You gave me a chance. I wanted to do the best for my fam-ily, and you gave me the opportunity.' It's true, I stayed in that apartment jumping and screaming and crying."

Almost three years after arriving at JFK, Si Zhi felt he was finally gain-ing ground. Like José's family when they moved into Jefferson Houses, Si Zhi felt a sense of empowerment living at 1199 Plaza—a literal rising above that was exhilarating.

"This was the first thing that made me feel happy when I came to America. The first day I was happy. Before, life was too tired. Everything was on my shoulders, heavy. That day everything was light." Si Zhi stayed there for six years. "I kept my house beautiful. The floor shined like water."

Work at the hotel brought little of the same satisfaction. As he had at the Shanghai shipyard and the New Jersey welding company, Si Zhi wasted little time before streamlining work at the hotel, despite his struggle to learn English. "When I started, I could see the building and maintenance sucked, but when they gave me the job, I couldn't talk. So later on, when I could talk, I helped the engineering people a lot. They didn't even know how to use the right tools."

Si Zhi became increasingly frustrated with his position at the hotel as these contributions went unacknowledged. "In China, I was in a very high position, so when I got here, I felt bad."

On his long commute home at 4:00 A.M., Si Zhi would ask himself, "I'm gonna clean toilets all my life in America?"

Si Zhi sought a transfer to the maintenance department but quickly ran into resistance. "I applied, but I didn't get it," Si Zhi explains. "I al-most got it, but my manager said, 'No, I need him in my department.'" Si Zhi continued to work beyond his job description, earning praise for a manager who would not let him transfer departments. Eventually, a new maintenance manager was hired.

"I knew, when he got this position, I could not transfer departments. This guy was Puerto Rican. This sucked. I said, 'Oh, I have no chance.'" Si Zhi's pessimism, born of thinly drawn stereotypes from life in East Harlem, became a filter for what happened next. "As soon as he got that job, all these people got fired—an Italian, two Russians, another European, a Filipino. All these people had licenses, electrician, air conditioning, he fired all of them. He hired all Puerto Rican people, but they were not good, they didn't have any licenses." Si Zhi continued to press his case but to no avail. "So I gave up. And one year later, we had a different local union. So if I moved departments, I would lose my seniority."

The perception of ethnic exclusion at work was exacerbated by several incidents that occurred when he was making his way back to East Harlem in the early morning hours. "A couple of times, waiting for the bus, a car came full of young people, white kids, asking, 'Hey, can you tell me how to get to Lincoln Tunnel?' I tell them, and finally they hit me with a beer bottle, 'Fuck you, go back to China!'"

According to Si Zhi, 90 percent of his coworkers in housekeeping were Asian, most of whom were Mandarin-speaking ethnic Chinese from China, Vietnam, and Cambodia. Si Zhi avoided socializing with many of them, preferring to distance himself from what he called the "Asian community."

"I have coworkers, and at the job I talk to them, but I don't want to know them outside the job. It doesn't mean I look down on them, but they are always talking about casinos or girlfriends when they already have families. They are always talking about how easy it is to get welfare. They don't care about enjoying this country. I can't tell them they are wrong. I can't judge them. But I don't want to do it."

That night at the bus stop, with the stink of beer and the sting of "Go back to China!" still pungent, Si Zhi could not disassociate himself from the "Asian community." Despite differences of history, nation, and language, Si Zhi was part of that community, and he would not be bullied.

"I picked up the bottle, and I threw it back."

Despite the best efforts of substandard housing, underemployment, and racist joyriders, Si Zhi had no intention of going back to China. Five years into his stay at 1199 Plaza, Si Zhi heard from a friend about a new housing development in the neighborhood. "So I went and I looked, but the date already passed. I applied anyway, just to take a chance."

The development was La Esperanza Homes, a string of twenty three-family homes on 111th and 112th Streets built by New York City Housing Partnership and a private real estate development company. After half a century of high-rise, high-density subsidized housing, the city changed course to meet the needs of middle-income residents in what the Department of Housing and Urban Development (HUD) described as "one of the poorest communities in Manhattan, characterized by poverty, high unemployment, poor educational facilities, and a high number of single-parent households."[24] The innovative program won the Housing and Urban Development Secretary's Best in American Living Award for 1998.

Si Zhi's application was accepted, and, like nineteen others, he was obligated to contribute 5 percent of the subsidized cost of the new home as a down payment. The total cost of the three-family townhouse was listed at $340,900, but a $100,900 subsidy reduced the purchase price to $240,000. Si Zhi would need $12,000 for a down payment.

"Ever since I come to this country, I never buy clothes, never buy anything for myself," says Si Zhi. "I always put my money away, waiting to make a better life for my family."

After eight years in New York, Si Zhi emptied his savings, just over $12,000, and signed a contract on his new home. The subsidy would gradually be reduced by 4 percent annually, encouraging the new home owners to remain residents for at least twenty-five years. The mortgage payments, though high, would be covered by rental income from two apartments in each building.

The arrangement was ideal for Si Zhi and many of his new neighbors, but the elegance of the financing, all designed to anchor home owners to East Harlem and provide quality, low-density housing had its own, perhaps unintended consequences. The subsidy, set at around $100,000, was in place to discourage selling out early but could not compete with a booming real estate market. In less than four years, one of Si Zhi's neighbors sold his home for more than half a million dollars, realizing a profit of more than $100,000—even after repaying the subsidy for selling early.

Two others have since placed their homes on the market at even higher prices, prohibitively high for long-term residents of East Harlem. Moreover, the high mortgage rates forced many home owners to price their rental properties out of reach for local residents, attracting young, upwardly mobile professionals who too often had little or no interest in the life of the community.[25]

The long-term implications for East Harlem were not foremost in his mind when Si Zhi moved into his new home in 1998. In less than ten years, he was a home owner and a landlord in Manhattan, and he quickly got to know his neighbors and fellow home owners—a new experience for all of them. Their yards divided by chain-link fencing, they traded gardening tips and the cherished woes of home ownership. It did not take long for Si Zhi to distinguish himself, not only for his immaculate garden but for his do-it-yourself prowess as well. He was the first to design and construct a garden, to install a doorbell on his gate, and to tile the bland concrete stoop in front.

The neighbor whose backyard faced his own was Maria. Not long after Si Zhi moved in, he met Maria's first tenant—a Puerto Rican named José just back from an errant sojourn in Florida.

.   .   .   .   .

Fourth of July. Independence Day. Si Zhi's in-laws have come for a backyard barbecue. Four generations of a Shanghai family gather in Si Zhi's home: all of them in-laws, mother and father, aunt and uncle, brothers, nieces and nephews. At one hundred, Sharon's grandfather is the oldest and, trailed by his wife, the earliest to leave.

As the fading light of a summer's day turns the backyard into a secret garden of color, Si Zhi ambles down the metal staircase for a break from the festivities. Sharon's relatives have said their good-byes to Grandfather in the house but have not yet returned to the yard.

"Don't ask me the name of the plants. I don't know. I know all the Chinese names, I just don't know the names in English," Si Zhi says, squatting beside a young plant pushing up through the soil. "This one has flowers, all these have flowers." Then another, thick-trunked shrub gets a tender examination. "You see this, this is oranges. But they can't stay in winter, it's too cold. But if you keep it inside, it can't get bigger, you have to put it in the ground."

Si Zhi fills a plate with barbecued chicken, beef, and lamb and opens a can of beer. "If a gardener, someone hired me to do that job, I would like it. If I had a big place, I would plant trees."

He settles into one of the empty chairs and thinks of Alison. She would have been here, playing with her cousins on the small, immaculate patch of grass, but West Point has her jumping out of airplanes somewhere over Georgia.

Alison started West Point in fall 2002, one year after the terrorist attacks of September 11. She wanted the "experience" of military training, and Si Zhi liked the idea of an imposed discipline. Since seventh grade, Alison had been part of Prep for Prep, a privately funded program to help underserved students in New York City attend elite private high schools. With their help, Alison attended the Brearley School, an elite private school for girls. Brearley, on East 83d Street, is not far from the once all-girl high school, Julia Richman, that José's sister and Lucille attended in the 1960s and 1970s. In Alison's junior year at the Brearley School, she earned a near-perfect score on the Scholastic Aptitude Test.

"After that, she got lazy," says Si Zhi.

Alison was in an awkward social position. She was an immigrant herself (though largely socialized in the United States) and attended an elite private school but lived in one of New York's most underserved communities. The complexity of Alison's position was not unique, though that was small consolation at the time.[26] Not surprisingly, there was tension in the household, and Si Zhi often felt at a loss about how to guide his daughter. "I know my daughter. She does just enough to stay on top, but she never continues to push." Si Zhi has done nothing but push since the Cultural Revolution.

If Si Zhi was overbearing with Alison, he had a startling cautionary tale to inspire strict measures. Two years after he moved his family into their new home, the bodies of a Chinese couple were found floating in the East River near 102nd Street. They were Stephen and Chilin Leung, friends of Si Zhi's, both murdered by their daughter, Connie, and her African American boyfriend, Eric Louissaint.[27]

"Connie was the same age as my daughter. They used to play together at 1199." Si Zhi remembers seeing Connie and her boyfriend at Jefferson Park, where he would exercise in the evening before heading to work. They both attended Manhattan Center for Science and Mathematics on Pleasant Avenue—formerly Leonard Covello's Benjamin Franklin High School, an early emblem of ethnic unity in East Harlem. "I would tell my daughter, 'Look at these kids. That's bad.'"

According to news reports surrounding the murders, Connie's parents felt the same way about her relationship with Eric. They forbade Connie to see Eric and allegedly threatened to arrange a marriage for her. Desperate, the young couple met at Aguilar Library on 110th Street, a refuge for many young people over the past century, to plan her parents' murder, which they carried out on November 2, 2000. In the weeks and months after the murders, the city was gripped by what appeared to be a tragic response to her parents' rejection of an interracial relationship.

But according to Si Zhi, it was not ethnic prejudice that set Connie's parents against her relationship; it was their hopes for her future. "A lot of newspapers said the parents didn't like it because the boy was black. This is not true." In fact, several news accounts reported that Mr. Leung went to Connie's school the day before the murders to discuss her poor attendance. Detectives on the case confirmed that the Leungs seemed most concerned about Eric's lack of employment and bad influence on Connie's work ethic.[28] According to Si Zhi, "They said, 'You have a boyfriend. I don't care his color, but when you met him, you never go to school.' That's why he didn't like it. So they killed them. They waited for them to come home and killed them. That's the problem. They didn't like that she didn't go to school."[29]

Si Zhi's defense of the young woman's parents touched on his own concern about the importance of education, but his denial of any racially motivated condemnation led to other concerns about his daughter, himself, and East Harlem. "In the beginning, I didn't care," he says in response to questions about ethnic conflict. "For me, personally, I am not against black people, but it's hard for me to get close to them because a lot of bad experiences have made me like that."

One of those bad experiences involved a group of young African American girls. Si Zhi was walking along Second Avenue, on his way to

Franklin Plaza to visit his in-laws. "They started throwing ice at me," remembers Si Zhi. "I told them to stop, that this was not nice, but they wouldn't stop." Eventually, two adults joined the girls and, according to Si Zhi, defended their actions. "They said, 'Go back to your place.' I said, 'My place is here!' They said, 'No, you're Chinese.' "

The remark echoed the taunts of the drunken white kids downtown, and Si Zhi lost his temper. In the multiethnic wonder that is East Harlem, a Latina approached from across the street to intervene. "One Spanish lady, from across the street, she saw everything. So she came running, and said, 'These girls are bad. Why are you doing that?' She said to me, 'Go, go, go. Don't bother with these nasty people.' "

Unfortunately, "Go back to China" was not the only dark memory rekindled in that event. "At 106th Street I saw a police car sitting there," remembers Si Zhi. Just as on that rain-swept night on Second Avenue and 28th Street, Si Zhi approached the patrol car and saw two officers, "drinking coffee." He knocked on the window, explained the situation, and asked the officers to reprimand the girls. " 'Could you go over there with me, and tell them to stop doing this.' The police looked at me, he said, 'If nothing bothering you, don't make a big deal.' "

Si Zhi's voice still tightens at the telling. "But it did bother me! And he stayed in his car."

Eventually, Si Zhi walked away but not before widening the gap between himself and most of his neighbors. His response now is not altogether different from that of Pete or José, or countless others who confront the inevitable cleavages that erupt in a diverse community: the myriad variations on "I'm not racist but . . ." In his words, "I can't figure out between black people and Puerto Ricans, that's why I don't rent to any of them."

When Alison enrolled at West Point Academy, Si Zhi was pleased. His pristine minivan was soon festooned with West Point ephemera, and he and Sharon made frequent trips to visit her at the academy not far north on the Hudson River. "For me, I'm happy, because I know West Point will give her discipline." But the choice of a U.S. military academy has little effect on Si Zhi's own patriotism or sense of civic duty. "It's free, and I know it's a good education. It will give her a lot of opportunities. I don't think about patriotism, or the United States. It is just a job that Alison signed up for."

This issue is a particularly sensitive one for family back in Shanghai, all of whom know about Alison's achievement. One of Si Zhi's brothers, who had spent some time in the Chinese army, remembered watching training videos from West Point, designed to strike fear in the hearts of young soldiers preparing for potential war with the United States.

"He was worried it was no place for a girl. He even offered money to send her to some other university." On a recent visit to Shanghai, Si Zhi, Sharon, and Alison all faced questions about her choice: "What would you do if America declares war on China?" According to Si Zhi, Alison replied, "I would have no choice. I would have to serve my country."

Alison's patriotic feelings about her adopted country have not necessarily trickled up to her parents, though Si Zhi became a citizen in 1994. Because he and his family arrived in the United States as legal residents, sponsored by his in-laws, they could have remained so indefinitely.

"For me, I really didn't need citizenship. But it was for my daughter. I knew that when she grew up, and didn't have citizenship, it would bother her." Sharon, however, failed the language test and did not reapply. Si Zhi contends that the language test was unfairly administered: "If my wife had argued, she might have passed, but she was scared. After that, she said, 'I don't want it. It doesn't bother me.'"

Despite Si Zhi's ambivalence about his citizenship, he recognizes the privilege that accompanies his status. This is especially salient in light of recent global resistance to the unilateralism of U.S. foreign policy, which Si Zhi sees as contradictory, especially in China. "Even now there are a lot of college students protesting America for bombing, and the next day they wait in a big, huge line at the American embassy to get a visa. They protest a lot, but what they want to do is go to America. I am lucky I came here."

Even Sharon, after nearly a decade in the garment district sweatshops, has found life in the United States, and even East Harlem, preferable to life in Shanghai. Si Zhi remembers with some pride a recent trip to China, when Sharon was asked by some childhood friends why they would not return to Shanghai to stay.

"They said, 'You see how China has changed, beautiful buildings. So how do you feel now?' She said, 'I love it in America, and for just one reason. My husband has just a basic job, and he can buy a house and support a family. Even if your husband has some position, can he do that? We've been gone fifteen years, how about you? Do you own a house? No. That's it.' "

Si Zhi sums up his brand of patriotism in one succinct statement, not altogether foreign or necessarily new: "We don't talk about politics or freedom. We don't care. Only one thing, America gave me an opportunity."

In the years since Si Zhi left Shanghai, China has experienced unprecedented economic growth—creating opportunities mostly for urban Chinese that Si Zhi could have only dreamed about. By 2002 China's economy was growing 8 percent per year, and China had outmaneuvered Japan to become the largest Asian exporter to the United States.[30] Shanghai and other cities were exploding with new construction and foreign investment. Shanghai alone constructed more than twenty-five hundred buildings taller than eighteen stories throughout the 1990s, including Jin Mao Tower, the fourth-largest building in the world.[31] Throughout the boom, the once all-encompassing Communist Party was hemorrhaging members and quickly becoming irrelevant to the lives of many young mainland Chinese.[32]

Si Zhi invested in Shanghai's economic boom in 2002 by buying an apartment in a new high-rise tower. "Long ago, the government took all property, so I wanted to get a place where Sharon's parents could stay. Their little money gives just a basic life here, but take that money over there, they will live like kings. This was the first reason, to give it to them to use."

But honoring his in-laws was not the only motivation. Si Zhi was investing in his future—a future predicated on transnational ties and divided loyalties. "I feel like I have two homes," he says with some conviction. But then conviction falters, and he continues, "I don't think I would want to be in Shanghai. I don't know. Maybe. In China a lot of people can't make it. When I retire, I will spend more time in China. But I would not move there. If the government system doesn't change, I cannot stay there."

Despite all of the changes in Shanghai and throughout China, Si Zhi recognizes too much that has not changed. The economic boom has left many behind, and expatriates like himself are some of the only investors wealthy enough to buy into the new luxury residential buildings of his hometown. Two years after Si Zhi purchased his apartment, one-sixth of residential real estate in Shanghai remains vacant, and most Chinese would have to pay a price equivalent to ten to fifteen times their annual income to buy into the boom.[33]

"I enjoy it, but at the same time a lot of things bother me that I can't enjoy," Si Zhi explains. "Like people that have no job." For Si Zhi, the service economy of bustling cities like Shanghai consists of men and women not unlike himself when he arrived in New York. They come to work in the hotels and restaurants that cater to tourists and the urban elite but earn a small fraction of the wages Si Zhi earns in the United States. "They leave their family, leave their kids for the whole year. They get so little money, and they don't spend it, they don't eat. You can see it. This is a bad life, and it bothers me. Over here, people respect me, but over there, it's too low, they won't even look at you."

Si Zhi recounts his visits to Shanghai, socializing with those he left behind and who now enjoy the benefits of a more open economy. It is always a trip fraught with conflict, torn as he is between the two worlds he inhabits. "I enjoy it there, with my friends, with my community, but at the same time I go to a restaurant and I see a lot of people working, waitress and waiter, they treat them like shit. I don't like it. I always say, 'You do that again, I won't have anything to do with you.' I always say that because I have the same kind of job. 'What would you do if that were me?'"

First one, then another, and soon the backyard is full of family again. Sliding in and out of Mandarin and English with practiced ease, laughing about the neighbor's dogs or the pranks of the youngest of the cousins.

"I feel good being here. I feel very, very good. I feel America is the best country. It's not perfect, but of all the countries I have seen or know, I feel this is a good country. I feel like home here. Shanghai feels like home also, because I have a community there. Not like here."

Si Zhi eats quickly, then makes sure everyone is happy—plying them with more food and drink. One brother-in-law points up through the thick, leafy grapevine toward a few American flags hanging from Si Zhi's terrace.

"You see my American flags?" asks Si Zhi with some pride.

His brother-in-law smiles and says, "They're probably made in China."

EIGHT Urban "Renewal" and
the Final Migration

June 12, 2004. It's my birthday.

It's also the day of the 116th Street Festival, a neighborhood-wide block party on the Saturday before the Puerto Rican Day parade. Outside, a half block from my front door, Third Avenue is throbbing. Live music from two outdoor venues almost drowns out competing portable stereos and the mildly offensive taunts emanating from a carnival dunking booth. Steam from roasting pork, grilled corn, and boiling stew filters through the crowd, blending with the sickly sweet smell of spilled soda, cotton candy, and contraband liquor. There is no escape from East Harlem's biggest party, stretching from below 106th Street to beyond 120th Street.

I'm standing in the galley kitchen of my ground-floor, one-bedroom apartment in Si Zhi's building frying chicken for forty or so guests. It's the second time I've subjected myself to this culinary ordeal, rising early and frying for hours, and for the second time it is well worth it. By the end of the day, most of those who populate my rather disjointed social world will have stood in the same room, or at least the same vicinity, for a couple of hours. Corporate lawyers and hairdressers, Ph.D.'s and shop-keepers, janitors and accountants—a microcosm of the city that cuts through the many boundaries, social and geographic, New Yorkers work hard to maintain.

The thick haze of grease has effectively masked the smells coming from the street, and once the chicken is done and piled high on platters, I step through our two front doors and out into the gated front patio. Cheryl, my wife, is greeting friends from Washington, and a few others are already sitting at a large folding table we borrowed from Si Zhi for the occasion. Maria and Eduardo are there, as well as a few more friends from down the street. Mohamed will join us after he closes up the store, and Si Zhi seems to be hiding upstairs.

Pete won't make it over from 114th Street. He doesn't like the crowds. José said he would come, but Saturdays are better for holing up and tin-kering on the computer. Lucille also wants to come, but her intestinal condition is flaring up—within the week she will be in the hospital, again.

I open a beer and take a seat, waiting while guests file inside for chicken. In the brief solitude of our patio, Si Zhi peers out his window above and then quickly scurries down.

"You need more tables?" he asks.

"No, no, but you should get a plate," I answer. "And take one to Sharon."

"No, that's all right," he says shyly, afraid of intruding.

"You should both come down and join us."

"No, no, I just want to make sure everything is all right," he says, shak-ing his head and waving his hands. "It's your party."

"But it's your house," I argue.

"No," Si Zhi answers, retreating up the stairs. "Maybe later."

Si Zhi is not necessarily a shy man. I've seen him red-faced and swear-ing at the injustices of the police or his employers, and I've seen him weep over an Americanized daughter he doesn't always understand. I've been his tenant for more than five years, and he has welcomed me into his home more times than I can count. But he still seems uncomfortable as a guest in my home.

Before I can formulate a theory, one by one the guests return to fill their plates with southern fried chicken, rice and cream gravy, green beans, and biscuits. My mother would be proud.

.   .   .   .   .

I was not born in East Harlem. I was not even born in New York. As the son of a very successful doctor, in Houston, Texas, I could hardly have had an upbringing more different from that of the individuals in the preceding chapters. For me, opportunity was a given, along with a myopic, privileged worldview.

But something, somewhere, snapped.

Through years of Catholic school, travels in Latin America, a startling religious conversion, and marriage to Cheryl at just twenty-one, my worldview widened with little fanfare and no great epiphany. By the time I graduated from college, I had accepted the orthodox theology of salvation that has been the foundation of Christianity since the first-century church. It is a faith born of practice and reflection, constantly testing institutional tradition against what I consider biblical authority. It was my faith that informed a creeping realization that life was not as it should be, despite or even because of the comforts it afforded. It was my faith that made personal responsibility for social change a moral imperative. However unintended, it was also an efficient way to alienate most of my family and many of my old friends.

I enrolled in graduate programs in cultural anthropology as far from Texas as I could manage. Studies took us to Boston, Massachusetts, and Oxford, England—where I felt as out of place as I later would in East Harlem—and fieldwork took us even farther, to a Caribbean port city in Costa Rica. Every assumption was challenged, and, as I neared the completion of my degree, a vision emerged for some practical application of our accumulated passions.

We wanted to bridge the worlds we had crisscrossed on our journeys, especially back in the States, and we thought the most engaging medium would be the creative arts. The idea was to create a synergistic artist residency and education organization that would encourage aspiring artists to connect their work to urban issues of social justice, as well as provide free training in the arts to local residents. In exchange for living and studio space, artists from within the neighborhood and around the country would teach their trades to children and adults in the community.

We also wanted to bridge the worlds of faith we had moved in and out of over the years. We were as nondenominational as we were orthodox in our Christianity, and we hoped to provide a space for Catholics and Protestants, conservatives and charismatics to work together. The project was not an evangelical one—the art classes would be a service to the community free of any religious content—but it was ecumenical. This position, unfortunately, would cost us some support.

It was a vision that would eventually plant us in East Harlem. As should be clear, Cheryl and I did not choose East Harlem as a field site for anthropological research. We chose it as a place to challenge our beliefs, to sharpen our convictions about the way the world works, and often doesn't work, and to test how our faith can inform our response. In the end, I'm not convinced the motivations are distinguishable, and perhaps the writing of this book was in some ways inevitable. I am, after all, a Christian *and* an anthropologist (and male and white and from the South—all of which inform my identity). Regardless of our reason for being, our project was ill-fated and would slowly, surely bring us to our knees—disillusioned but no less committed to the patch of Manhattan between 96th and 125th Streets.

Like Maria, Mohamed, and Si Zhi, I arrived in New York, and East Harlem, by way of JFK airport. In June 1999, after bouncing from the United States to England to Costa Rica and back again, our travels came to a skidding stop on a tarmac that had welcomed so many other sojourners. We had very little money, few friends, and no jobs, but we had a grand vision for art education in the city.

Our first introduction to East Harlem came in our first weeks in New York. The 116th Street Festival that would bring my friends for fried chicken five years later brought Cheryl and me up the #6 train to 110th Street. We emerged to a sun-drenched, music-filled version of the neighborhood that resonated with every aspect of our vision. It was in Manhattan, convenient enough to the downtown art world we hoped to engage, and yet diverse enough to challenge the stereotypes often generated by the mainstream media. But if it was going to work, we had to work from the inside. We had to build something local through the residents themselves.

José was first. We met him through his website, a loving homage to El Barrio. It was José who invited two strangers into his home and introduced us to his family and then to his neighborhood in all its idiosyncratic charms.[1] It was José who served as one of our organization's first board members, and it was José who found our apartment with Si Zhi.

Next came Carla. Carla, an oversized African American woman with a personality to match, lived in a railroad apartment in a tenement across from Jefferson Park with her husband and their two children. Born and raised in the Bronx, Carla had long ago settled her family in East Harlem, and as our second board member, she became a tireless champion of our organization.

By February 2000 we had a board of directors made up of East Harlem residents, we were incorporated in the state of New York, and we received nonprofit status from the federal government. It was a whirlwind of success that raised our expectations far beyond what was reasonable. We still had few resources, worked out of our one-bedroom apartment, and had no connection with larger, more established institutions.

Our early success, perhaps, should not have been so surprising. Ever since Irish and German laborers had settled near the Hell Gate section of the East River, outsiders had focused their philanthropic patronage on the tenants of East Harlem. The earliest social welfare organizations, such as Settlement House, were founded by white, usually Protestant, outsiders. It was a tradition that continued even through the tumultuous 1960s and 1970s, when the Puerto Rican community became more actively involved in their own social and political movements.[2] Figures like Norman Eddy, a Protestant clergyman and mentor to José and many other young Puerto Rican activists, settled in East Harlem, committed to a social justice agenda that included personal involvement and responsibility, not merely philanthropic distance.[3] But even Eddy, after decades of activism in the community, would be considered an outsider by some and accused of pursuing his own agenda.

Another engaged outsider to East Harlem was a young woman, Jo Adler, who helped to organize the Upper Park Avenue Community Association with Mary Iemma and Margaret Jenkins in the 1960s. Adler moved to East Harlem in 1963, working on behalf of the Block Development Organization. For two years, she tried unsuccessfully to organize tenant associations in the neighborhood. Neighbors thought her work was "suspicious at worst and noncommittal at best." Iemma remembered watching Adler through the blinds of her window and listening to her neighbors: "They said she was a communist, a spy, and horrible things." Ultimately, UPACA took shape a year later not because of Adler's reaching out to the community but because Iemma and Jenkins reached out to her. As Iemma remembered, "All of a sudden I looked at her and I felt a great bit of pity and sympathy for her."[4]

Jo Adler and Norman Eddy were never able to fully overcome their outsider status, and their stories are as inspiring as they are cautionary. By 1968 Adler had left UPACA and East Harlem, disappointed with the organization's ties to city government and the Federal Housing Administration. By 1970 she had moved to Brooklyn, where she committed suicide.[5]

Taking on the burden of "saving" the inner city, especially as an outsider, is as presumptuous as it is doomed to fail. We did not consider ourselves pioneers on the new urban frontier,[6] nor were we under the impression that East Harlem *needed* another social service organization. Faced with the megalopolis of New York City, we were intent on actively engaging the life of the city, not passively consuming what was on offer. If anyone needed saving, it was ourselves, and there seemed no better place to start than a neighborhood that had tested the mettle of newcomers for generations. But we knew our intentions meant little if our neighbors were content to watch us through the blinds.

Despite our hopes of remaining subordinate to the direction of locals and to movements already in place, we were keenly aware of the access we had to resources largely unavailable to local residents, even those working tirelessly to create and maintain their own grassroots solutions to endemic problems in the community. Because of a contact at a large law firm, we received incorporation and nonprofit status in a matter of months—at no cost. Countless other East Harlem organizations had struggled to achieve that milestone of legitimacy for years.

Determined to use this cultural capital in service to the neighborhood, we built into the organization a plan to raise up local leadership to take over the project as soon as possible. I attended as many community board meetings as my schedule allowed and began discussing collaborations with other local organizations. By the end of our first year, in 2000, we raised enough money to provide art classes for two hundred schoolchildren in the East Harlem El Faro Beacon Community Center.[7]

Unfortunately, we were also beginning to see the edges of a vision that once extended to the horizon. Throughout our first year, we approached several churches in the neighborhood in the hope that they might host art classes in the summer. After months of discussion, neither Catholic nor Protestant congregations would allow outsiders to teach art to their children. El Faro, a city-run program, welcomed our volunteers, but our application to the city's Department of Cultural Affairs for funding to buy art supplies was denied because we were a "religious" organization. In addition, Christians often refused to contribute funds because we were not evangelical enough, and those hostile to religion refused because we were too religious.

After more than a year, we had the same small group of local support, no one to take over leadership, and only a fraction of the capital we would need to acquire a residential facility that was central to the mission of the organization. And after more than a year in East Harlem, we still felt out of place—in the community and in the city. Downtown, we were the social masochists, actually choosing to live anywhere north of 96th Street. Uptown, despite constant affirmation from individuals within the community, we could not shake our fear that we were interlopers, the advance guard of those who would cross that real estate boundary soon enough.

Living betwixt and between two worlds had its moments.

When I wasn't attending community board meetings, contacting local organizations, or trying to raise money, I was adjunct teaching in anthropology departments around the city. The farthest-flung classes would have me walking home through the neighborhood well past midnight. I had read Bourgois's *In Search of Respect*—a crash course in developing a relative sense of safety.

One night, while walking through Jefferson and Johnson Houses on my way home from the subway, I noticed a group of young men standing in the shadows. It was late, as usual, and I steeled myself against making any assumptions. As I passed, I heard one of them call out to me. I tensed, cursed my own fear, and kept walking. He called out again. I kept moving, eyes forward.

Then it occurred to me. The man had called out, "Praise the Lord!"

I stopped, turned, and met a familiar face jogging to catch up with me. It was Robert, a bear of a young man whom I had met one Sunday at Bethel Gospel Assembly, the church that now occupies James Fennimore Cooper Junior High School, Lucille's alma mater. It was our first visit to the church, and as parishioners processed to the altar to make an offering, I realized to my embarrassment that I had no money. Robert, sitting next to me, sized up the situation and silently handed me a couple of bills to carry to the front. It was a singularly humbling experience, and eternally endearing to the man whom I had just assumed was out to get me.

When Robert finally reached me, he said, "I couldn't remember your name, so I just called out, 'Praise the Lord,' and hoped you would recognize me."

Humility, it seemed, was East Harlem's greatest lesson. And on more than one occasion it involved my name.

Still early in our time in East Harlem, I met Aki, the Guinean vendor who rented space from the laundromat next door to Mohamed's store. As I was killing time waiting for my clothes to dry, we spoke about how we both had arrived in New York and our hopes for the future. Aki dreamed of cashing in his vending business for a gypsy cab, and he listened with all due sympathy to my attempts to find a full-time teaching job.

There was one problem. Aki insisted on calling me "Boss Man."

No doubt a bit of friendly slang Aki picked up trying to fit in, it was nevertheless awkward for someone also trying to fit in to have a very dark-skinned African calling a very light-skinned southerner "Boss Man." I did my best to teach him to pronounce my first name. Unfortunately, in Aki's peculiar blend of English, French, and Guinean dialect, "Russell" came out something like "Ah-sole," very much like "Asshole." Thereafter, instead of "Boss Man," I had a beaming Aki calling out a half block away, "How are you today, Asshole?!"

We compromised on an innocuous nickname, but the episode gave me pause. As an outsider, especially a white outsider, I carried with me a whole history of difference that engendered either a mislaid and unearned deference or a personalized animosity. Despite my best intentions, would I always be either the Boss Man or the Asshole?

·   ·   ·   ·   ·

"Is Russell Sharman here?" a familiar voice asked. I turned to see Norma and her wheelchair-bound mother arriving for fried chicken. No taller than five feet, Norma smiled behind thick-rimmed glasses. "There he is!" she said, catching my eye.

I met Norma in our first few months in the neighborhood. She worked the front desk at the community board office on 115th Street. As she maneuvered her mother into our patio, she said, "I'm sorry I'm so late. We were here and there, you know."

"No one is late today," I assured her.

Norma had always made me feel welcome in the neighborhood, even at the first few community board meetings where I felt keenly out of place. When voting members had all picked up their packets of information, she would slip me any extra copies to keep me up-to-date. Still hopeful that we could acquire a facility to house an artist residency, I frequented all the meetings dealing with city properties and real estate.

In the beginning, our plan for 20,000 square feet of residential and public art space seemed ambitious but possible. As I walked the streets of East Harlem, it was clear that a large percentage of properties were empty or abandoned. Surely it would be in the best interest of the city and the neighborhood to rehabilitate some of them for the purposes of free art classes. Unfortunately, our purposes, along with those of many local prospective home owners and nonprofit organizations, were not what the city or private developers had in mind.

It was only after several trips downtown to identify the owners of abandoned buildings in East Harlem that I began to recognize a pattern of warehousing properties in preparation for a real estate boom. Records often listed owners as nonexistent businesses or indicated the last known address as that of a burned-out shell of a building.[8] It was apparent that many of the abandoned and deteriorating properties in East Harlem, the same "blighted" spaces that reaffirmed an image of decay, were intentionally left undeveloped and unproductive.

But this "disinvestment" in East Harlem, which excluded local residents and organizations from revitalizing their own real estate market, would eventually lead to massive reinvestment by development corporations once conditions ripened for profit. That critical moment, when the potential rate of return justifies capital reinvestment in rental properties long since abandoned, seemed to occur in East Harlem in the late 1990s, though the full effects would not be felt for several years.[9] At that point the phenomenon took on its more familiar label—gentrification.

Gentrification is a relatively modern term for an old concept. Used by Ruth Glass in 1964, the term applied to the displacement of working-class residents from certain sections of London by an emergent middle class eager to invest in urban real estate.[10] It was, from its first use, a negative term meant to critique the political, economic, and social structures that allowed the process to unfold to the detriment of the working class and the urban poor. In the intervening years, gentrification has taken on a more ambiguous definition. Co-opted by city planners and real estate developers, gentrification is often portrayed as a positive process of urban renewal that brings new life to "blighted" communities. Redefined as the process of reinvesting in abandoned real estate, gentrification becomes value-neutral if not an outright moral obligation.[11]

But the effect of gentrification on people already living in those allegedly blighted communities is not value-neutral, and it is rarely positive. For example, one of the clearest indicators that gentrification has taken root in East Harlem is the attempt by real estate brokers and developers to rebrand the neighborhood. Documented by Arlene Dávila in her book *Barrio Dreams,* this process has a direct impact on the cultural claim Puerto Ricans have maintained on the neighborhood since displacing

Italians more than sixty years ago. Despite local movements to promote "El Barrio" and "Spanish Harlem" as distinctive labels for the community, real estate listings in city newspapers have conspicuously avoided those terms. At least as early as 1981, developers have tried to push the 96th Street boundary northward, referring to properties as far as 106th Street as "Upper Yorkville."[12] It is a thinly veiled attempt to disassociate East Harlem from its own history and present the neat grid of streets as a cultural void waiting to be filled with "qualified" applicants. In the socially and politically loaded terms of gentrification, developers and brokers market 96th Street as a real estate frontier, hoping to draw intrepid homesteaders into the northern wilderness.

What is happening in East Harlem and the debates over gentrification's relative moral value are not necessarily new. When Glass was discussing "gentrification" in London, social critics in the United States were bemoaning the failure of urban planning in cities like New York, especially in regard to public housing.[13] In 1961 Jane Jacobs cited East Harlem specifically as a neighborhood well on its way to "unslumming" on its own before private lenders undermined investment and the city destroyed what progress had been made by erecting massive housing projects. Like contemporary critics of gentrification, Jacobs ridiculed the idea of city officials wanting to "bring back the middle class," arguing that cities themselves "grow the middle class" precisely in neighborhoods like East Harlem so long as they value its residents and consider them worth retaining.[14]

Despite the popularity of Jacobs's work, no one involved with city planning or real estate development seemed to be doing much reading. In the past forty years, long periods of disinvestment were followed by cataclysmic amounts of reinvestment that displaced thousands of working-class residents throughout Queens and Brooklyn along the banks of the East River, as well as on the Lower East Side, in Harlem, and, most recently, in East Harlem.[15] Rather than nurture an emergent middle class, investors and developers preferred to warehouse abandoned properties or allow inhabited buildings to deteriorate. As long-term tenants moved up in terms of education and employment, they most often moved out rather than remain in substandard housing. The process produces

large tracts of abandoned or substandard housing stock that can be purchased and redeveloped as one large site, usually with the help of public
subsidies to private developers. It is precisely the process that precipitated massive slum clearance in East Harlem in the 1940s to make way for
the public housing projects that now dominate the cityscape. Sixty years
later, however, the state has ceded control to private industry, hoping market forces will correct the mistakes of urban planners at midcentury.

The flagship project of this new approach to urban renewal in East
Harlem is La Esperanza Homes, where Si Zhi lives as a home owner and
landlord. Five years after its completion, the neat rows of faux tenements
were heralded as a massive success. Plans were drawn up to duplicate
the development throughout the neighborhood. In a matter of months
several city blocks between Madison Avenue and Fifth Avenue south of
Marcus Garvey Park were reduced to rubble. The tenements of Lucille's
childhood were cleared away like cobwebs to make way for row after
row of new three-family homes.

In one of our last attempts to find some anchor for our organization in East
Harlem real estate, I attended a town hall meeting to introduce one of
these new housing developments on 119th Street between Third and Second Avenues. I folded myself into the wooden theater seats of a public
school auditorium along with several hundred other neighbors to learn
how to apply for one of the new buildings. Most of those around me had
seen the block of new construction along 111th and 112th Streets where I
rented my one-bedroom apartment. Dozens of passersby had stopped me
over the years to ask about them, assuming I was the owner. We were all
eager to take advantage of something similar in the community.

As the presentation began, it was soon clear that this development
was going to be very different from La Esperanza Homes. Architec-
turally, the design was almost identical to Si Zhi's building, but the
unsubsidized cost was nearly triple. In five years the market had radically changed. According to the offering, the $30,000 lots would be sub-
sidized over twenty-five years, but a 5 percent down payment on the
$750,000 three-family home would be required. If the $37,500 down payment was not daunting, the prospect of charging hundreds of dollars

more in rent than other apartments in the area just to cover mortgage payments did not sit well with the audience. Some began to leave, shaking their heads in dismay. When challenged on the unseemly mortgage payments, the representatives of the development corporation suggested making a higher down payment, say, $100,000. There was audible laughter, and another wave of early departures.

The development, now complete and awaiting new tenants, is indicative of changes in East Harlem and changes in the way the city and private corporations are approaching urban renewal. Known as neoliberalism, it is a philosophy of privatization that applies market principles to social services, reducing government responsibility for social welfare.[16] But since the "market" in question, that is, the highly regulated sphere of social services, is never "free" or unencumbered, its effects are uneven at best. By offering a small subsidy on the cost of land, the development on 119th Street was already removed from the "free market" and able to artificially set the total cost of the three-family home at a fixed price of $750,000, well above the resources of local residents.[17] After initially offering the homes to local residents, as required, the offer could be extended to outsiders, effectively excluding those at the town hall meeting. Once the homes were occupied, high rents would also exclude local residents, creating another foothold for gentrification in the community and driving poorer tenants to the margins of East Harlem or out of the neighborhood altogether. Meanwhile, the city and private developers could promote another successful attempt to create "affordable" housing.

In 2003 I rented a car and carted the remains of our fledgling organization to a storage facility in Washington Heights. It was over. After four years it was clear that our little nonprofit could never buy into the escalating real estate market of East Harlem.

On my way home, I drove down Fifth Avenue, around Marcus Garvey Park, and over to Madison Avenue. A friend from downtown had recently purchased a three-bedroom apartment in a co-op on Madison Avenue and 117th Street, and he was excited to show me his new home. As I pulled to the curb in front of his building and stepped from the car, I realized I had not been to this section of the neighborhood in a couple of years. The last time, I stood on the same street wondering at the acres of rubble left by developers to make way for new construction. Now, townhouses and apartment buildings lined the streets, gleaming in the afternoon sun.

I stepped into the lobby of my friend's building, and a doorman called up to his apartment. A few minutes later I stood in his living room, looking out over Madison Avenue at the dozens of new homes built in the last two years, trying to remember what it was like when they were still open lots, never knowing what it was like when they were the tenements mostly housing African Americans.

My friend, an actor in his first role on a popular television series filmed in Los Angeles, only used the apartment during the summer. "Isn't it a great view?" he asked.

I agreed, and then it hit me—Lucille lived on this block. But her world was razed so I could stand in my friend's apartment and admire the view.

·   ·   ·   ·   ·

Mohamed has arrived at my party, wading through the debris of the 116th Street Festival to reach my front gate. For a few more hours revelers will own the streets, corralled between pale blue police barricades and stoic officers but jubilant nonetheless. By morning the sidewalks will be empty of the vendors and their booths and the streets will be swept clean. The neighborhood will be eerily empty for a Sunday as thousands gather on Fifth Avenue for the Puerto Rican Day Parade.

Philippe Bourgois has stopped by as well, and as the sun begins to set behind Johnson Houses to the west, he plays jump rope with a little girl from the neighborhood. Philippe is passing through East Harlem nearly ten years after the crack epidemic described in his book has given way to upscale restaurants and moderate-income housing developments. East Harlem's total population actually increased during the 1990s for the first time since the 1970s, and medium household income, though still low, increased by 10 percent between 1990 and 2000, to $22,110.[18]

Indeed, the East Harlem of the preceding pages stands in stark contrast to the East Harlem of Bourgois's *In Search of Respect*. Two books in ten years by two anthropologists offering two different narratives of the same community. A lot can happen in a decade, but perhaps there is more at work here than time. Perhaps it is the same parallax effect that makes Pete's East Harlem different from José's or Lucille's, or that of any of the newer tenants of the previous few chapters. Bourgois claimed he was forced into crack against his will; that is, his attempt to study a generalized informal economy became an ethnography of drug dealing as it unfolded on his doorstep (not far from my own). All the while, Pete, José, Lucille, Mohamed, Si Zhi, and tens of thousands of other residents went to work, cared for their families, attended festivals, churches, and mosques.[19] I suppose, like Bourgois, I was forced into their lives by living beside them.

I met Mohamed early on; his store is around the corner. Maria cuts hair nearby; she's cut mine since I moved here. Most of the individuals who populate this book are part of the block-based micro-community that surrounds my building. As if there were an informal zoning ordinance, every few blocks there seems to be a supermarket, a vegetable stand, a 99-cent store, a hair salon, a liquor store, and at least two bodegas. As I engaged in their lives, in the lives of my neighbors, it became apparent that the changes I was witnessing in East Harlem affected everyone. And not just in the real estate market but in demographics as well. It was a change that implicated Cheryl and me in a way I could not ignore professionally or personally.

According to the 2000 census, non-Hispanic whites in East Harlem increased by 20 percent, to just over 8,300, between 1990 and 2000. In a population of more than 100,000 it is a small percentage, but halfway through the next decade it is showing every sign of increasing rapidly. Once a statistical anomaly, we are no longer the only white people exiting the subway at 110th Street. Reluctant to recognize a verifiable trend, we find ourselves avoiding eye contact with those who look like us.

If real estate developers can erase the history of East Harlem simply by changing its name, could the recent arrival of white tenants mark the beginning of a final migration that would end two centuries of ethnic succession?

Mohamed is already thinking about the implications of a new white influx. "I have a lot of white friends in the neighborhood," he explains.

"They are moving up here, and if I am here in the next five years, I will definitely have to change the type of merchandise that I put in my store." Mohamed argues that nonwhites expect low-cost goods, regardless of quality, forcing him to stock merchandise he himself would never use. "A lot of Caucasians don't buy this type of merchandise," he continues, "so if Caucasians start moving up here, I think I have to stock nice stuff. It's not the money that matters, they want good quality."

José, who lives behind us, has also noticed the neighborhood changing. He predicts it won't be long until 106th Street is indistinguishable from 86th Street, though for José this trend is not necessarily an ominous one. When Cheryl and I first moved to East Harlem and discussed our ideas, particularly in regard to how outsiders would be received in the neighborhood, José argued, "The only people who will have a problem with you being white is you."

For a community that has always been more diverse than its various ethnic blocs might have preferred or acknowledged, the perennial demographic changes are certainly not new, and neither is the resistance to those changes. Though more frequent sightings of whites on the streets of the neighborhood herald a new, perhaps more affluent population, the arrival of middle-class and wealthier tenants is not characterized by any one phenotype. As with the return of middle-class African American residents to Central Harlem, one of the most publicized aspects of East Harlem's gentrification is its ability to attract successful third- and fourth-generation Puerto Ricans back to the heart of Spanish Harlem.[20] José finds these changes exciting, especially in regard to local politics. As he says, "It will be an interesting dynamic seeing more people, more affluent and middle-class people mix in at the activist level. Actually, it might help our group, 'cause they tend to do things better, they're more efficient. It might help lift that political awareness."

Like most changes in East Harlem, time will tell. Germans feared the influx of Italians, Italians the influx of Puerto Ricans, and Puerto Ricans the influx of Mexicans—and all with good reason. But as newcomers have changed the dynamic of the neighborhood, so, too, have changes in the neighborhood changed the composition of newcomers. Public housing uprooted Italians and drew in African Americans, disinvestment displaced Puerto Ricans and attracted Mexicans, and gentrification now draws a new middle class of whites, Puerto Ricans, and blacks. The people transform the streets, and the streets transform the people.

.   .   .   .   .

It is dark now, and most of the guests have gone. I am sitting out front watching groups of festival-goers drift away from Third Avenue, heading home. Si Zhi appears at his doorway at the top of the stairs, and without a word I gather up a plate of food I prepared for him.

"Oh, thank you very much," he responds. We meet halfway up his front steps, and he takes my offering with a little nod and a broad smile. "You are a very good tenant. A very good friend."

I thank Si Zhi for his kindness and watch him step back inside his home. He never did join the party, and I still do not know why. The answer is probably more complex than I can know. The English language is still a bit of a struggle for him, and perhaps the variety of guests I so relish seems incongruous and impossible to navigate for him. Perhaps it is the incongruity of my own social position that seems daunting.

Whatever the reason, it is clear that my attempts to engage in the lives of my neighbors will not always succeed. To some, I will always be either the Boss Man or the Asshole; to others, I will be known only by a single thread of connection, a shared faith, a common backyard, or the nearest bodega. But I suspect my experience is not peculiar to my whiteness, just as the experiences of Pete, José, Lucille, Maria, Mohamed, and Si Zhi are not peculiar to their respective ethnic identities. Each one of us feels in and out of place as we move through the streets of our neighborhood and the lives of our neighbors. Each one of us bears the burden of a collective, unchosen history—the Italians, the Puerto Ricans, the African Americans, the Mexicans, the West Africans, the Chinese, the whites— competing with our own individual choices, our own individual stories.

For generations, East Harlem has played host to our stories, carving them into the concrete fabric like notches in a tree. I think I first realized this some years ago, while standing on the corner of 115th Street and First Avenue on a warm July evening. Our organization was in its death throes, a difficult, demoralizing time, and I needed a break. Walking through the maze of tenements and housing projects, bodegas and liquor stores, I stumbled upon the garish lights of a street fair and an overweight Italian crooner singing Sinatra on the back of a flatbed truck.

The Feast of Our Lady of Mt. Carmel was in full swing around Pleasant Avenue, with carnival rides lining the streets, vendors hawking Italian sausage, pizza, espresso, and cotton candy. In the midst of the chaos, lost somewhere in the darkness of night, a few hundred Haitians trailed slowly behind a statue of Our Lady as it wound through the streets of East Harlem's east side. But back on 115th Street, it was all a jubilant riot—the Italians had come home, at least for a weekend.

The halfhearted rendition of "New York, New York" came to a close, and the singer began snapping his fingers to the first few bars of the next song. It was "Rose in Spanish Harlem," an anthem for the neighborhood since its first recording in the early 1960s by Ben E. King. I scanned the small crowd that had gathered around the makeshift stage. There were Italians to be sure, but there were also Puerto Ricans, Mexicans, African Americans, Asians, and me—all lost in the lyrics about a rose struggling to take root in the cracked pavement of East Harlem.

And as I watched the crowd, it occurred to me that each of us, all of us, sang the words as if it were *our* song. And always would be.

Notes

PREFACE

1.   This is by no means an exhaustive list. Attentive readers will note various threads running through each chapter, including discussions of public housing, the urban public education system, immigration policy, and the informal economy. My hope is that, especially in a classroom setting, these threads can be used to great effect.

2.   Plato, *The Republic,* trans. F. M. Cornford (Oxford: Oxford University Press, 1941), p. 321.

3.   At least as early as Franz Boas and his approach to exhaustive data collection, the life history has proven a powerful if problematic contribution to ethnographic method. This was especially true of fieldwork among North American Indians, such as Leo Simmons, *Sun Chief: The Autobiography of a Hopi Indian* (New Haven, CT: Yale University Press, 1942). Other well-known examples of life history are Sidney Mintz, *Worker in the Cane: A Puerto Rican Life History* (New

York: Norton, 1974); and Ruth Behar, *Translated Woman: Crossing the Border with Esperanza's Story* (Boston: Beacon Press, 1993). Contemporary scholars are also finding innovative ways to use life histories in analysis; see, for example, Henry Delcore, "Development and the Life Story of a Thai Farmer Leader," *Ethnology* 43, no. 1 (2004): 33–50; and Vieda Skultans, "Arguing with the KGB Archives: Archival and Narrative Memory in Post-Soviet Latvia," *Ethnos* 66, no. 3 (2001): 320–43.

4. There are at least as many critiques of the life history method as there are examples of its use. For a discussion of the relationship between investigator and subject in the recording and writing of life histories, see Geyla Frank, "Finding the Common Denominator: A Phenomenological Critique of Life History Method," *Ethos* 7, no. 1 (1979): 68–94; Vincent Crapanzano, "The Life History in Anthropological Field Work," *Anthropology and Humanism Quarterly* 2, nos. 2–3 (1977): 3–7; and Behar, *Translated Woman.*

5. Matti Bunzl, "Boas, Foucault, and the 'Native Anthropologist': Notes toward a New-Boasian Anthropology," *American Anthropologist* 106, no. 3 (2004): 441.

6. Lila Abu-Lughod, "Writing against Culture," in *Recapturing Anthropology: Working in the Present,* ed. Richard Fox (Santa Fe, NM: School of American Research Press, 1991), pp. 137–61. See also Martin Sokefeld, "Debating Self, Identity, and Culture in Anthropology," *Current Anthropology* 40, no. 4 (1999): 417–77: "This entity—culture—is only our construction from countless encounters, dialogues, and interactions with actual selves or individuals" (p. 431).

7. Mintz, *Worker in the Cane,* p. ix.

CHAPTER 1

1. "Pete," "Lucille," and "Maria" are pseudonyms, and some identifying characteristics of their living and working locations have been changed.

2. See note 1.

3. See note 1.

4. See Jane Jacobs, *The Death and Life of Great American Cities* (New York: Random House, 1961).

5. Nancy Foner, *From Ellis Island to JFK: New York's Two Great Waves of Immigration* (New Haven, CT: Yale University Press, 2000).

6. Robert Orsi, *The Madonna of 115th Street: Faith and Community in Italian Harlem, 1880–1950* (New Haven, CT: Yale University Press, 2002).

7. Dan Wakefield, *Island in the City* (Boston: Houghton Mifflin, 1957); Philippe Bourgois, *In Search of Respect: Selling Crack in El Barrio* (Cambridge: Cambridge University Press, 1995).

8. Ronald Fernandez, *The Disenchanted Island* (Westport, CT: Praeger, 1996).

9. Clara Rodríguez, *Puerto Ricans: Born in the USA* (New York: Routledge, 1990).

10. According to U.S. Census reports, the number of Puerto Ricans in East Harlem declined from 42,013 to 34,673 between 1990 and 2000. During the same period, the number of non-Hispanic black residents of East Harlem increased from 29,843 to 36,134.

11. Robert C. Smith, "Mexicans: Social, Educational, Economic, and Political Problems and Prospects in New York," in *New Immigrants in New York*, ed. Nancy Foner (New York: Columbia University Press, 2001), pp. 275–300.

12. Paul Stoller, *Money Has No Smell* (Chicago: University of Chicago Press, 2002).

13. Min Zhou, "Chinese: Divergent Destinies in Immigrant New York," in Foner, ed., *New Immigrants in New York*, pp. 141–72.

14. Bourgois, *In Search of Respect.*

CHAPTER 2

1. Nancy Foner, *From Ellis Island to JFK: New York's Two Great Waves of Immigration* (New Haven, CT: Yale University Press, 2000), p. 10.

2. See, Foner, *From Ellis Island to JFK;* and Thomas Kessner, *The Golden Door: Italian and Jewish Immigrant Mobility in New York City, 1880–1915* (New York: Oxford University Press, 1977).

3. Philippe Bourgois, *In Search of Respect: Selling Crack in El Barrio* (Cambridge: Cambridge University Press, 1995), p. 57.

4. It is important to note that much of the quota system was directed at Europe. The Chinese Exclusion Act already barred ethnic Chinese immigrants, and similar exceptions applied to Japanese and other non-European nationalities (see chap. 7). Ironically, given discussion to follow in chapter 5, the Western Hemisphere, that is, Latin America, was not included in the quota system because the United States desperately needed Mexican agricultural labor at the time. See Roger Daniels, *Guarding the Golden Door* (New York: Hill and Wang, 2004); and Foner, *From Ellis Island to JFK.*

5. Robert Orsi, *The Madonna of 115th Street: Faith and Community in Italian Harlem, 1880–1950* (New Haven, CT: Yale University Press, 2002), p. 29.

6. For a detailed examination of the history of New York City housing, see Richard Plunz, *A History of Housing in New York City: Dwelling Type and Social Change in the American Metropolis* (New York: Columbia University Press, 1990). See also Ronald Lawson, ed., *The Tenant Movement in New York City, 1904–1984* (New Brunswick, NJ: Rutgers University Press, 1986).

7. Orsi, *The Madonna of 115th Street*, p. 21; Foner, *From Ellis Island to JFK*, p. 121.

8. See Leonard Covello, *The Heart Is the Teacher* (New York: McGraw-Hill, 1958), pp. 188–89, 237–43, for another firsthand account of Italian Harlem's unfounded reputation.

9. Covello, *The Heart Is the Teacher,* p. 181.

10. Christopher Gray, "A Library Branch That Wasn't Designed by the Book," *New York Times,* June 9, 1996, p. R7.

11. Jeffery Gurock, *When Harlem Was Jewish, 1870–1930* (New York: Columbia University Press, 1979), p. 182n23.

12. Gurock, *When Harlem Was Jewish,* pp. 145–46.

13. Plunz, *A History of Housing in New York City,* p. 227.

14. Covello, *The Heart Is the Teacher,* p. 206.

15. Covello, *The Heart Is the Teacher,* p. 220.

16. See Jacobs, *The Death and Life of Great American Cities;* and Plunz, *A History of Housing in New York City.*

17. See Rosalie Genevro, "Site Selection and the New York City Housing Authority, 1934–1939," *Journal of Urban History* 12, no. 4 (1986): 334–52.

18. Jacobs, *The Death and Life of Great American Cities,* p. 4.

19. Oscar Newman, *Defensible Space: Crime Prevention through Urban Design* (New York: Macmillan, 1972).

20. Plunz, *A History of Housing in New York City,* p. 245. See also Peter Marcuse, "The Beginnings of Public Housing in New York," *Journal of Urban History* 12, no. 4 (1986): 353–90; and Genevro, "Site Selection and the New York City Housing Authority."

21. Wayne Barrett, "Dark Angels of a Bogus Catholic Museum," *Village Voice,* June 19, 2001, p. 47.

22. James Dao, "Anthony (Fat Tony) Salerno, 80, a Top Crime Boss, Dies in Prison," *New York Times,* July 29, 1992, p. D19.

23. "FBI Expects New Mob Indictments," *The Record* (Bergen County), February 20, 1986, p. C37.

24. Al Baker and Linda Stasi, "Landmark East Harlem Eatery Torched," *New York Daily News,* June 6, 1995, p. 10; "Man Is Shot to Death," *New York Times,* December 23, 2003, p. B2; Alex Witchel, "A Table at Rao's? Forgetaboutit," *New York Times,* February 14, 1996, p. C1.

25. Covello, *The Heart Is the Teacher,* p. 46.

26. Orsi, *The Madonna of 115th Street.*

CHAPTER 3

1. The estimates of Puerto Rican settlement on the mainland, especially in the first half of the twentieth century, are a source of constant controversy. Accusations of undercounting, or outright noncounting, including admissions from

the U.S. Census Bureau itself, have helped to obscure a clear statistical picture of Puerto Rican migration to New York City. This is especially true of East Harlem, where the figures given for the mid-1950s (based on Francesco Cordasco and Rocco Galatioto, "Ethnic Displacement in the Interstitial Community: The East Harlem [New York City] Experience," in *The Puerto Rican Experience,* ed. Francesco Cordasco and Eugene Bucchioni [Totowa, NJ: Rowman and Littlefield, 1973], pp. 171–85) seem improbably low and no doubt result from statistical confusion over the racial, ethnic, and national status of Puerto Ricans at the time. The only clear consensus seems to be that migration before the Jones Act of 1917 was statistically insignificant, spiked through the 1920s, tapered in the 1930s during the Great Depression, and hit all-time highs in the 1940s and 1950s. For a sample of various estimates, see Lawrence Chenault, *The Puerto Rican Migrant in New York City* (New York: Columbia University Press, 1938); Kal Wagenhaim, *A Survey of Puerto Ricans on the U.S. Mainland in the 1970s* (New York: Praeger, 1975); and Virginia Sánchez-Korrol, *From Colonia to Community: The History of Puerto Ricans in New York City, 1917–1948* (Westport, CT: Greenwood Press, 1983).

2. Sánchez-Korrol, *From Colonia to Community.*

3. U.S. military service had been part of the Puerto Rican experience since the same Jones Act that conferred citizenship in 1917 made military service compulsory for Puerto Rican men.

4. Practitioners themselves reject the label "Santería" as it literally means the worship of saints, a reductive, Eurocentric view of their beliefs. For a compelling critique of scholarship regarding Afro-Cuban religion as well as Puerto Rican spiritualism, see Andrés Isidoro Pérez y Mena, *Speaking with the Dead* (New York: AMS Press, 1991); and Andrés Isidoro Pérez y Mena, "Cuban Santería, Haitian Vodun, Puerto Rican Spiritualism: A Multiculturalist Inquiry into Syncretism," *Journal for the Scientific Study of Religion* 37, no. 1 (1998): 15–27. See also Steven Gregory's account, *Santería in New York City* (New York: Garland, 1999).

5. These phenomena, known respectively as *mestizaje* and *blanqueamiento* by many scholars, appear throughout Latin America. For further discussion of race in Latin America and the Caribbean, see Peter Wade, *Race and Ethnicity in Latin America* (London: Pluto Press, 1997); and Norman Whitten and Arlene Torres, *Blackness in Latin America and the Caribbean,* 2 vols. (Bloomington: Indiana University Press, 1998). For a discussion of Puerto Ricans in particular, see Clara Rodríguez, "Puerto Ricans: Between Black and White," in *Historical Perspectives on Puerto Rican Survival in the United States,* ed. Clara Rodríguez and Virginia Sánchez-Korrol (Princeton, NJ: Markus Wiener, 1996), pp. 25–35; Juan Flores, *From Bomba to Hip Hop: Puerto Rican Culture and Latino Identity* (New York: Columbia University Press, 2000); Clara Rodríguez, *Puerto Ricans: Born in the USA;* and Arlene Dávila, *Sponsored Identities: Cultural Politics in Puerto Rico* (Philadelphia: Temple University Press, 1997).

6. Piri Thomas, *Down These Mean Streets* (New York: Random House, 1967), p. 156. "Paddy" refers to whites.

7. http://www.east-harlem.com.

8. Thomas W. Ennis, "Harlem Changed by Public Housing," *New York Times,* June 23, 1957, p. 225.

9. Dan Wakefield, *Island in the City* (Boston: Houghton Mifflin, 1957), p. 235.

10. Charles Grutzner, "City Housing Unit Bars Race Quota," *New York Times,* July 5, 1959, p. 27.

11. Alexander Feinberg, "Gains in Harlem Cited by Wagner," *New York Times,* October 26, 1957, p. 11.

12. Grutzner, "City Housing Unit Bars Race Quota."

13. Grutzner, "City Housing Unit Bars Race Quota."

14. Grutzner, "City Housing Unit Bars Race Quota."

15. "Bias Laid to City in Tenant Choice," *New York Times,* July 4, 1960, p. 1.

16. Patricia Cayo Sexton, *Spanish Harlem: An Anatomy of Poverty* (New York: Harper and Row, 1965), pp. 9, 23, 24, 35.

17. Interestingly, the Spanish Methodist Church was built on the site of one of the last synagogues in East Harlem. José can still remember the day the old temple burned to the ground: "When I was five, I remember coming up the stairs of the subway on 110th Street and there was smoke everywhere. I think it was their way of getting the congregation's money back. Everyone moved out, and well, you know, you get the insurance money." There is no evidence of any fraud, just the inevitable deterioration of unused space in so crowded a community. And like the library, the market, and the streets themselves, the mark of old tenants was replaced by the new: from the ashes of that synagogue rose the Spanish Methodist Church.

18. Joseph P. Fried, "East Harlem Youths Explain Garbage-Dumping Demonstration," *New York Times,* August 19, 1969, p. 86.

19. Michael T. Kaufman, "Puerto Rican Group Seizes Church in East Harlem in Demand for Space," *New York Times,* December 29, 1969, p. 26; Michael T. Kaufman, "105 Members of Young Lords Submit to Arrest," *New York Times,* January 8, 1970, p. 28.

20. Michael T. Kaufman, "200 Armed Young Lords Seize Church after Taking Body There," *New York Times,* October 19, 1970, p. 26; "Young Lords Start to Evacuate Church," *New York Times,* December 10, 1970, p. 36.

21. Francis X. Clines, "About New York," *New York Times,* May 25, 1978, p. B9.

22. For a detailed historical analysis of decentralization in New York City politics, see Robert Pecorella, *Community Power in a Postreform City* (Armonk, NY: M. E. Sharpe, 1994). Roger Sanjek, *The Future of Us All: Race and Neighborhood Pol-*

itics in New York City (Ithaca, NY: Cornell University Press, 1998), also offers important insights into the effects of these changes at the local level.

23. For more information on political organizations in East Harlem during this time, see Monte Rivera, "Organizational Politics of the East Harlem Barrio in the 1970s," in *Puerto Rican Politics in Urban America,* ed. James Jennings and Monte Rivera (Westport, CT: Greenwood Press, 1984), pp. 61–72.

24. Sanjek, *The Future of Us All,* p. 85.

25. Philippe Bourgois, *In Search of Respect: Selling Crack in El Barrio* (Cambridge: Cambridge University Press, 1995), p. 138.

26. Sanjek, *The Future of Us All,* p. 85.

27. See Bourgois, *In Search of Respect,* for a stunning account of infrastructural breakdown and the cultural politics of crack dealing in East Harlem during this time.

28. For the years between 1993 and 2002, both the Twenty-fifth and Twenty-third Precincts, which include all of East Harlem, reported decreases of 64 and 58 percent respectively in reported crimes (murder, rape, robbery, assault, larceny, and grand larceny). Many credit the New York City Police Department (NYPD) under the Giuliani administration for quelling the violence that most residents still talk about, though it should be noted that these statistics are based solely on data provided by the NYPD and do not include unreported criminal activity.

29. For more detailed accounts of the transformation of El Museo del Barrio, see Arlene Dávila, "Latinizing Culture: Art, Museums, and the Politics of U.S. Multicultural Encompassment," *Cultural Anthropology* 14, no. 2 (1999): 180–202; Russell Leigh Sharman, "Duke versus Tito: Aesthetic Conflict in East Harlem, NY," *Visual Anthropology Review* 18, nos. 1–2 (2001): 3–21; or Mireya Navarro, "El Museo Is Thinking Outside the Barrio," *New York Times,* November 8, 2002, p. B1.

30. See Sharman, "Duke versus Tito."

CHAPTER 4

1. See Gilbert Osofsky, *Harlem: The Making of a Ghetto* (New York: Harper and Row, 1963).

2. Quoted in Jervis Anderson, *This Was Harlem: A Cultural Portrait, 1900–1950* (New York: Farrar, Straus and Giroux, 1981), pp. 61–62. Anderson adds: "In other words, Harlem would be almost any place uptown, above 110th Street, where there were noticeable concentrations of Blacks" (p. 61).

3. These statistics come from Patricia Cayo Sexton, *Spanish Harlem: An Anatomy of Poverty* (New York: Harper and Row, 1965), p. 9, and like many of the statistics specific to East Harlem, especially before the 1990 census, they are diffi-

cult to verify. However, these demographic snapshots give us some idea of what life was like on the street for Pete, José, and Lucille during the mid-twentieth century.

4.   Jane Jacobs, *The Death and Life of Great American Cities* (New York: Random House, 1961), p. 72.

5.   See Diane Ravitch, *The Great School Wars: New York City, 1805–1973* (New York: Basic Books, 1974), p. 251.

6.   See Ravitch, *The Great School Wars*, p. 259; see also Steven Gregory, *Black Corona: Race and the Politics of Place in an Urban Community* (Princeton, NJ: Princeton University Press, 1998), p. 75.

7.   Leonard Buder, "5 Yorkville Schools Welcome 340 Harlem Transfer Pupils," *New York Times*, February 2, 1960, p. 37.

8.   See Ravitch, *The Great School Wars*, p. 261.

9.   See Ravitch, *The Great School Wars*, p. 276.

10.   Leonard Buder, "P.S. 6 Rezoning Stirs East Side," *New York Times*, May 9, 1960, p. 31; Leonard Buder, "Shifts in Schools Set on East Side," *New York Times*, June 10, 1960, p. 32.

11.   See Ravitch, *The Great School Wars*, p. 262.

12.   Julia Richman High School is in many ways an object lesson in the convoluted history of New York City public education. Founded in 1913 to relieve pressure on Manhattan high schools, Julia Richman was a scattered-site school, housing three thousand students in six separate buildings throughout the borough. In 1917 students began a campaign that filled the mailboxes of politicians, women's club members, doctors, lawyers, and a host of other prominent citizens with thirty thousand letters demanding a new building. Finally, in 1924, a new building was dedicated on Manhattan's Upper East Side by the mayor himself. By the 1950s and 1960s Richman was the school of choice for many young women in East Harlem. After zoning laws were changed to allow for school choice, a stopgap measure in the face of demands for desegregation, parents and children entered a kind of free market for public schools. By the 1990s the school had become a large, overcrowded, coeducational complex, emblematic of the deteriorating public school system. The solution: divide the building into six small schools. Eighty years after three thousand schoolchildren lobbied for their six buildings to be housed together, their one building was split apart into six separate schools and held up as a national model for educational innovation. See "Schools Open with 850,000 Attending," *New York Times*, September 9, 1913, p. 5; "Write for a High School," *New York Times*, February 11, 1917, p. 11; "Hylan Lauds Smith for Aiding Schools," *New York Times*, October 2, 1924, p. 13; and Michael Winerip, "Students Pass but Schools Fail?" *New York Times*, January 21, 2004, p. B11.

13.   "32-Story Building with over 300 Units Dedicated in Harlem," *New York Times*, December 5, 1974, p. 93.

14.   See John Goering, Maynard Robinson, and Knight Hoover, *The Best Eight Blocks in Harlem: The Last Decade of Urban Reform* (Washington, DC: University Press of America, 1977).

15.   Charlayne Hunter, "Women's Self-Help Plan Is Working in East Harlem," *New York Times,* July 5, 1970, p. 38.

16.   Charlayne Hunter, "Mutual Effort Produces Harlem Housing," *New York Times,* May 28, 1972, p. 34.

17.   Goering, Robinson, and Hoover, *The Best Eight Blocks in Harlem.*

18.   See Richard Plunz, *A History of Housing in New York City: Dwelling Type and Social Change in the Metropolis* (New York: Columbia University Press, 1990). See also Ronald Lawson, ed., *The Tenant Movement in New York City, 1904–1984* (New Brunswick, NJ: Rutgers University Press, 1986).

19.   For an insightful critique of this same phenomenon in Chicago, see Sudhir Alladi Venkatesh, *American Project: The Rise and Fall of a Modern Ghetto* (Cambridge, MA: Harvard University Press, 2000).

20.   The most comprehensive description and analysis of the crack cocaine phenomenon can be found in Philippe Bourgois, *In Search of Respect: Selling Crack in El Barrio* (Cambridge: Cambridge University Press, 1995). His ethnographic investigation of the drug trade in East Harlem during the 1980s and 1990s pays particular attention to the intersection of 110th Street and Lexington Avenue.

21.   Federal spending on subsidized housing programs dropped from $31 billion in 1981 to $8 billion in 1988. In the first two years of Reagan's administration, federal aid to New York City fell 21 percent, public assistance to 1.1 million New Yorkers was reduced or eliminated, and rent increases affected public housing throughout the city. See Clyde Haberman, "Reality Check during a Time of Mourning," *New York Times,* June 8, 2004, p. B1.

CHAPTER 5

1.   According to the 1910 census, more than 96 percent of rural households in Mexico owned no land. By 1920 the annual number of Mexican migrants crossing the U.S. border had reached 68,000. Between 1920 and 1929 more than 600,000 Mexicans crossed the border into the United States. See James Cockcroft, *Mexico: Class Formation, Capital Accumulations and the State* (New York: Monthly Review Press, 1983); Jorge Durand, Douglas S. Massey, and René M. Zenteno, "Mexican Migration to the United States: Continuities and Changes," *Latin American Research Review* 36, no. 1 (2001): 107–27; Jorge Durand, Douglas S. Massey, and Fernando Charvet, "The Changing Geography of Mexican Immigration to the United States: 1910–1996," *Social Science Quarterly* 81, no. 1 (2000): 1–15.

2.   See Lynn Stephen, "Pro-Zapatista and Pro-PRI: Resolving the Contradic-

tions of Zapatismo in Rural Oaxaca," *Latin American Research Review* 32, no. 1 (2001): 41–70.

3.   Samuel Brunk, "Remembering Emiliano Zapata: Three Moments in the Posthumous Career of the Martyr of Chinameca," *Hispanic American Historical Review* 78, no. 3 (1998): 457–90.

4.   John Ross, "The Zapatistas at Ten," *North American Congress on Latin America* 37, no. 3 (2003): 11–15.

5.   For a fascinating discussion of how the Mexican government, under the leadership of President Salinas de Gortari, enacted these changes using the very same legacy of Zapata that Zapatistas would use to combat their implementation, see Stephen, "Pro-Zapatista and Pro-PRI."

6.   Wayne Cornelius, "Death at the Border: The Efficacy and Unintended Consequences of U.S. Immigration Control Policy," *Population and Development Review* 27, no. 4 (2001): 661–85.

7.   Miriam Davidson, *Lives on the Line: Dispatches from the U.S.-Mexico Border* (Tucson: University of Arizona Press, 2000), p. 10. See also Lawrence Taylor and Maeve Hickey, *Tunnel Kids* (Tucson: University of Arizona Press, 2001).

8.   Davidson, *Lives on the Line,* p. 10.

9.   Kathryn Kopinak, "Household, Gender and Migration in Mexican Maquiladoras: The Case of Nogales," in *International Migration, Refugee Flows and Human Rights in North America: The Impact of Trade and Restructuring,* ed. Alan B. Simmons (New York: Center for Migration Studies, 1996), pp. 214–28.

10.   One of the most tragic implications of this phenomenon was the epidemic of unsolved murders in Ciudad Juárez during the 1990s. An estimated 258 women were raped, murdered, and left by the side of the road between 1993 and 2003. See Davidson, *Lives on the Line,* p. 39; and "258 Killed in Border City," *New York Times,* May 22, 2003, p. A4.

11.   Kopinak's study found that only 1 percent of her respondents, all of whom worked in the maquiladoras, claimed they had come to Nogales in order to cross into the United States. Kopinak, "Household, Gender and Migration in Mexican Maquiladoras," p. 223.

12.   This turnstile effect at the U.S.-Mexico border has long antagonized U.S. attempts to control unauthorized immigration. Advocates of amnesty argue that more open borders would actually reduce the total number of migrants, not to mention the mortality rate of those attempting to cross in isolated areas, by allowing for the cyclical nature of labor migration. Indeed, research indicates that tighter border controls result in longer periods of undocumented residency. Durand and colleagues note that the two periods of highest return migration in the past half century occurred immediately after "massive waves of legalization": "The shift of large segments of the Mexican migratory workforce from undocumented to documented status ironically facilitates circulation back and

forth across the border. Paradoxically, granting a visa for 'permanent residence' makes it easier and less costly for a migrant to return home" (Durand, Massey, and Zenteno, "Mexican Migration to the United States," p. 122).

13.   See Joseph Nevins, *Operation Gatekeeper: The Rise of the 'Illegal Alien' and the Making of the U.S.-Mexico Boundary* (New York: Routledge, 2002).

14.   See Durand, Massey, and Zenteno, "Mexican Migration to the United States." See also Katherine M. Donato, "U.S. Policy and Mexican Migration to the United States, 1942–1992," *Social Science Quarterly* 75, no. 4 (1994): 705–29.

15.   Kevin R. Johnson, "The Continuing Latino Quest for Full Membership and Equal Citizenship: Legal Progress, Social Setbacks, and Political Promise," in *The Columbia History of Latinos in the U.S. since 1960,* ed. David G. Gutiérrez (New York: Columbia University Press, 2004), pp. 391–420.

16.   The effects of the 1986 Immigration Act, the IRCA, were short-lived. According to one study: "While IRCA temporarily changed the stock of undocumented migrants through the legalization program, in the long run it did not change the basic dynamic of undocumented migration to the United States. By the 1990s, migration flows had returned to their pre-IRCA levels" (Karl Eschbach, Jacqueline Hagan, and Néstor Rodríguez, "Deaths during Undocumented Migration: Trends and Policy Implications in the New Era of Homeland Security," paper presented at the 26th Annual National Legal Conference on Immigration and Refugee Policy, Washington, DC, April 2003, p. 3). For more detail on the militarization of the U.S.-Mexico border, see Timothy J. Dunn, *The Militarization of the U.S.-Mexico Border, 1978–1992: Low-Intensity Conflict Doctrine Comes Home* (Austin, TX: CMAS Books, 1996); and Tom Barry, *Crossing the Line: Immigrants, Economic Integration and Drug Enforcement on the U.S.-Mexico Border* (Albuquerque, NM: Resource Center Press, 1994).

17.   Karl Eschbach, Jacqueline Hagan, and Néstor Rodríguez, "Death at the Border," *International Migration Review* 33, no. 2 (1999): 430–54.

18.   U.S. Immigration and Naturalization Service, *Statistical Yearbook of the Immigration and Naturalization Service, 1997* (Washington, DC: Government Printing Office, 1999).

19.   Eschbach, Hagan, and Rodríguez, "Death at the Border."

20.   Rita J. Simon and Margo Corona DeLey, "Undocumented Mexican Women: Their Work and Personal Experiences," in *International Migration: The Female Experience,* ed. Rita J. Simon and Caroline B. Brettell (Totowa, NJ: Rowman and Allanheld, 1986), pp. 113–32.

21.   See Douglas S. Massey, "Why Does Immigration Occur? A Theoretical Synthesis," in *Handbook of International Migration: The American Experience,* ed. Charles Hirschman, Philip Kasinitz, and Josh DeWind (New York: Russell Sage Foundation, 1999), pp. 34–52. See also Michael Piore, *Birds of Passage: Migrant Labor and Industrial Societies* (Cambridge: Cambridge University Press, 1979).

22.   See Gordon H. Hanson, Raymond Robertson, and Antonio Spilimbergo, "Does Border Enforcement Protect U.S. Workers from Illegal Immigration?" *Review of Economics and Statistics* 84, no. 1 (2002): 73–92; and Frank D. Bean, B. Lindsay Lowell, and Lowell J. Taylor, "Undocumented Mexican Immigrants and the Earnings of Other Workers in the United States," *Demography* 25 (1988): 35–52.

23.   This was most clearly stated during a hearing before the U.S. House of Representatives Subcommittee on Immigration, Border Security, and Claims. During the hearing, Texas representative Lamar Smith used the following analogy to argue against "regularizing illegal immigration": "If, for example, you have a lot of people trying to break into your house . . . the answer isn't to open your doors and say, well, whoever wants to come in, come in or make it easier for people to do so. That is going to even lead to more dire consequences, for, in this case, the homeowner, or for the United States. . . . The other things [*sic*] that I have also heard some people say, that somehow this is the United States's [*sic*] fault because we are a prosperous country and have jobs for people. . . . Well, again the analogy to me is like a homeowner who might have some nice possessions in his house, he might have a big screen TV, he might have some jewelry. And, if is [*sic*] someone is trying to break into that house, I don't consider that to be the fault of the home-owner with the nice things in his house. I think you still need to prevent people from taking illegal actions and protect the people who have a right to live under the laws of their country" (Subcommittee on Immigration, Border Security, and Claims, House of Representatives, 108th Cong., *Deadly Consequences of Illegal Alien Smuggling* [Washington, DC: Government Printing Office, June 24, 2003], p. 10).

24.   Robert Suro, "Remittance Senders and Receivers: Tracking the Transnational Channels," report prepared by the Pew Hispanic Center, Washington, DC, November 24, 2003.

25.   David G. Gutiérrez, "Demography and the Shifting Boundaries of 'Community': Reflections on 'U.S. Latinos' and the Evolution of Latino Studies," in Gutiérrez, ed., *The Columbia History of Latinos in the U.S. since 1960*, pp. 1–42.

26.   U.S. Immigration and Naturalization Service, *Statistical Yearbook of the Immigration and Naturalization Service, 2002* (Washington, DC: Government Printing Office, 2003).

27.   Smith, "Mexicans," pp. 275–300. According to the U.S. Census, New York City alone counted just under 62,000 Mexicans in 1990 and just over 186,000 in 2000.

28.   See Jane H. Lii, "Mexico Blooms in a 116th Street Barrio," *New York Times*, June 1, 1997, p. CY6; and Nina Siegal, "Four Corners," *New York Times*, July 30, 2000, p. CY1.

29.   For a somewhat dated but still informative article on formal and informal marriages in Mexico and among Mexican nationals in the United States, see

Woodrow Borah and Sherburne F. Cook, "Marriage and Legitimacy in Mexican Culture: Mexico and California," *California Law Review* 54, no. 2 (1966): 946–1008.

30.   The unidentified body was one of more than three hundred annual fatalities among unauthorized migrants since 2001. The inevitable emphasis on border security that followed the terrorist attacks of September 11, 2001, caused a short-lived decrease in apprehension by the U.S. Border Patrol but did little to slow overall migration from Mexico in the long term. See Eschbach, Hagan, and Rodríguez, "Deaths during Undocumented Migration." See also Jim Yardley, "Mexicans' Bids to Enter U.S. Rebound to Pre-9/11 Levels," *New York Times,* November 24, 2002, pp. 1, 24; and Evelyn Nieves, "Illegal Immigrant Death Rate Rises Sharply in Barren Areas," *New York Times,* August 6, 2002, p. A1.

31.   See Nancy Foner, *From Ellis Island to JFK: New York's Two Great Waves of Immigration* (New Haven, CT: Yale University Press, 2000); and Michael Piore, *Birds of Passage: Migrant Labor and Industrial Societies* (Cambridge: Cambridge University Press, 1979).

32.   See Nancy Foner, "Transnationalism Then and Now: New York Immigrants Today and at the Turn of the Twentieth Century," in *Migration, Transnationalization, and Race in a Changing New York,* ed. Héctor R. Cordero-Guzmán, Robert C. Smith, and Ramón Grosfoguel (Philadelphia: Temple University Press, 2001), pp. 35–57. See also Nina Glick Schiller, "Transmigrants and Nation-States: Something Old and Something New in the U.S. Immigrant Experience," in Hirschman, Kasinitz, and DeWind, eds., *Handbook of International Migration.*

33.   "It is the Lord that accompanies us on the way, with his tenderness always at our side. If dangers lie in wait for us everywhere, our friend Jesus will save us" (my translation).

34.   Mireya Navarro, "Multiple Shrines to Patron Saints Testify to a Rivalry of the Devout," *New York Times,* May 29, 2002, p. B1.

35.   See Alan Feuer, "Mexicans and Puerto Ricans Quarrel in East Harlem," *New York Times,* September 6, 2003, p. B1.

36.   See Smith, "Mexicans." For more insight into immigrant youth gang formation, see James Diego Vigil, *A Rainbow of Gangs: Street Cultures in the Mega-City* (Austin: University of Texas Press, 2002); and Tony Waters, *Immigration and Crime* (Thousand Oaks, CA: Sage, 1999).

CHAPTER 6

1.   See H. L. Wesseling, *Divide and Rule: The Partition of Africa, 1880–1914,* trans. Arnold J. Pomerans (London: Praeger, 1996); and Thomas Pakenham, *The Scramble for Africa: The White Man's Conquest of the Dark Continent from 1876 to 1912* (New York: Random House, 1991).

2. Statistics are based on SIL International's *Ethnologue: Languages of the World,* 14th ed.: http://www.ethnologue.com.

3. Greg Campbell, *Blood Diamonds* (Boulder, CO: Westview Press, 2002).

4. J. Anyu Ndumbe, "Diamonds, Ethnicity and Power: The Case of Sierra Leone," *Mediterranean Quarterly* 12, no. 4 (2001): 90–105.

5. See Toma J. Makannah and Mohamed Bailey, "Sierra Leone," in *Urbanization in Africa: A Handbook,* ed. James D. Tarver (Westport, CT: Greenwood Press, 1994), pp. 298–314. See also Arthur Abraham, "Amistad Revolt: An Historical Legacy of Sierra Leone and the United States," in *Sierra Leone: Current Issues and Background,* ed. Brett Sillinger (New York: Nova Science Publishers, 2003), pp. 1–16; and Campbell, *Blood Diamonds.*

6. See Adekeye Adebajo, *Building Peace in West Africa: Liberia, Sierra Leone, and Guinea-Bissau* (London: Lynne Rienner, 2002). See also Ndumbe, "Diamonds, Ethnicity and Power."

7. Adebajo, *Building Peace in West Africa.*

8. There are many accounts of the atrocities in Sierra Leone during the 1990s, some of which are referenced above. Additional sources include Human Rights Watch, *We'll Kill You If You Cry: Sexual Violence in the Sierra Leone Conflict* (Washington, DC: Human Rights Watch, 2003); and Sillinger, ed., *Sierra Leone.*

9. Andrew Jacobs, " 'Walkers' Make a Tentative Stand," *New York Times,* November 10, 1999, p. B1.

10. New York City Department of City Planning, *The Newest New Yorkers, 1990–1994* (New York: Department of City Planning, 1996). See also Paul Stoller, "West Africans: Trading Places in New York," in *New Immigrants in New York,* ed. Nancy Foner (New York: Columbia University Press, 2001), pp. 229–50.

11. Adam Nossiter, "A Shabby Welcome Mat," *New York Times,* February 11, 1995, p. 21.

12. Paul Stoller, *Money Has No Smell* (Chicago: University of Chicago Press, 2002).

13. See Stoller, *Money Has No Smell;* and Stoller, "West Africans." See also Ronald Sullivan, "Crackdown on Vendors in the Streets," *New York Times,* April 13, 1993, p. B1; Emily Bernstein, "Rousting the Peddlers of 125th Street," *New York Times,* September 12, 1993, p. 779; Steven Lee Myers, "Mayor Reveals Plan to End Illegal Vendors in Harlem," *New York Times,* October 12, 1994, p. B3; Jonathan P. Hicks, "Police Move Street Vendors in Harlem," *New York Times,* October 18, 1994, p. B1.

14. Roger Waldinger, Howard Aldrich, Robin Ward, and Associates, *Ethnic Entrepreneurs: Immigrant Business in Industrial Societies* (London: Sage, 1990).

15. See Waldinger et al., *Ethnic Entrepreneurs;* and Jan Rath, ed., *Immigrant Businesses* (New York: St. Martin's Press, 2000).

NOTES TO PAGES 152–168

16. Douglas Martin, "When $75 Holdup Equals Cabby's Life," *New York Times,* November 22, 1993, p. A1.

17. Rachel L. Swarns, "Hispanic Mothers Lagging as Others Leave Welfare," *New York Times,* September 15, 1998, p. A1.

18. Arlene Dávila, *Barrio Dreams: Puerto Ricans, Latinos, and the Neoliberal City* (Berkeley: University of California Press, 2004), p. 7.

19. Francis X. Clines, "Clinton Signs Bill Cutting Welfare; States in New Role," *New York Times,* August 23, 1996, p. A1.

20. Somini Sengupta, "State's Poorest Facing Loss of U.S. Aid," *New York Times,* February 10, 2001, p. B1. See also LynNell Hancock, *Hands to Work: The Stories of Three Families Racing the Welfare Clock* (New York: William Morrow, 2002); Nina Bernstein, "As Welfare Deadline Looms, Answers Don't Seem So Easy," *New York Times,* June 25, 2001, p. A1; Nina Bernstein, "Uncertainties Loom as New Yorkers Hit Welfare Time Limit," *New York Times,* November 30, 2001, p. A1.

21. Alan Finder, "Evidence Is Scant That Workfare Leads to Full-Time Jobs," *New York Times,* April 12, 1998, p. 1.

22. Joe Sexton, "Welfare Cuts Don't Dash the Optimism of Store Owners," *New York Times,* July 19, 1997, pp. 1, 21.

23. See Stoller, *Money Has No Smell.* See also Tina Kelley, "Police Seize Cache of Thousands of Counterfeit CD's and Videos," *New York Times,* February 20, 2002, p. B2; C. J. Chivers, "Bronx Man Is Accused of Running a Videocassette Counterfeiting Operation," *New York Times,* January 24, 2000, p. B3; Kit R. Roane, "Police Smash Piracy Ring for Videos, Arresting 43," *New York Times,* May 6, 1998, p. B4.

24. Carter B. Horsley, "Softening the Edge of East Harlem," *New York Times,* July 30, 1978, p. E6.

CHAPTER 7

1. John King Fairbank, *China: A New History* (Cambridge, MA: Harvard University Press, 1992); J. A. G. Roberts, *A Concise History of China* (Cambridge, MA: Harvard University Press, 1999).

2. Fairbank, *China;* Roberts, *A Concise History of China.* See also Feng Jical, *Voices from the Whirlwind: An Oral History of the Chinese Cultural Revolution* (New York: Pantheon Books, 1991); and for accounts specific to Shanghai, see Zi-Ping Luo, *A Generation Lost: China under the Cultural Revolution* (New York: Holt, 1990); and Nien Cheng, *Life and Death in Shanghai* (New York: Grove Press, 1986).

3. Fairbank, *China.*

4. Bernard Wong, *A Chinese American Community: Ethnicity and Survival Strategies* (Singapore: Chopmen Enterprises, 1979).

5. Scholarship on immigration law and its effect on Asian immigration in particular is ubiquitous. For a concise summary, see Harry Kitano and Roger Daniels, *Asian Americans: Emerging Minorities* (Englewood Cliffs, NJ: Prentice Hall, 1988).

6. See Zhang Liang, *The Tiananmen Papers* (New York: Public Affairs Press, 2001); Fairbank, *China*; Roberts, *A Concise History of China*; and Harrison Salisbury, *Tiananmen Diary: Thirteen Days in June* (Boston: Little, Brown, 1989).

7. New York City Department of City Planning, *The Newest New Yorkers: An Analysis of Immigration into New York City during the 1980s* (New York: Department of City Planning, 1992), p. 24.

8. Herbert Barringer, Robert Gardner, and Michael Levin, *Asians and Pacific Islanders in the United States* (New York: Russell Sage Foundation, 1993).

9. See Zhou, "Chinese"; and New York City Department of City Planning, *The Newest New Yorkers*. Typically, data on "ethnic Chinese" include Taiwan and Hong Kong along with mainland Chinese. These three sending regions have interconnected but very different histories of migration, and, where possible, the statistical distinctions will be made.

10. Zhou, "Chinese."

11. Paul Crowell, "6,406 Apartments Slated for City," *New York Times,* July 22, 1961, p. 1; Sam Kaplan, "New Cooperative Spur to Renewal," *New York Times,* October 8, 1961, p. R1.

12. Martin Arnold, "Prospective Tenants Avoiding 4 Co-op Projects Built by City," *New York Times,* November 12, 1961, p. 84.

13. Martin Arnold, "Relocation Plagues Merchants Forced Out by Urban Renewal," *New York Times,* March 5, 1962, p. 1.

14. "Fraud Investigated in Housing Project," *New York Times,* June 10, 1966, p. 33.

15. Xiaolan Bao, *Holding Up More than Half the Sky: Chinese Women Garment Workers in New York City, 1948–1992* (Chicago: University of Illinois Press, 2001); See also Roger Waldinger, *Through the Eye of the Needle: Immigrants and Enterprise in New York's Garment Trades* (New York: New York University Press, 1986).

16. Dave Von Drehle, *Triangle: The Fire That Changed America* (New York: Atlantic Monthly Press, 2003).

17. Bao, *Holding Up More than Half the Sky*.

18. Zhou, "Chinese."

19. The Chinese garment industry in New York has a long history of organized labor, marked most notably by a massive strike in 1982 that forced Chinatown garment producers to sign union contracts. See Bao, *Holding Up More than Half the Sky*; and Xinyang Wang, *Surviving the City: The Chinese Immigrant Experience in New York City, 1890–1970* (New York: Rowman and Littlefield, 2001).

20. Paul Goldberger, "First-Rate Housing Opens in Harlem," *New York Times,*

November 2, 1974, p. 33; Charlayne Hunter, "Hopes and Fears on Rise with New Harlem Skyline," *New York Times,* November 20, 1973, p. 41; Orde Coombs, "Three Faces of Harlem," *New York Times,* November 3, 1974, p. 300.

21.   Carter Horsley, "New Skyline Emerging on East Side North of 86th," *New York Times,* June 23, 1974, p. 336.

22.   "Urban Oases Hailed in Annual Bard Awards," *New York Times,* June 16, 1976, p. 35.

23.   See Coombs, "Three Faces of Harlem."

24.   Quoted from the HUD website in its description of the award-winning La Esperanza Homes: www.huduser.org/research/1998awrds7.html.

25.   The apparent success of La Esperanza Homes led to several duplicate developments throughout East Harlem, each at higher and higher cost to home owners. They include Fifth Avenue Homes, which razed Lucille's childhood block to make way for townhouses and condominiums priced well out of her reach. See chapter 8 for further discussions of these changes.

26.   Much has been written concerning the generation gap of assimilation for immigrant parents and their children, particularly among Chinese. For some examples, see May Paomay Tung, *Chinese Americans and Their Immigrant Parents* (New York: Haworth Press, 2000); and Betty Lee Sung, *The Adjustment Experience of Chinese Immigrant Children in New York City* (New York: Center for Migration Studies, 1987).

27.   "Slay Rap for Teen," *Daily News,* November 17, 2000, p. 7; "Teen, Boyfriend Admit Killing Parents in Video Confessions," *Daily News,* November 18, 2000, p. 14; Andy Newman, "Body Found in River Is Thought to Be That of Strangling Victim," *New York Times,* November 20, 2000, p. B5.

28.   "Chinatown Remembers Slain Couple," *Daily News,* November 25, 2000, p. 19; "Slay Rap for Teen"; "Teen, Boyfriend Admit Killing Parents in Video Confessions."

29.   Both Eric Louissaint and Connie Leung were sentenced to thirty years to life in prison for the murder of her parents. "Strangling Guilty Plea," *Daily News,* March 19, 2002, p. 7; "Woman Sentenced in Parents' Deaths," *New York Times,* May 8, 2003, p. B10.

30.   Joseph Kahn, "China's Hot, at Least for Now," *New York Times,* December 16, 2002, p. C10.

31.   Jim Yardley, "Splendid Skyline, Do You Feel Something Sinking?" *New York Times,* October 14, 2003, p. A4.

32.   Eric Eckholm, "As China's Economy Shines, the Party Line Loses Luster," *New York Times,* November 5, 2002, p. A1.

33.   That is, compared to the U.S. average of 3.5 times annual income. Keith Bradsher, "China's Buildings: In Pink, and in the Red," *New York Times,* August 15, 2004, p. 12.

CHAPTER 8

1. www.east-harlem.com/sharmans.htm.

2. See Patricia Cayo Sexton, *Spanish Harlem: An Anatomy of Poverty* (New York: Harper and Row, 1965); and Arlene Dávila, *Barrio Dreams: Puerto Ricans, Latinos, and the Neoliberal City* (Berkeley: University of California Press, 2004).

3. See Dan Wakefield, *Island in the City* (Boston: Houghton Mifflin, 1957).

4. John Goering, Maynard Robinson, and Knight Hoover, *The Best Eight Blocks in Harlem: The Last Decade of Urban Reform* (Washington, DC: University Press of America, 1977), pp. 7–8.

5. Charlayne Hunter, "Women's Self-Help Plan Is Working in East Harlem," *New York Times,* July 5, 1970, p. 38.

6. This concept is taken from Neil Smith's book by the same name, a compelling analysis of urban renewal in the past half century and an indispensable primer on gentrification in the United States and around the globe: Neil Smith, *The New Urban Frontier: Gentrification and the Revanchist City* (New York: Routledge, 1996).

7. The children at El Faro were dependents of those in the "workfare" program. Their parents worked minimum-wage jobs to meet employment requirements but did not earn enough to pay for day care in the summer or after school while they worked. A citywide system of Beacon Community Centers was established to fill the gap, but, at least at El Faro in East Harlem, they were woefully understaffed, had no air-conditioning in the summer, and were given almost no supplies.

8. I did find one property actually inhabited by its owner, a massive public school building on First Avenue that appeared abandoned. Inside, a reclusive, rather eccentric man named Greg had converted the second level into Ray Rock Studios and marketed the space as a "mansion movie set." Greg, a white southern transplant to New York, had decorated the interior with tapestries, vintage books, fake mantels, and even full suits of armor. When asked about the building itself, Greg let me know that it was for sale, $15 million, but that the real owner lived elsewhere and preferred to remain anonymous.

9. Neil Smith refers to this moment as the "rent gap" and considers it a precursor to gentrification (Smith, *The New Urban Frontier*).

10. Ruth Glass, *London: Aspects of Change* (London: Center for Urban Studies, 1964).

11. For more in-depth contemporary analysis of the phenomenon of gentrification, see Smith, *The New Urban Frontier;* J. John Palen and Bruce London, eds., *Gentrification, Displacement and Neighborhood Revitalization* (Albany: State University of New York Press, 1984); Neil Smith and Peter Williams, eds., *Gentrification of the City* (Boston: Allen and Unwin, 1986).

12. Carter B. Horsley, "In East Harlem, Interest Focuses on Housing Sites," *New York Times,* March 22, 1981, p. R1; Joseph Berger, "After Exodus, Gentrification Changes Face of East Harlem," *New York Times,* December 10, 2002, p. B1.

13. See Jewel Bellush and Murray Hausknecht, eds., *Urban Renewal: People, Politics, and Planning* (Garden City, NY: Anchor Books, 1961). See in particular the essay by Herbert J. Gans, "The Failure of Urban Renewal: A Critique and Some Proposals," pp. 465–84.

14. Jane Jacobs, *The Death and Life of Great American Cities* (New York: Random House, 1961).

15. While these trajectories suggest a market led by the preferences of upwardly mobile Manhattanites pushing outward, changes in East New York, a beleaguered community near the eastern edge of the city, suggest it is a systemwide process. See Janet L. Abu-Lughod, ed., *From Urban Village to East Village: The Battle for New York's Lower East Side* (Oxford: Blackwell, 1994); Peter Marcuse, "Abandonment, Gentrification, and Displacement: The Linkages in New York City," in Smith and Williams, eds., *Gentrification of the City,* pp. 153–77; Smith, *The New Urban Frontier;* Dávila, *Barrio Dreams.*

16. For a more in-depth examination of this process in East Harlem, see Dávila, *Barrio Dreams.* See also Noam Chomsky, *Profits over People: Neoliberalism and the Global Order* (New York: Seven Stories Press, 1999).

17. See Chomsky, *Profits over People.*

18. Berger, "After Exodus, Gentrification Changes Face of East Harlem."

19. Maria arrived after the period covered in Bourgois's book.

20. Berger, "After Exodus, Gentrification Changes Face of East Harlem"; Dávila, *Barrio Dreams.*

Bibliography

Abraham, Arthur. "Amistad Revolt: An Historical Legacy of Sierra Leone and the United States." In *Sierra Leone: Current Issues and Background*, ed. Brett Sillinger, pp. 1–16. New York: Nova Science Publishers, 2003.

Abu-Lughod, Janet L., ed. *From Urban Village to East Village: The Battle for New York's Lower East Side*. Oxford: Blackwell, 1994.

Abu-Lughod, Lila. "Writing against Culture." In *Recapturing Anthropology: Working in the Present*, ed. Richard Fox, pp. 137–61. Santa Fe, NM: School of American Research Press, 1991.

Adebajo, Adekeye. *Building Peace in West Africa: Liberia, Sierra Leone, and Guinea-Bissau*. London: Lynne Rienner, 2002.

Anderson, Jervis. *This Was Harlem: A Cultural Portrait, 1900–1950*. New York: Farrar, Straus and Giroux, 1981.

Bao, Xiaolan. *Holding Up More than Half the Sky: Chinese Women Garment Workers in New York City, 1948–1992*. Chicago: University of Illinois Press, 2001.

Barringer, Herbert, Robert Gardner, and Michael Levin. *Asians and Pacific Islanders in the United States.* New York: Russell Sage Foundation, 1993.

Barry, Tom. *Crossing the Line: Immigrants, Economic Integration and Drug Enforcement on the U.S.-Mexico Border.* Albuquerque, NM: Resource Center Press, 1994.

Bean, Frank D., B. Lindsay Lowell, and Lowell J. Taylor. "Undocumented Mexican Immigrants and the Earnings of Other Workers in the United States." *Demography* 25 (1988): 35–52.

Behar, Ruth. *Translated Woman: Crossing the Border with Esperanza's Story.* Boston: Beacon Press, 1993.

Bellush, Jewel, and Murray Hausknecht, eds. *Urban Renewal: People, Politics, and Planning.* Garden City, NY: Anchor Books, 1961.

Borah, Woodrow, and Sherburne F. Cook. "Marriage and Legitimacy in Mexican Culture: Mexico and California." *California Law Review* 54, no. 2 (1966): 946–1008.

Bourgois, Philippe. *In Search of Respect: Selling Crack in El Barrio.* Cambridge: Cambridge University Press, 1995.

Brunk, Samuel. "Remembering Emiliano Zapata: Three Moments in the Posthumous Career of the Martyr of Chinameca." *Hispanic American Historical Review* 8, no. 3 (1998): 457–90.

Bunzl, Matti. "Boas, Foucault, and the 'Native Anthropologist': Notes toward a New-Boasian Anthropology." *American Anthropologist* 6, no. 3 (2002): 435–42.

Campbell, Greg. *Blood Diamonds.* Boulder, CO: Westview Press, 2002.

Chenault, Lawrence. *The Puerto Rican Migrant in New York City.* New York: Columbia University Press, 1938.

Cheng, Nien. *Life and Death in Shanghai.* New York: Grove Press, 1986.

Chomsky, Noam. *Profits over People: Neoliberalism and the Global Order.* New York: Seven Stories Press, 1999.

Cockcroft, James. *Mexico: Class Formation, Capital Accumulations and the State.* New York: Monthly Review Press, 1983.

Cordasco, Francesco, and Rocco Galatioto. "Ethnic Displacement in the Interstitial Community: The East Harlem [New York City] Experience." In *The Puerto Rican Experience,* ed. Francesco Cordasco and Eugene Bucchioni, pp. 171–85. Totowa, NJ: Rowman and Littlefield, 1973.

Cornelius, Wayne. "Death at the Border: The Efficacy and Unintended Consequences of U.S. Immigration Control Policy." *Population and Development Review* 27, no. 4 (2001): 661–85.

Covello, Leonard. *The Heart Is the Teacher.* New York: McGraw-Hill, 1958.

Crapanzano, Vincent. "The Life History in Anthropological Field Work." *Anthropology and Humanism Quarterly* 2, nos. 2–3 (1977): 3–7.

Daniels, Roger. *Guarding the Golden Door.* New York: Hill and Wang, 2004.

Davidson, Miriam. *Lives on the Line: Dispatches from the U.S.-Mexico Border.* Tucson: University of Arizona Press, 2000.

Dávila, Arlene. *Barrio Dreams: Puerto Ricans, Latinos, and the Neoliberal City.* Berkeley: University of California Press, 2004.

———. "Latinizing Culture: Art, Museums, and the Politics of U.S. Multicultural Encompassment." *Cultural Anthropology* 14, no. 2 (1999): 180–202.

———. *Sponsored Identities: Cultural Politics in Puerto Rico.* Philadelphia: Temple University Press, 1997.

Delcore, Henry. "Development and the Life Story of a Thai Farmer Leader." *Ethnology* 43, no. 1 (2004): 33–50.

Donato, Katherine M. "U.S. Policy and Mexican Migration to the United States, 1942–1992." *Social Science Quarterly* 75, no. 4 (1994): 705–29.

Dunn, Timothy J. *The Militarization of the U.S.-Mexico Border, 1978–1992: Low-Intensity Conflict Doctrine Comes Home.* Austin, TX: CMAS Books, 1996.

Durand, Jorge, Douglas S. Massey, and Fernando Charvet. "The Changing Geography of Mexican Immigration to the United States: 1910–1996." *Social Science Quarterly* 81, no. 1 (2000): 1–15.

Durand, Jorge, Douglas S. Massey, and René M. Zenteno. "Mexican Migration to the United States: Continuities and Changes." *Latin American Research Review* 36, no. 1 (2001): 107–27.

Eschbach, Karl, Jacqueline Hagan, and Néstor Rodríguez. "Death at the Border." *International Migration Review* 33, no. 2 (1999): 430–54.

———. "Deaths during Undocumented Migration: Trends and Policy Implications in the New Era of Homeland Security." Paper presented at the 26th Annual National Legal Conference on Immigration and Refugee Policy, Washington, DC, 2003.

Fairbank, John King. *China: A New History.* Cambridge, MA: Harvard University Press, 1992.

Fernandez, Ronald. *The Disenchanted Island.* Westport, CT: Praeger Press, 1996.

Flores, Juan. *From Bomba to Hip Hop: Puerto Rican Culture and Latino Identity.* New York: Columbia University Press, 2000.

Foner, Nancy. *From Ellis Island to JFK: New York's Two Great Waves of Immigration.* New Haven, CT: Yale University Press, 2000.

———. "Transnationalism Then and Now: New York Immigrants Today and at the Turn of the Twentieth Century." In *Migration, Transnationalization, and Race in a Changing New York,* ed. Héctor R. Cordero-Guzmán, Robert C. Smith, and Ramón Grosfoguel, pp. 35–57. Philadelphia: Temple University Press, 2001.

Frank, Geyla. "Finding the Common Denominator: A Phenomenological Critique of Life History Method." *Ethos* 7, no. 1 (1979): 68–94.

Gans, Herbert J. "The Failure of Urban Renewal: A Critique and Some Proposals." In *Urban Renewal: People, Politics, and Planning,* ed. Jewel Bellush and Murray Hausknecht, pp. 465–84. Garden City, NY: Anchor Books, 1961.

Genevro, Rosalie. "Site Selection and the New York City Housing Authority, 1934–1939." *Journal of Urban History* 12, no. 4 (1986): 334–52.

Glass, Ruth. *London: Aspects of Change.* London: Center for Urban Studies, 1964.

Glick Schiller, Nina. "Transmigrants and Nation-States: Something Old and Something New in the U.S. Immigrant Experience." In *Handbook of International Migration: The American Experience,* ed. Charles Hirschman, Philip Kasinitz, and Josh DeWind, pp. 94–119. New York: Russell Sage Foundation, 1999.

Goering, John, Maynard Robinson, and Knight Hoover. *The Best Eight Blocks in Harlem: The Last Decade of Urban Reform.* Washington, DC: University Press of America, 1977.

Gregory, Steven. *Black Corona: Race and the Politics of Place in an Urban Community.* Princeton, NJ: Princeton University Press, 1998.

——— . *Santería in New York City.* New York: Garland, 1999.

Gurock, Jeffery. *When Harlem Was Jewish, 1870–1930.* New York: Columbia University Press, 1979.

Gutiérrez, David G. "Demography and the Shifting Boundaries of 'Community': Reflections on 'U.S. Latinos' and the Evolution of Latino Studies." In *The Columbia History of Latinos in the U.S. since 1960,* ed. David G. Gutiérrez, pp. 1–42. New York: Columbia University Press, 2004.

Hancock, LynNell. *Hands to Work: The Stories of Three Families Racing the Welfare Clock.* New York: William Morrow, 2002.

Hanson, Gordon H., Raymond Robertson, and Antonio Spilimbergo. "Does Border Enforcement Protect U.S. Workers from Illegal Immigration?" *Review of Economics and Statistics* 84, no. 1 (2002): 73–92.

Human Rights Watch. *We'll Kill You If You Cry: Sexual Violence in the Sierra Leone Conflict.* Washington, DC: Human Rights Watch, 2003.

Jacobs, Jane. *The Death and Life of Great American Cities.* New York: Random House, 1961.

Jical, Feng. *Voices from the Whirlwind: An Oral History of the Chinese Cultural Revolution.* New York: Pantheon Books, 1991.

Johnson, Kevin R. "The Continuing Latino Quest for Full Membership and Equal Citizenship: Legal Progress, Social Setbacks, and Political Promise." In *The Columbia History of Latinos in the U.S. since 1960,* ed. David G. Gutiérrez, pp. 391–420. New York: Columbia University Press, 2004.

Kessner, Thomas. *The Golden Door: Italian and Jewish Immigrant Mobility in New York City, 1880–1915.* New York: Oxford University Press, 1977.

Kitano, Harry, and Roger Daniels. *Asian Americans: Emerging Minorities.* Englewood Cliffs, NJ: Prentice Hall, 1988.

Kopinak, Kathryn. "Household, Gender and Migration in Mexican Maquiladoras: The Case of Nogales." In *International Migration, Refugee Flows and Human Rights in North America: The Impact of Trade and Restructuring,* ed. Alan B. Simmons, pp. 214–28. New York: Center for Migration Studies, 1996.

Lawson, Ronald, ed. *The Tenant Movement in New York City, 1904–1984.* New Brunswick, NJ: Rutgers University Press, 1986.

Liang, Zhang. *The Tiananmen Papers.* New York: Public Affairs Press, 2001.

Luo, Zi-Ping. *A Generation Lost: China under the Cultural Revolution.* New York: Holt, 1990.

Makannah, Toma J., and Mohamed Bailey. 1994. "Sierra Leone." In *Urbanization in Africa: A Handbook,* ed. James D. Tarver, pp. 298–314. Westport, CT: Greenwood Press, 1994.

Marcuse, Peter. "Abandonment, Gentrification, and Displacement: The Linkages in New York City." In *Gentrification of the City,* ed. Neil Smith and Peter Williams, pp. 153–77. Boston: Allen and Unwin, 1986.

——— . "The Beginnings of Public Housing in New York." *Journal of Urban History* 12, no. 4 (1986): 353–90.

Massey, Douglas S. "Why Does Immigration Occur? A Theoretical Synthesis." In *Handbook of International Migration: The American Experience,* ed. Charles Hirschman, Philip Kasinitz, and Josh DeWind, pp. 34–52. New York: Russell Sage Foundation, 1999.

Mintz, Sidney. *Worker in the Cane: A Puerto Rican Life History.* New York: Norton, 1974.

Ndumbe, J. Anyu. "Diamonds, Ethnicity and Power: The Case of Sierra Leone." *Mediterranean Quarterly* 12, no. 4 (2001): 90–105.

Nevins, Joseph. *Operation Gatekeeper: The Rise of the 'Illegal Alien' and the Making of the U.S.-Mexico Boundary.* New York: Routledge, 2002.

New York City Department of City Planning. *The Newest New Yorkers: An Analysis of Immigration into New York City during the 1980s.* New York: Department of City Planning, 1992.

——— . *The Newest New Yorkers, 1990–1994.* New York: Department of City Planning, 1996.

New York Daily News, June 6, 1995–March 19, 2002.

New York Times, September 9, 1913–January 21, 2004.

Newman, Oscar. *Defensible Space: Crime Prevention through Urban Design.* New York: Macmillan, 1972.

Orsi, Robert. *The Madonna of 115th Street: Faith and Community in Italian Harlem, 1880–1950.* New Haven, CT: Yale University Press, 2002.

Osofsky, Gilbert. *Harlem: The Making of a Ghetto.* New York: Harper and Row, 1963.

Pakenham, Thomas. *The Scramble for Africa: The White Man's Conquest of the Dark Continent from 1876 to 1912.* New York: Random House, 1991.

Palen, J. John, and Bruce London, eds. *Gentrification, Displacement and Neighborhood Revitalization.* Albany: State University of New York Press, 1984.

Pecorella, Robert. *Community Power in a Postreform City.* Armonk, NY: M. E. Sharpe, 1994.

Pérez y Mena, Andrés Isidoro. "Cuban Santería, Haitian Vodun, Puerto Rican Spiritualism: A Multiculturalist Inquiry into Syncretism." *Journal for the Scientific Study of Religion* 37, no. 1 (1998): 15–27.

——— . *Speaking with the Dead.* New York: AMS Press, 1991.

Piore, Michael. *Birds of Passage: Migrant Labor and Industrial Societies.* Cambridge: Cambridge University Press, 1979.

Plato. *The Republic.* Trans. F. M. Cornford. Oxford: Oxford University Press, 1941.

Plunz, Richard. *A History of Housing in New York City: Dwelling Type and Social Change in the American Metropolis.* New York: Columbia University Press, 1990.

Rath, Jan, ed. *Immigrant Businesses.* New York: St. Martin's Press, 2000.

Ravitch, Diane. *The Great School Wars: New York City, 1805–1973.* New York: Basic Books, 1974.

Rivera, Monte. "Organizational Politics of the East Harlem Barrio in the 1970s." In *Puerto Rican Politics in Urban America,* ed. James Jennings and Monte Rivera, pp. 61–72. Westport, CT: Greenwood Press, 1984.

Roberts, J. A. G. *A Concise History of China.* Cambridge, MA: Harvard University Press, 1999.

Rodríguez, Clara. "Puerto Ricans: Between Black and White." In *Historical Perspectives on Puerto Rican Survival in the United States,* ed. Clara Rodríguez and Virginia Sánchez-Korrol, pp. 25–35. Princeton, NJ: Markus Wiener, 1996.

——— . *Puerto Ricans: Born in the USA.* New York: Routledge, 1990.

Ross, John. "The Zapatistas at Ten." *North American Congress on Latin America* 37, no. 3 (2003): 11–15.

Salisbury, Harrison. *Tiananmen Diary: Thirteen Days in June.* Boston: Little, Brown, 1989.

Sánchez-Korrol, Virginia. *From Colonia to Community: The History of Puerto Ricans in New York City, 1917–1948.* Westport, CT: Greenwood Press, 1983.

Sanjek, Roger. *The Future of Us All: Race and Neighborhood Politics in New York City.* Ithaca, NY: Cornell University Press, 1998.

Sexton, Patricia Cayo. *Spanish Harlem: An Anatomy of Poverty.* New York: Harper and Row, 1965.

Sharman, Russell Leigh. "Duke versus Tito: Aesthetic Conflict in East Harlem, NY." *Visual Anthropology Review* 18, nos. 1–2 (2001): 3–21.

Sillinger, Brett, ed. *Sierra Leone: Current Issues and Background.* New York: Nova Science Publishers, 2003.

Simmons, Leo. *Sun Chief: The Autobiography of a Hopi Indian.* New Haven, CT: Yale University Press, 1942.

Simon, Rita J., and Margo Corona DeLey. "Undocumented Mexican Women: Their Work and Personal Experiences." In *International Migration: The Female Experience*, ed. Rita J. Simon and Caroline B. Brettell, pp. 113–32. Totowa, NJ: Rowman and Allanheld, 1986.

Skultans, Vieda. "Arguing with the KGB Archives: Archival and Narrative Memory in Post-Soviet Latvia." *Ethnos* 66, no. 3 (2001): 320–43.

Smith, Neil. *The New Urban Frontier: Gentrification and the Revanchist City*. New York: Routledge, 1996.

Smith, Neil, and Peter Williams, eds. *Gentrification of the City*. Boston: Allen and Unwin, 1986.

Smith, Robert C. "Mexicans: Social, Educational, Economic, and Political Problems and Prospects in New York." In *New Immigrants in New York*, ed. Nancy Foner, pp. 275–300. New York: Columbia University Press, 2001.

Sokefeld, Martin. "Debating Self, Identity, and Culture in Anthropology." *Current Anthropology* 40, no. 4 (1999): 417–77.

Stephen, Lynn. "Pro-Zapatista and Pro-PRI: Resolving the Contradictions of Zapatismo in Rural Oaxaca." *Latin American Research Review* 32, no. 2 (2001): 41–70.

Stoller, Paul. *Money Has No Smell*. Chicago: University of Chicago Press, 2002.

———. "West Africans: Trading Places in New York." In *New Immigrants in New York*, ed. Nancy Foner, pp. 229–50. New York: Columbia University Press, 2001.

Sung, Betty Lee. *The Adjustment Experience of Chinese Immigrant Children in New York City*. New York: Center for Migration Studies, 1987.

Suro, Robert. "Remittance Senders and Receivers: Tracking the Transnational Channels." Report prepared by the Pew Hispanic Center, Washington, DC, 2003.

Taylor, Lawrence, and Maeve Hickey. *Tunnel Kids*. Tucson: University of Arizona Press, 2001.

Thomas, Piri. *Down These Mean Streets*. New York: Random House, 1967.

Tung, May Paomay. *Chinese Americans and Their Immigrant Parents*. New York: Haworth Press, 2000.

U.S. Congress. House of Representatives. Subcommittee on Immigration, Border Security, and Claims. 108th Cong. *Deadly Consequences of Illegal Alien Smuggling*. Washington DC: Government Printing Office, 2003.

U.S. Immigration and Naturalization Service. *Statistical Yearbook of the Immigration and Naturalization Service, 1997*. Washington, DC: Government Printing Office, 1999.

———. *Statistical Yearbook of the Immigration and Naturalization Service, 2002*. Washington, DC: Government Printing Office, 2003.

Venkatesh, Sudhir Alladi. *American Project: The Rise and Fall of a Modern Ghetto*. Cambridge, MA: Harvard University Press, 2001.

Vigil, James Diego. *A Rainbow of Gangs: Street Cultures in the Mega-City.* Austin: University of Texas Press, 2002.

Von Drehle, Dave. *Triangle: The Fire That Changed America.* New York: Atlantic Monthly Press, 2003.

Wade, Peter. *Race and Ethnicity in Latin America.* London: Pluto Press, 1997.

Wagenhaim, Kal. *A Survey of Puerto Ricans on the U.S. Mainland in the 1970s.* New York: Praeger, 1975.

Wakefield, Dan. *Island in the City.* Boston: Houghton Mifflin, 1957.

Waldinger, Roger. *Through the Eye of the Needle: Immigrants and Enterprise in New York's Garment Trades.* New York: New York University Press, 1986.

Waldinger, Roger, Howard Aldrich, Robin Ward, and Associates. *Ethnic Entrepreneurs: Immigrant Business in Industrial Societies.* London: Sage, 1990.

Wang, Xinyang. *Surviving the City: The Chinese Immigrant Experience in New York City, 1890–1970.* New York: Rowman and Littlefield, 2001.

Waters, Tony. *Immigration and Crime.* Thousand Oaks, CA: Sage, 1999.

Wesseling, H. L. *Divide and Rule: The Partition of Africa, 1880–1914.* Trans. Arnold J. Pomerans. London: Praeger, 1996.

Whitten, Norman, and Arlene Torres. *Blackness in Latin America and the Caribbean.* 2 vols. Bloomington: Indiana University Press, 1998.

Wong, Bernard. *A Chinese American Community: Ethnicity and Survival Strategies.* Singapore: Chopmen Enterprises, 1979.

Zhou, Min. "Chinese: Divergent Destinies in Immigrant New York." In *New Immigrants in New York,* ed. Nancy Foner, pp. 141–72. New York: Columbia University Press, 2001.

Index

Pleasant Avenue, 9–10, 12–13, 37, 38, 44, 46–47

Plexiglas walls, 8

population statistics: on African Americans, 15, 62, 74, 81–82, 211n10, 215–16n3; on Asian Americans, 171; on Chinese, 18, 171; on Italians, 23; on Mexicans, 16, 74, 121; on non-Hispanic whites, 205; on Puerto Ricans, 15, 51, 62, 68–69, 82, 121, 211n10, 215–16n3; on Russian Jews, 33, 34; on sub-Saharan Africans, 143; on undocumented immigrants, 114–15; on West Africans, 17. *See also* immigration statistics

Powell, Adam Clayton, Jr., 85

prenatal care statistics, 62

Prep for Prep program, 184

privatization: of *ejido* land grants, 108–9; of public housing, 45–46, 102–3, 202–3

Protestant church, 195–96, 197

public education, 89–91, 177, 216n12. *See also* schools

public housing: cooperative types of, 172–73, 178–80; criminal activity in, 98–99, 175; description of buildings, 4–5; desegregation in, 58–59; federal funding cuts on, 99–100, 217n21; map locations of, *ii*; neighborhood impact of, 13, 36, 38, 43–44, 76–77; NYCHA's construction of, 34–36; percent of families in, xii; privatization of, 45–46, 102–3, 202–3; tenancy qualifications for, 56, 101–2; under Title I of FHA, 95; of UPACA, 93–94, 95–96

Public Works Administration (PWA), 34–35

Puente, Tito, 4, 7, 76

Puerto Rican Day Parade, 204

Puerto Ricans: botanicas of, 8; citizenship status of, 13–14, 51; community activism of, 63–65, 74–76; culinary delicacies of, 50; factory job losses of, 66–67, 69; gang activities of, 57–58, 62–63, 91, 94; gentrification's impact on, 200–201, 206; immigration statistics on, 13, 51–52, 56–57, 212–13n1; Italians' relations with, 32–33, 44–45, 57; life story representing, 2, 13; Mexicans' relations with, 77, 130–31; in military service, 52, 68, 213n3; parish church of, 60–61; population statistics on, 15, 51, 62, 68–69, 82, 121, 211n10, 215–16n3; public housing for, 58–59; race categories of, 54–55; Santería practice of, 53–54. *See also* José

Puerto Rico: political status of, 13–14, 63; statistics on migration from, 51, 212–13n1

racism: of African American kids, 185–86; in employment, 180–81; of police, 178; as Puerto Rican issue, 54–55; of white kids, 181

Ramadan, 157–58

Rao, Vincent, 39

Rao's Italian Restaurant, *ii*, 10, 37, 39–40

Reagan administration, 97, 99–100, 114, 217n21

Regla de Ocha (Lucumí), 53, 213n4

remittances, 119, 128–29

Revolutionary United Front (RUF), 140, 143

"Rose in Spanish Harlem" (song), 208

Russian Jews, 33–34

Salerno, Anthony "Fat Tony," 30, 37, 39

Santería practice, 53–54, 213n4

Schomburg Towers, 179

schools: for alternative education, 99; during Cultural Revolution, 164, 165–66; desegregation of, 89–91, 216n12; in Italian Harlem, 31–32; in Prep for Prep program, 184; quality of education in, 177; of St. Cecilia's Church, 60–61

Second Avenue and 28th Street, 176

Senegalese street vendors, 145–46

September 11, 154

Settlement House, 195

Shanghai (China), 18, 163, 171, 188–89

Sharman, Russell Leigh: art organization of, 19, 195, 196–97, 199, 203; background of, 193–94; East Harlem experience of, xii–xiii, 198–99, 207–8; ethnographic style of, xiii–xiv, 209–10n3, 210n6; party guests of, 191–93, 204

Sierra Leone (West Africa), 137–41, 143, 146, 159

Sierra Leone Selection Trust, 138

Si Zhi (Chinese tenant), 2, 17–18; on American factories, 173; citizenship issues of, 186–88; co-op residence of, 178–80; during Cultural Revolution, 164–66; education priority of, 177–78, 184–85; on garment industry, 174–75; hotel housekeeping jobs of, 162–63, 176–77, 180–81; on in-law relationship, 175–76; on moving to America, 167–68, 169, 170–71; on racism, 181, 185–86; Shanghai shipyard job of, 166–67; socializing with, 192–93, 207; townhouse property of, 161–62, 169–70, 182–83; transnationalism of, 188–89. *See also* Chinese

slum clearance projects, 35–36, 56, 95

social clubs: of Central Harlem, 83; of Italian Harlem, 29–30, 38–40
Spanish-American War (1898), 51
Spanish Methodist Church, 62–63, 214n17
St. Cecilia's Church, *ii*, 5, 60–61, 129–30
Stevens, Siaka, 140
street vendors, 136, 145–46, 150–52, 157
sub-Saharan Africans, 143, 145
superblocks, 5, 35–36
Susu language, 137

Taiwan, 18
Temple Number 7 (Harlem), 85
Tenement House Act (1867), 25
Tenement House Act (1879), 26
Tenement House Act (1901), 26
tenements: description of, 44; deterioration/abandonment of, 199–200, 201–2, 227n15; legislative regulation of, 25–26; market rent in, 55; replaced by public housing, 35–37, 56–57; replaced by townhouses, 103–4, 161, 204
Third Avenue, 16; gypsy cabs on, 3; from 96th to 106th Street, 3–5; 99-cent store on, 135–37; street vendors on, 150–51
Thomas, Piri, 51, 55, 57
Tiananmen Square massacre (1989), 168–69
Title I of Federal Housing Act, 95
Tito Puente Way (110th Street), 7, 76
townhouse developments: cost of homes in, 182–83, 202–3, 225n25; description of, 161, 169–70; tenements replaced by, 103–4, 202–4
transnationalism, 128–29, 134, 188–89
travel agencies, 122, 128
Triangle Shirtwaist Company fire (1911), 174
28th Street and Second Avenue, 176

undocumented Mexican immigrants: arrest of, in 1997, 109; border crossings by, 111–12, 113, 125–28, 221n30; funds for migration of, 120; gender of, 133; open border approach to, 218–19n12; statistics on, 114–15, 121; in U.S. labor market, 117–18, 220n23; U.S. strategies against, 114, 219n16
undocumented West African immigrants, 143

UPACA (Upper Park Avenue Community Association), 93–94, 95, 196
UPACA (Upper Park Avenue Community Association) Gardens, 14; financing/construction of, 93–94; gangs in, 98–99; insulated tenants of, 96; map location of, *ii*; tenant patrol of, 79–81
UPACA (Upper Park Avenue Community Association) Towers, 93, 94, 96
Upper Manhattan Empowerment Zone, 71
Urban Action Task Force (New York City), 64
urban renewal. *See* gentrification
U.S. Border Patrol, 109, 114–15, 126, 221n30
U.S. Housing Authority (USHA), 34
U.S. Immigration Commission, 24
U.S.-Mexico border: arrests on, in 1997, 109; Border Patrol enforcement at, 114–15, 219n16, 221n30; crossings of, 1920–1929, 217n1; difficulties in crossing, 111–12, 113, 125–28; open border approach to, 218–19n12

wages: remittances from, 119, 128–29; of undocumented workers, 117–18, 220n23. *See also* income statistics
welfare recipients, 92, 153–55
West Africans: and African Americans, 44; colonized background of, 137; counterfeiting operations of, 156–57; in diamond trade, 137–38; as gypsy cab drivers, 3, 151–52, 157–58; life story representing, 2, 16; religious practices of, 157–58; status of, in Britain, 140–41; street vendor businesses of, 136, 145–46, 150–51; transient presence of, 17, 145. *See also* Mohamed
West Point Academy, 184, 186–87
whites: desegregated schools of, 90; East Harlem migration of, 2, 19–20; merchandising to, 206; population of, 1990–2000, 205; as public housing tenants, 58, 59
workfare program, 154–55, 226n7

Yoruba religion, 53–54, 213n4
Young Lords street gang, 62–63, 64, 91, 94

Zapata, Emiliano, 107
Zapatistas, 108–9

Designer: Jessica Grunwald
Text: 10/14 Palatino
Display: Univers Condensed Light 47 and Bauer Bodoni
Compositor: Sheridan Books, Inc.
Indexer: Patricia Deminna
Printer and binder: Sheridan Books, Inc.